FAMILY TREATMENT
The Sibling Bond and Other Relationship Issues

FAMILY TREATMENT

The Sibling Bond and Other Relationship Issues

By

EDITH M. FREEMAN, PH.D.
*University of Kansas
School of Social Welfare*

CHARLES C THOMAS • PUBLISHER
Springfield • Illinois • U.S.A.

Published and Distributed Throughout the World by

CHARLES C THOMAS • PUBLISHER
2600 South First Street
Springfield, Illinois 62794-9265

This book is protected by copyright. No part of
it may be reproduced in any manner without
written permission from the publisher.

© *1993 by* CHARLES C THOMAS • PUBLISHER
ISBN 0-398-05859-8
Library of Congress Catalog Card Number: 93-12387

With THOMAS BOOKS *careful attention is given to all details of manufacturing and design. It is the Publisher's desire to present books that are satisfactory as to their physical qualities and artistic possibilities and appropriate for their particular use.* THOMAS BOOKS *will be true to those laws of quality that assure a good name and good will.*

Printed in the United States of America
SC-R-3

Library of Congress Cataloging-in-Publication Data

Freeman, Edith M.
    Family treatment : the sibling bond and other relationship issues
/ by Edith M. Freeman.
      p.   cm.
    Includes bibliographical references and index.
    ISBN 0-398-05859-8
    1. Family psychotherapy.   2. Brothers and sisters.   I. Title.
RC488.5.F744   1993
616.89'156—dc20
                                                            93-12387
                                                            CIP

To Gloria
My sister in joy and sorrow,
may our sibling bond endure.

FOREWORD

Siblings... the very word conjures up multiple images, images of loyalty and betrayal, bondedness and distance, mutual pride and competitiveness. Sometimes these images are of intense romance, of incest, sometimes of rage and even murder. Sibling bonds, sibling relationships, are often at the literary center of the fictional narrative, at the heart of the play, the film, the poem. From Greek mythology to Shakespeare to Chekhov to Woody Allen, powerful and complex relationships among siblings often serve as the pole around which the story pivots.

The sibling story is an extraordinarily timely one for a professional book, as the very meanings of "family" itself are being constantly rescrutinized in our technologically "saturated" society. As Kenneth Gergen (1991) points out in his troubling vision of American life today, changes in communication, transportation, and other low- and hi-tech areas have greatly affected not only our own senses of self or, more accurately, the ways we go about constructing our identities, but the possibilities for relatedness to others, inside and outside of the family. The demands on us for "relating," Gergen believes, as we face increasing and unremitting stimuli and are deluged daily with more and more people and paper, have increased exponentially even in the last decade. We are asked to fragment ourselves just to keep up.

How does the frenetic pace of family life today, the wide geographic dispersion of family members, impact on family and, in this case, on sibling relationships? In earlier times, in the family life of the village, the farm, the small town, brothers and sisters often occupied the center of our peer universes; the nature of the surround compelled a more centripetal sibling experience. Today, we have the possibility of having relatives and close friends all over the world, of linking by air travel, phone, FAX, express mail, and the like. We can even chat with our friends or our siblings as we travel to and from work. The jet age has produced a paradox; it has allowed us to both move away, it has decentered the family, but at the same time we can reconnect instantly even from down under. Sibling relationships are being transformed even as we read this book. Do they have the potential for being part of the solution to the threat of family fragmentation?

Why, in the professional literature, in this case in the family field, have sibs and particularly contemporary sibling relationship patterns, gotten such short shrift? And why are such relationships pathologized, most often portrayed as problematic and competitive? These are the kinds of questions that Edith Freeman begins with in this excellent and comprehensive examination of sibling relationships over the life span. This book is an effort to redress what has been a serious lack of attention to the sibling phenomenon in the family therapy field in general and in family-centered social work practice in particular.

Freeman takes a wholistic approach to the topic of siblings. She is, in my view, an integrative thinker. With a perspective informed by ecological and systemic ideas as well as developmental and life span metaphors, Freeman does not observe the usual rather rigid boundaries erected between psychodynamic and systems paradigms for understanding human development and functioning, nor does she separate the roles of practitioner and researcher. In other words, her perspective and her presentation are complexly transactional and circular as she moves comfortably among individual, couple, family, and group theory and modality; and between theory, practice, and research, her own as well as the research of others. Even her approach to research and evaluation is inclusive rather than exclusive, as she welcomes evaluation tools from both positivist and naturalistic research. Her own research serves as laboratory for her practice wisdom and vice versa.

Freeman is an integrative and wholistic thinker in yet another way. She believes very strongly that the sibling rivalry and sibling pathology themes have been greatly overemphasized in the clinical literature. Bringing to this volume what has been called a "strengths" perspective, while she does not ignore the ways that sibling relationships can be implicated in individual and family troubles, she explores the ways in which siblings have and can serve as natural helping networks for each other, as sources of support and nurturance. Weaving the strengths idea with changing individual and family roles and tasks over the life span, she explores how sibling relationships shift in response to changing needs and circumstances, particularly at critical junctures such as leaving home or in caring for aging parents. Of particular interest is the amazing individual resilience she finds, even in adults who endured highly traumatic family contexts growing up. The potential damage, she believes, is frequently mediated by the ingenuity and support of siblings.

The family field may also be faulted for its overemphasis on faulty families and its lack of attention to the social circumstances and social discourses that shape individual and family functioning. Freeman does not make this error. Not only is she sensitive to issues of race, class, gender, and ecology, but she envisions the practice role in work with individuals, whole families, or with autonomous sibling groups broadly; for her, each of the cases she presents has implications not only for clinical intervention, but also for research, policy-making, advocacy, and prevention.

This comprehensive portrait of family and sibling relationships is rich with extended case examples, helpful assessment tools, charts, intergenerational maps, and suggestions for evaluation. It is both educational (incorporating an up-to-date review of relevant theoretical, clinical, and research literature) and practical. Health and mental health professionals, educators, and others who work with today's families and family members will find a dazzling array of ideas here for how to use the emergent possibilities in sibling relationships for growth and change.

Gergen K. (1991). *The Saturated Self: Dilemmas of Identity in Contemporary Life.* New York: Basic Books.

JOAN LAIRD
Smith College
School of Social Work

PREFACE

The members of each sibling subsystem are unique and yet similar in many ways. Certainly each child "is born into a different family," i.e., each is born at a different time, when the family is experiencing different issues and is at a different stage of its development. Moreover, each sibling is born with a different perspective, temperament, and combination of strengths and needs. Thus, siblings may experience even their common environmental conditions within and outside the family differently.

Yet, each sibling subsystem integrates these similarities and differences in a manner that provides the members with a common history, consisting of significant experiences during childhood and adolescence. Individuals are never far away from that common history during later years, whether their brothers and sisters are living or deceased, close or cut-off, caring and/or antagonistic. This integration of unique and common experiences into their lives over time is an important part of the sibling bond. The quality of this bond may reflect also the resiliency of the individuals, family, or the sibling subsystem itself as a unique social support network. The network performs important autonomous functions for the members' growth and development (e.g., for handling parental authority and managing the members' differences) that are independent of the parents and other systems. The network's influence is intense during various developmental stages and it is enduring across the life span, characteristics that make it unique in comparison to other significant relationships.

In what ways is this book useful to the range of helping professionals in clarifying the nature of the sibling bond and these unique aspects of the relationship? The purpose of this book summarizes how it may be useful to practitioners. First, the book is designed to clarify the nature of sibling relationships and their effects on the formation of other intimate relationships throughout the life span. To this end, the book analyzes research on the sibling bond, along with the developmental issues that are manifested and handled at various developmental stages. The book also points out parallels between how some of those issues are handled between siblings and how they are managed in other significant relationships.

A second purpose of the book is to explain how such knowledge about the developmental experiences of siblings is useful to social workers and other helping professionals. For instance, it helps to distinguish between "normative" sibling relationships that involve typical conflicts and pressures and those sibling relationships in which more severe, chronic problems have developed. Little has been written about how more severe problems such as sibling incest can be resolved, even within the family therapy practice area. Much of the available information in that area is focused on the family as a unit or on the marital and parental subsystems. Some of the family therapy literature highlights treatment of siblings as a way of enhancing how that subsystem copes with family problems such as parental alcoholism or the loss of a parent through death or divorce. This literature is beneficial because it focuses on how the family's generational history impacts on those problems. But it does not often examine those situations from a life span developmental perspective, or across the life cycle of individuals and their sibling subsystems and in terms of resiliency.

The focus on resiliency and strengths within the context of exploring how needs can be resolved is consistent throughout the chapters of this book. As the reader will observe from these chapters, all sibling subsystems involve some aspects of normal interactions or a natural history. Chapter 1 describes some examples of issues that are addressed as part of the natural history of sibling relationships. Such issues may be activated or reactivated by a number of events, whether they are normative or unusual. Those events include natural developmental transitions over the life span, crises, family traditions and dysruptions, and dynamics within the sibling subsystem.

During natural developmental transitions, critical developmental tasks must be addressed by the individual, sibling subsystem, and family. The resources for addressing those tasks may come from natural helping activities involving modeling and problem-solving. The sources of mutual and self-help activities may be the sibship, the parent generation's sibling relationships, the extended family network, or alternative (substitute) siblings. The use of such resources is described in Chapters 2 and 3 in which the developmental tasks and relationships of siblings over the life span are detailed. It is clear from these discussions that the sibling subsystem, like the family unit itself, provides a subcontext within which the stages of the life cycle and tasks are played out, influenced, and managed.

In some situations, however, these developmental tasks and the natural course of sibling relationships are disrupted due to crises and other problems in the situation. Those instances require more formalized services to manage developmental tasks and the family and sibling subsystem issues that may be involved. Both current and unresolved issues are often the focus. Chapter 4 discusses the need to expand the family treatment field (beyond traditional family therapy) for these purposes, while Chapters 5–11 describe specifically how to apply the family treatment perspective to sibling issues to effectively assess situations, intervene, and evaluate the work.

It must be acknowledged that family therapy has successfully spanned the boundaries between the various helping professions and family approaches by providing a common framework for treatment based on systems theory. By emphasizing systems theory, family therapy has moved these professions from the limitations of the medical model to a perspective that does not require judgements about blame. Both positive and negative situations are assumed to develop from multiple variables, and thus, change can take place in any part of a system. In family therapy, the process of change is best facilitated with the total system present, the family unit. This book expands the traditional focus of family therapy by recognizing that the independence and interdependence of the sibling subsystem in relation to the total unit is similar to that of the marital subsystem.

The benefits of this expanded field include increased opportunities to observe and enhance the functioning of families through attention to the sibling subsystem. The focus is on the sibling subsystem in relation to the family as well as in relation to systems outside the family, for example, in the workplace, school, and peer relationships. The chapters of this book illustrate how requirements of these external systems influence a sibship's or family's path to treatment. For children and youth, the school and church may be obvious paths to services while public housing associations and adult day care centers may be less obvious paths for adults and the elderly. Table 1.1 in Chapter 1 describes the developmental tasks for each stage, sibling issues, appropriate family treatment modalities, and typical settings or paths to treatment. Both these traditional and nontraditional paths to treatment and the natural points in the life cycle where sibling and individual issues arise highlight when and where services may be needed. Practitioners in these and other settings should develop creative and aggressive outreach activities in providing the expanded family treatment services.

This book can assist helping professionals in providing those services due to its' ecological and systems-based framework. The book was designed as a primary text for courses in family therapy and treatment, child welfare, mental health, and adult and life span development in graduate schools of social work, psychology, psychiatry, nursing, guidance counseling and human resources. It may also serve as a supplementary text for general practice courses in those disciplines as well as child and family specializations.

E.M.F.

ACKNOWLEDGMENTS

Considering who can benefit from this book and how has clarified in what ways writing the book has assisted me both professionally and personally. I am certainly more respectful and in awe of the power of sibling relationships throughout the life span. I thank my siblings, living and deceased, for our meaningful common history. My appreciation goes to Sadye Logan who reviewed and commented on parts of the manuscript, and to Nancie Palmer and Susana Carrizosa who assisted in researching the literature. Nancie Jenkins helped in conducting some of the research interviews which are the basis for the case studies included in this book. I am indebted to Kim Ray who completed many of the tables and illustrations in the book.

And I am most thankful to my family for their continuous and enthusiastic support.

E. M. F.

CONTENTS

	Page
Foreword: Joan Laird	vii
Preface and Acknowledgments	xi
Chapter 1. The Sibling Bond: An Introduction to the Social Network Experience	3

Part One: The Sibling Bond: Conceptual, Research, and Treatment Issues

Introduction	19
Chapter 2. The Sibling Bond in Childhood and Adolescence: Coping Patterns From a Strengths Perspective	21
Chapter 3. The Sibling Bond in Adulthood: Lifelong Adaptations in Close, Tenuous, and Alienated Relationships	47
Chapter 4. Siblings and Family Therapy: An Historical Perspective	73

Part Two: Approaches to Family Treatment for Resolving Sibling and Other Relationship Issues

Introduction	99
Chapter 5. Family Network Therapy to Enhance Young Siblings' Strategies for Coping with Racial Stress	101
Chapter 6. Combining Strategic Family and Sibling Therapy in Treatment for Blended Families	119
Chapter 7. Communication and Task Centered Family Treatment for Adolescent Sibling Loyalty and Community Violence Issues	137
Chapter 8. Family Group Work with Young Adults Who Have Sibling Control Issues	161
Chapter 9. Family Treatment with Individuals: ACOA's with Sibling Issues and Peer Conflicts in the Workplace	179
Chapter 10. Sibling Therapy for Intergenerational Caretaking Issues in Middle Adulthood	201

Chapter 11.	Cognitive-Behavioral Family Treatment and RET: Sibling Issues and Life Review in the Elderly	221
Epilogue	The Family Treatment Process: Why Evaluate?	239
Author Index		247
Subject Index		253

FAMILY TREATMENT
The Sibling Bond and Other Relationship Issues

*If I could hear my brothers' voices
perhaps they would say,
rejoice
we are not so far away
and all is well.*

From "The Living Heart"
by Edith M. Freeman

Chapter 1

THE SIBLING BOND:
AN INTRODUCTION TO THE
SOCIAL NETWORK EXPERIENCE

The purpose of this book is to explore an aspect of family life and relationships that has been addressed inadequately in the literature until recently: the sibling relationship and social network. One tendency has been to de-emphasize the importance of these relationships by viewing them only as a direct outcome of parent-child relationships. This tendency has obscured important information about the significant roles and autonomous activities that sibling subsystems perform (Bank and Kahn, 1982). Another trend has been to distort the nature of sibling relationships by concentrating on status variables such as birth order or on negative dynamics such as sibling rivalry. The failure to focus more wholistically on such relationships across the lifespan has led to lost opportunities to understand and utilize them more fully in family treatment and prevention (Riskin and Faunce, 1972; McKeever, 1983).

It is not clear how or why this pattern has developed in the literature or why it is now changing. One contributing factor to the changes may be the efforts within social work, psychology, and other helping professions to more effectively help clients resolve environmental problems (Nulman, 1983). This can be seen in the increasing emphasis on identifying risk and protective factors related to the policies and practices of large social systems (e.g., health, education, housing), the immediate neighborhood, social support networks, the extended family, and the immediate family including siblings. Siblings are now viewed as an important subsystem within the family and as a unique social support network. The emphasis on risk and protective factors helps to clarify factors in these networks and other areas that have either created/helped to maintain the problems or that can provide important resources for resolving them (Hawkins, Catalano, and Miller, 1992).

As part of the natural environment, the significant role of siblings across the lifespan has been documented through research (Mosatche, Brady, and Noberini, 1983). Sibling relationships provide individuals with their earliest experiences in social support networks. These relationships are unique in **how** they provide that introduction to social supports, the way they model parallel relationships and the handling of authority issues, and in their longevity across the lifespan (Freeman, 1989; Minuchin, 1974; Dunn, 1983; Goetting, 1986). What then is the natural history of such relationships as well as the process of growth and development that occurs within them? And what assumptions and theories are useful for understanding this naturally occurring phenomenon?

This chapter summarizes important philosophical assumptions and theories about sibling relationships, including what makes them unique in comparison to other family and social relationships. The natural history of sibling relationships is described to identify some of the common characteristics involved. Finally, the effects of normative issues and problems in the sibling subsystem on the members and on other relationships are discussed.

Overview of Sibling Relationships and Networks

Although sibling relationships are the focus of this book, those relationships should be viewed within the context of the family rather than in isolation. In this vein, McKeever (1983) indicates "sibships" serve significant functions and provide critical resources to individual members that are not addressed by other family relationships. This basic premise implys that, in the best circumstances, an intricate choreography takes place within the sibling subsystem that complements the dance within the family as a total system (Compher, 1984).

Philosophical Assumptions

The above premise also serves as a foundation for the following philosophical assumptions about the unique role of sibling relationships in the growth and development of individuals (Freeman, 1989; Bank and Kahn, 1975, 1982; Mostache et al., 1986; Dunn, 1983; Goetting, 1986; Cicirelli, 1980; Feldman, 1981):

1. Sibling relationships are a significant influence on all other relationships (e.g., friendships), because they are generally the indi-

vidual's introduction to parallel or lateral relationships and social networks.
2. There are unique qualities involved in sibling relationships that may not be totally present in other significant relationships, or that differ in terms of the timing and intensity in which they are experienced.
3. Particular positive and negative issues that may dominate early relationships within a sibling subsystem tend to be repeated and expanded on in those relationships during adulthood even though the developmental and family tasks around which those issues manifest themselves may be different over time.
4. There are a series of common and predictable issues that confront members of sibling subsystems across diverse family circumstances, while there are different issues that confront those in particular circumstances (e.g., the family with an alcoholic member or the family in which one child is a replacement for another sibling).
5. In families in which there are three or more children, one sibling relationship may have greater impact on the life of each child than the other relationships—either a primarily positive or negative influence during childhood and/or adulthood.
6. In some circumstances involving only children, where there is a significant age difference between siblings, or where there is a loss of sibling contact, those children may attempt to simulate sibling relationships or networks with alternative siblings in terms of the issues addressed and the continuity of those relationships over time.
7. One primary source of modeling for sibling relationships may be the parents' families-of-origin (their sibling relationships). Issues in the current generation may interact with intergenerational issues and then be passed down to the next generation through family "secrets," rules, myths, ghosts, and traditions.

These assumptions provide the underpinnings for the discussions about sibling relationships in different chapters throughout this book. They raise other questions yet to be researched and documented, for instance, whether sibling relationships in childhood can predict the nature of those relationships in adulthood and what is the context in which sibling relationships develop mostly positive or negative qualities?

An explanatory model is needed to frame these assumptions and questions about sibling relationships.

A Conceptual Framework

Figure 1.1 illustrates the conceptual framework for clarifying sibling relationships based on family systems theory and an ecological perspective. As noted by Hartman and Laird (1983), such a theoretical approach helps to keep "... an eye fixed on the total family system in context" (p. ix). Furthermore, this approach emphasizes strengths, coping, and resiliency within a developmental framework that considers individual, sibling, and family life cycle developmental phases and the quality of the match or lack of match between needs and resources (Mostache et al., 1986; Rhodes, 1980; Anthony, 1987; Germain, 1979). Movement within the framework is circular rather than linear, with the flow between significant factors, manifestations in childhood/youth, and manifestations in adulthood going in multiple directions. In addition to systems theory, role, developmental, communications, crisis, and stress/coping theories are part of this framework (Davis, 1986; Bloom, 1985; Nelson, 1986; Garrison and Weber, 1981; Pearlin, 1981; Tolman and Rose, 1985).

Some important concepts are integral to this conceptual framework and need to be defined clearly. For instance, in terms of significant factors, family structure refers to how a family organizes itself related to subsystems and boundaries (Goldenberg and Goldenberg, 1984). Boundaries reflect degrees of distance or closeness between family members, between subsystems within the family (e.g., the parental and sibling subsystems), and between the family and its' external relationships. Another important quality of boundaries is the degree of permeability or flexibility as needed. Does the outer boundary permit outsiders to enter the family system and members to invest in relationships outside the family as well as utilize necessary environmental resources (Hepworth and Larson, 1986)? Does the sibling subsystem boundary protect its members' autonomous functions from unwarranted input by others? Hartman and Laird (1983) note "It is important that children have the opportunity to experiment in this laboratory (this natural social network) without undue adult interference" (p. 89).

According to Hartman (1985), relationships are the quality of emotional connections between family members that may be either supportive, strained, or emotionally charged in a negative way. Relationships are

Significant Factors	Manifestations in Childhood and Adolescence	Manifestations in Adulthood
Identity (individual, sibship, family, ethnic)	*Coping Patterns* (concentrated individually or deployed throughout the sibling social network)	*Current Adult to Adult Family-of-Origin Relationships/ Communications Patterns* (with parents, siblings, extended family members).
Structure (subsystems: marital, parental, sibling, extended family)	*Level of Resiliency* (individual, sibship network, or family unit)	*Level of Differentiation/ Individuation* (from parents, and within the sibship)
Functions (roles and relationships: parent-child, sibling to sibling, parent to parent).	*Issues Being Addressed* (in each relationship: dyads, coalitions, subsystems, networks)	*Other Significant Social Networks/Relationships* (as influenced by sibling relationships).
Resources (strengths and other assets: informal and formal)	*Developmental Transitions/ Tasks* (individual, sibling, family stages)	*Internal Well Being* (the individual's life satisfaction, self-esteem, adequacy of coping)
	Other Family Transitions, Disruptions, and Crises	*On-going Developmental Task Accomplishments* (individual as well as sibling networks, coalitions, and dyads)

Figure 1.1. Conceptual Framework for Sibling Relationships and Social Networks

influenced by the different subsystems within the family: non-nurturing relationships between parents and children may encourage closer relationships within the sibling subsystem and the adoption of a parent substitute role by one member of that subsystem. This role and other family roles involve behaviors that are prescribed by the family or sibling subsystem for members occupying a designated status and include specific rights and obligations. Roles within the family and sibling subsystem are often generalized for good or ill to relationships in other circumstances such as the workplace (Freeman, 1989). An informal resource or strength of the family is the ability to respond positively to differences in needs and skills among siblings, while a formal environmental resource might be the availability of medical or counseling services.

In addition to these significant factors, some of the early manifestations illustrated in the conceptual framework need further discussion (see Figure 1.1). Resiliency involves the ability to cope with adversity by withdrawing or "hibernating" strategically and then recovering or "bouncing back" in order to do creative problem-solving (Felsman and Vaillant, 1987; Taylor, 1983; Work and Cowen, 1988). Anthony (1987) has made an important distinction between resiliency at a survival level (just maintaining oneself) and thriving (continued growth and development beyond all expectations given the existing barriers). Resiliency and coping can be a function of individual, sibling subsystem, or family system variables.

The level of resiliency may be reflected in the issues that are addressed in a relationship and how they are addressed. Freeman (1989) defines issues as the content and intensity of what individuals in a relationship focus on, the areas they agree or disagree on either overtly or covertly. Issues are discussed in more detail in the next section of this chapter. Family dysruptions represent risks as well as opportunities for growth that stress the family unit beyond the "normal" requirements and upset the risk and protective factor balance. As an example, dysruptions can involve chronic conditions (e.g., family alcoholism, child sexual abuse, or sibling violence) and mismanaged developmental or other transitions (teenage pregnancy as a premature role assumption or a lack of support for mourning the loss of a sibling).

Similar to these childhood and adolescent manifestations related to the conceptual framework, outcomes in adulthood are reflected in a variety of ways (see Figure 1.1). The level of differentiation refers to individuation from parents **and** the sibling subsystem, with the level of differentiation from the one often influencing that process with the other. Basically, this process results in the ability to maintain a positive emotional connection in these relationships while developing a separate identity and life, both emotionally and physically (Bowen, 1974; Turrini, Ruskin, and Edward, 1981). Addressing differentiation and other developmental tasks can be accomplished by using sibling networks and coalitions. The handling of underlying issues can be facilitated as well. For instance, a sibling caretaking unit is needed during adulthood to handle the needs of aging parents and to address the issue of sibling loyalty (Mostache et al., 1986). This period and other developmental transitions over the lifespan are important for understanding the natural processes involved in sibling relationships.

The Natural History of Sibling Relationships

How does the sibling subsystem develop and how is it maintained in view of the assumptions and conceptual framework presented in the previous section? The concepts of circularity and multiple determinants from family systems theory are relevant for answering these questions. The common phenomena that occur over the life course within this subsystem do not involve a particular sequence or order nor do they occur in all sibling relationships. It can be assumed that when, how, and in what order these events occur depends on multiple variables that interact and make each situation somewhat unique. More specifically, these aspects of sibling relationships are influenced by individual, familial, and external factors (outside the family). Examples include personality characteristics, family strengths and dysruptions, social supports, and role modeling by peers and key adults in other systems as well as factors related to the sibling subsystem itself. Figure 1.2 reflects examples of some of the common phenomena that occur in the natural history of different sibling relationships (Scarr and Grajek, 1982; Goetting, 1986; Mostache et al., 1983).

Along with the natural history of relationships between brothers and sisters, certain normative issues are reflected in the focus and content of their interactions. These issues may be the primary focus during each stage of the sibling life cycle or they may vary during different stages based on which issues are in the foreground and which are in the background. For example, loyalty may be an issue during the young years and in middle age (when the sibling caretaking unit is usually formed), but affective perspectives may be the foreground issue during adulthood when sibling contacts are mostly voluntary (see Chapter 3 for a discussion on sibling solidarity) (Cicirelli, 1985; Mostache et al., 1983). The issues included in Figure 1.2 are not exhaustive; they represent some examples of areas on which siblings may focus their relationships over time. Nor does this list include the normative or problematic consequences that can develop during the course of handling such issues.

Natural History (of the development & maintenance of the sibling subsystem network)	Normative Issues/Problems (that stress and/or strengthen the sibling subsystem/network)
Attachment	Handling of Diversity in the Subsystem: age, gender, intellectual levels, special gifts/disabilities, ethnicity, identity, commitments, and lifestyles.
Secondary Bonding	
Subsystem Identity Development (through boundary clarification)	Developing Patterns in Affective Perspectives (friendliness and nonfriendliness toward one another).
	Deciding How to Allocate Resources: collaboration, compromise, competition.
Development of Reciprocal and Complementary Roles from Imitation to Role Modeling	Testing Loyalties and Supports
	Clarifying Areas of Value Consensus and Conflicts
Social Network Development and Maintenance	Establishing Patterns in Handling Transitions (individuation, separation, generativity, life review)
Solidarity (from maintaining contact to making a personal choice)	Handling Acculturation Experiences/Conflicts
Autonomous Subsystem Functions/Patterns	Responding to Subsystem Boundary Infringements (unity versus divisiveness experiences)
Differentiation	

Figure 1.2. Sibling Relationships & Subsystems

The Consequences of How Sibling Issues are Managed

It is important for helping professionals to distinguish between "normative" sibling relationships that involve typical conflicts and pressures and those relationships in which more severe, chronic problems have developed. In both types of circumstances, the issues of concern and how they are managed help to determine coping patterns and the sense of internal well being that were identified in the conceptual framework (see Figure 1.1). Over the natural history of such relationships the management and consequences of issues provide opportunities for individual growth and for the development of a sibling support network.

The impact of how issues are managed may be observable in sibling, parental, and other significant relationships under normal and problematic circumstances (a discussion on the historical context for sibling relationships in both types of circumstances can be found in Chapters 2 and 3, while Chapter 4 is focused on that context specifically related to family therapy).

Normative Consequences

As noted in Figure 1.2, the consequences of normative issues and problems can lead ultimately to the development and strengthening of the sibling social network and other relationships. Learning to manage diversity within the sibling subsystem is one example. Having a developmentally disabled child in the family can result in other siblings learning to cope more effectively with stress (the stress can result from parents focusing too much attention on the needs of the one child and/or from the negative reactions of peers) (Ornic, Friedrich, and Greenberg, 1983). The brothers and sisters can grow also from helping their siblings to learn the activities of daily living as well as appropriate ways to interact socially (Berkovic, 1986; Dunn, 1983). Acquiring these competencies related to diversity can enhance the subsystem's function as a social network, thus contributing to it's growth along with that of the individual members (Dunn and Kendrick, 1981; Freeman and Palmer, 1989).

Another type of consequence is illustrated when changes in siblings' relationships with each other affect their relationships outside the subsystem. In terms of systems theory, such consequences must be related to the concept of circularity (where these factors influence each other) rather than to a one-to-one cause and effect process. The sibling social network's continuing growth may change the overall functioning of the family, enabling the parents to more effectively allocate the unit's psychological, financial, and other resources to all the siblings.

Another possible effect is the unit may be able to accept it's identity as a family with a disabled child through reframing the situation as an opportunity for growth. The reframing process can encourage siblings to become involved positively in the development of the disabled member and the reverse. The family can then mourn the loss of the members' expectations that this child would be "normal" (Lindsey and Stewart, 1989; Wilson, Blacher, and Baker, 1989). Other types of relationships can be affected as well. For instance, learning from the positive effects of diversity within the sibling subsystem increases the likelihood that this learning will be generalized to peers (Pepler, Corter, and Abramovitch, 1982; Greenfield and Weatherley, 1986), co-workers (Freeman and Palmer, 1989), and love relationships (Abend, 1984).

Problematic Consequences

More serious consequences can develop when the natural history of sibling relationships is disrupted by either internal or external factors. The development of sibling rivalry and/or violence are examples of internal factors (although external variables can affect these factors as well). An example of an external factor is when intergenerational coalitions develop (usually between one parent and child) to fill the gap from power differentials or a lack of intimacy between the parents. Table 1.1 includes some of the problematic consequences that are experienced in sibling relationships as well as developmental tasks and sibling issues that may be affected. The most appropriate treatment modalities for the different issues are also included. Those issues and treatment modalities will be discussed throughout the other chapters in this book to clarify the dynamics involved.

In these more serious situations, the social network **and** the subsystem's autonomy may be negatively affected and continue to create problems for the individual and subsystem across the lifespan (Bank and Kahn, 1975; Kahn and Bank, 1981; Goetting, 1986; Fishbein, 1981):

1. The social network is affected: Differentiation within the subsystem is difficult because attachment has not occurred and identity (individual and collective) cannot be addressed adequately. The members may not be able to help each other cope with these problems or they may exaccerbate each others' problems in this area through modeling, interference, or sibling coalitions formed to work against other children in the family. Later developmental tasks that require bonding/differentiation may be difficult for the person to accomplish individually, as part of the subsystem, or in other relationships as a result (see Chapters 6 and 9 of this book).
2. The autonomous activities of the subsystem are affected: Opportunities to teach/learn the rules about fair play, reciprocity, complementarity, how to handle authority issues, and giving reflected self-appraisal for identity development are reduced or eliminated. These autonomous functions need to be performed in reciprocal relationships such as those between siblings. If they are not, the

Table 1.1. Life Span Perspective on Sibling Issues and Family Treatment.

Age Range	Developmental Tasks	Sibling Issues	Family Treatment: Appropriate Modalities	Typical Practice Settings for Service Delivery
4–7 years mid/late childhood (chapter 5)	Identity (race, gender) Socialization Learn to play and interact in groups	Sibling acculturation Sibling bond	Family Network therapy Sibling therapy	Public and private schools Mental health/child guidance agencies
8–12 years Latency (Chapter 6)	Identity Trust Individuation	Sibling coalitions Sibling resiliency Sibling support networks	Sibling therapy Family therapy Sibling-oriented individual therapy	Child welfare agencies Family preservation programs Family Service agencies
13–19 years Adolescence (Chapter 7)	Separation/leaving family-of-origin home Values clarification/consolidation Friendship/loyalty	Sibling loyalty/value consensus Sibling achievement orientation Survivor guilt	Multiple family groups	Public Housing Associations Neighborhood/community organizations (e.g. crime watch)

Age/Stage	Developmental Tasks	Sibling Tasks	Intervention Modalities	Delivery Systems
20–25 years Young adulthood (Chapter 8)	Establish/maintain separate household Establish long term committed relationship	Sibling control/differentiation Sibling solidarity/de-identification	Multiple sibling groups Sibling-oriented groups	Mental Health Centers (prevention & treatment) Family Service Agencies Career Counseling programs Employee Assistance programs
26–39 years Adulthood (Chapter 9)	Career/work management Establish a family with or without children Consolidate lifestyle choices	Sibling rivalry Sibling cut-offs	Couple therapy	Employee Assistance programs Substance Abuse Treatment Programs Eating Disorder Clinics
40–55 years Midlife (Chapter 10)	Generativity Acceptance of one's biological/psychological/social changes	Sibling bond Sibling role proscriptions	Sibling therapy (sibling care-taking unit)	Hospitals Adult Day Care Centers Home Health Care agencies
56 and above Old age (Chapter 11)	Accept one's own mortality Struggle with the meaning of one's experiences (life review)	Shared reminiscence Final resolution of sibling rivalry/solidarity	Sibling therapy Couple therapy Family Network therapy	Nursing Homes Senior Citizen Housing Employee Assistance Programs

members lack these competencies unless an alternative subsystem is developed (peers, cousins, or "fictive"-nonblood kin) (see Chapters 6, 7, and 8 of this book).

In summary, serious problems and consequences that affect sibling relationships will continue or be generalized to other significant relationships unless they are resolved. Resolution may come through self-help efforts or formal counseling. The earlier such efforts occur, the more growth opportunities will be available from an ecological and life span perspective. As noted by Bank and Kahn (1975), "Siblings continue to influence one another even when they are not physically together and even when they have had little or no communication" over time (p. 326).

Conclusion

The purpose of this introductory chapter has been to clarify how sibling relationships are important and yet different from other familial and social relationships. Although sibships perform many autonomous functions (such as reciprocal interactions) that are not handled with the same timing and intensity in other relationships, perhaps the subsystem's most important role is as a social network. Over the natural course of sibling relationships, the network develops from the point of attachment and bonding to the accomplishment of development tasks such as individuation during childhood and youth and the shared life review in old age. In support of this assumption, Goetting (1986) concluded that "Some siblingship tasks are constant, weaving threads of consistency from birth to death, while others stand out as idiosyncratic to the context of the particular stage of the life cycle" (p. 703).

Some aspects of siblings' support networks are constant too under normal conditions. Those aspects, such as bonding and solidarity, are useful for coping with developmental transitions such as identity, individuation, and generativity. If the transitions can be coped with through individual and subsystem resources, they can provide opportunities for growth. Examples include the death of a sibling, the birth of a disabled sibling, ethnic identity conflicts between brothers and sisters, or sibling competition.

Other stresses are more serious or the necessary resources may not be available for coping. Sibling bonding and solidarity may not occur or may be diminished in those situations. Family violence, sibling incest, significant control issues, and sibling rivalry are some examples of serious and chronic problems that can prevent the development of the siblings' social network. The negative impact on later relationships and social networks can be assumed, but further research and practice analogs are needed to document this assumption. As a step in that direction, the other chapters in this book present and address some important questions related to this area.

REFERENCES

Abend, S. (1984). Sibling love and object choice. *Psychoanalytic Quarterly, LIII,* 425–430.

Anthony, E.J. (1987). Risk, vulnerability, and resilience: An overview. In E.J. Anthony and B.J. Cohler (Eds.), *The invulnerable child* (3–48). New York: Guilford Press.

Bank, S. and Kahn, M. (1982). *The sibling bond.* New York: Basic Books.

Bank, S. and Kahn, M.D. (1975). Sisterhood-brotherhood is powerful: Sibling subsystems and family therapy. *Family Process, 14,* 311–337.

Berkovic, S. (1986). Exploring the differences: A support group for brothers and sisters of children with intellectual disabilities. *Australian Social Work, 39,* 27–30.

Bloom, M. (1985). *Life span development: Bases for preventive and interventive helping* (Second Edition). New York: Macmillan.

Bowen, M. (1974). A family systems approach to alcoholism. *Addictions, 21,* 3–4.

Cicirelli, V.G. (1985). The role of siblings as family caregivers. In W.J. Sauer and R.T. Coward (Eds.), *Social support networks and care of the elderly* (93–107). New York: Springer.

Cicirelli, V.G. (1980). Sibling relationships in adulthood: A life span perspective. In Leonard W. Poon (Ed.), *Aging in the 1980's* (455–462). Washington, DC: American Psychological Association.

Compher, J.V. (1984). The dance within the family system. *Social Work, 29,* 361–365.

Davis, L.V. (1986). Role theory. In F.J. Turner (Ed.), *Social work treatment: Interlocking theoretical approaches* (541–563). New York: Free Press.

Dunn, J. (1983). Sibling relationships in early childhood. *Child Development, 54,* 787–811.

Dunn, J. and Kendrick, C. (1981). Social behavior of young siblings in the family context: Differences between same-sex and different-sex dyads. *Child Development, 52,* 1265–1273.

Feldman, G.C. (1981). Three's company: Family therapy with only-child families. *Journal of Marital and Family Therapy, 7,* 43–46.

Felsman, J.K. and Vaillant, G.E. (1987). Resilient children as adults: A 40-year study. In E.J. Anthony and B.J. Cohler (Eds.), *The invulnerable child* (289–313). New York: Guilford Press.

Fishbein, H.D. (1981). Sibling set configuration and family dysfunction. *The Family Process, 20,* 311–318.

Freeman, E.M. (1989). Adult children of alcoholics: Study of parental, sibling, and work relationships. Paper presented at the 34th Institute on the Prevention and Treatment of Alcoholism. Pontault-Combault, France: International Council on Alcohol and Addictions.

Freeman, E.M. and Palmer, N. (1989). Reconceptualizing dynamics in the alcoholic family: A secondary study in sibling relationships. Research report. Lawrence, KS: University of Kansas School of Social Welfare.

Garrison, C. and Weber, J. (1981). Family crisis intervention using multiple impact therapy. *Social Casework, 62,* 585-593.

Germain, C.B. (1979). Ecology and social work. In C.B. Germain (Ed.), *Social work practice: People and environments* (1-22). New York: Columbia University Press.

Goldenberg, I. and Goldenberg, H. (1984). *Family therapy: An overview* (Second Edition). Belmont, CA: Wadsworth.

Goetting, A. (1986). The development tasks of siblingships over the life cycle. *Journal of Marriage and The Family, 48,* 703-714.

Greenfield, G. and Weatherley, D. (1986). Sex-of-sibling effects on opposite and same-sex friendships. *Psychological Reports, 59,* 67-70.

Hartman, A. (1985). Summing up. In S. Sims, A. Hartman, and E. Saalberg (Eds.), *Empowering the Black Family.* Ann Arbor: University of Michigan School of Social Work.

Hartman, A. and Laird, J. (1983). *Family-centered social work practice.* New York: Free Press.

Hawkins, J.D., Catalano, R.F., and Miller, J.Y. (1992). Risk and protective factors for alcohol and other drug problems in adolescence and early adulthood: Implications for substance abuse prevention. *Planning for the future of prevention in Washington state.* Olympia: Washington Division of Substance Abuse.

Hepworth, D. and Larson, M. (1986). *Direct social work practice.* Chicago: Dorsey Press.

Kahn, M.D. and Bank, S. (1981). In pursuit of sisterhood: Adult siblings as a resource for combined individual and family therapy. *The Family Process, 20,* 85-95.

Lindsey, J.D. and Stewart, D.A. (1989). The guardian minority: Siblings of children with mental retardation. *Education and Training in Mental Retardation, 24,* 291-296.

McKeever, P. (1983). Siblings of chronically ill children: A literature review with implications for research and practice. *American Journal of Orthopsychiatry, 53,* 209-218.

Minuchin, S. (1974). *Families and family therapy.* Cambridge, MA: Harvard University Press.

Mosatche, H., Brady, E., and Noberini, M.R. (1983). A retrospective life span study of the closest sibling relationship. *The Journal of Psychology, 113,* 237-243.

Ornic, K., Friedrich, W.N., and Greenberg, M.T. (1983). Adaptation of families with mentally retarded children: A model of stress, coping, and family ecology. *American Journal of Mental Deficiency, 88,* 125-138.

Nelson, J.C. (1986). Communication theory and social work treatment. In F.J. Turner (Ed.), *Social work treatment: Interlocking theoretical approaches* (219–244). New York: Free Press.

Nulman, E. (1983). Family therapy and advocacy: Directions for the future. *Social Work, 28,* 19–23.

Pearlin, L. (1981). The stress process. *Journal of Health and Social Behavior, 22,* 337–356.

Pepler, D., Corter, C., and Abramovitch, R. (1982). Social relations among children: Siblings and peers. In K. Rubin and H. Ross (Eds.), *Peer relationships and social skills in childhood.* New York: Springer-Verlag.

Rhodes, S.L. (1980). A developmental approach to the life cycle of the family. In M. Bloom (Ed.), *Life span development: Bases for preventive and interventive helping.* New York: Macmillan.

Riskin, J.M. and Faunce, E.E. (1972). An evaluative review of family interaction research. *Family Process, 11,* 365–455.

Scarr, S. and Grajek, S. (1982). Similarities and differences among siblings. In M.E. Lamb and B. Sutton-Smith (Eds.), *Sibling relationships: Their nature and significance across the life span* (223–241). Hillsdale, N.J.: Erlbaum.

Taylor, S.E. (1983). Adjustment to threatening events: A theory of cognitive adaptation. *American Psychologist, 21,* 1161–1173.

Tolman, R. and Rose, S.D. (1985). Coping with stress. A multimodel approach. *Social Work, 30,* 151–158.

Turrini, P., Ruskin, N. and Edward, J. (1981). Separation-individuation: Theory and application. New York: Gardner Press.

Wilson, J., Blacher, J., and Baker, B.L. (1989). Siblings of children with severe handicaps. *Mental Retardation, 27,* 167–173.

Work, W.C. and Cowen, E.L. (1988). Resilient children, psychological wellness, and primary prevention. *American Journal of Community Psychology, 16,* 591–605.

PART I

THE SIBLING BOND: CONCEPTUAL, RESEARCH, AND TREATMENT ISSUES

The discussion in Chapter 1 on the sibling subsystem as the individual's introduction to social support networks involves an emphasis on resource sharing and strengths. This emphasis from Chapter 1 is reflected throughout the three chapters in Part I of this book. Chapter 2 is focused on research from the literature on sibling relationships during childhood and adolescence, while Chapter 3 addresses those relationships during adulthood. The life span developmental perspective in these chapters makes it possible to trace the common and unique themes and tasks that occur in sibling relationships through different stages of development.

Those two chapters also highlight what is known about resiliency and coping from the research literature, and how that knowledge clarifies both nurturing and non-nurturing aspects of the sibling bond. This unique bond is discussed within the context of other family relationships and life events highlighted in these chapters, particularly in the analysis of childhood and adolescence in Chapter 2. The author's original research on sibling relationships is included in the two chapters to further clarify how this process of coping and sibling dynamics tend to vary in a range of different circumstances over the life cycle.

Chapter 3 summarizes how sibling relationships have been addressed in the family therapy literature historically and presently. The benefits as well as the problems and gaps in that literature are identified in the chapter. This initial review and analysis of the literature lay a foundation for the second part of the chapter. In that section, the author recommends a broadening of the current family therapy practice area to a family treatment field. The broader field encompasses knowledge about sibling relationships within and outside the family, and as an autonomous subsystem with independent and interdependent functions.

Chapter 2

THE SIBLING BOND IN CHILDHOOD AND ADOLESCENCE: COPING PATTERNS FROM A STRENGTHS PERSPECTIVE

Sibling relationships have been ignored in the past as a significant factor in family life. Only gradually have researchers developed an awareness of the importance of such relationships. Bank & Kahn (1975), for example, attribute some aspects of individual development and family interactions to "autonomous activities within the sibling subsystem" (p. 311). A focus on such activities within adult sibling relationships can help to identify additional areas of exploration and more effective treatment strategies for resolving family problems.

Exploring such relationships during childhood and adolescence may be even more promising. Knowledge of early life experiences might highlight the following: (1) differences between the typical stresses and more severe problems which siblings experience as part of their developing relationships with each other, and (2) sources of effective and ineffective coping within sibling relationships in regard to family stresses. Thus, opportunities for prevention and early intervention may develop from new knowledge about sibling relationships in childhood and adolescence.

Often, however, when the needs of children and youth are addressed, the tendency is to focus on pathology. The emerging literature on sibling relationships and children in general is more useful because it highlights some of the positive coping patterns and resiliency that exist within this population. That emphasis encourages a more strengths-oriented approach to family treatment and prevention services for young people.

The current chapter reviews some of the historical and theoretical issues involved in this more positive approach to general functioning in childhood. It includes also a summary of the research literature on sibling relationships along with an analysis of how the coping and resiliency literature is applicable to those relationships. The author's retrospective research on childhood and adolescent sibling relationships is described within this context of resiliency and strengths. Finally, some implications are drawn from this discussion for prevention activities related to the field of family treatment.

The Historical, Social, and Theoretical Context: Assumptions About General Functioning in Childhood

As noted previously, much of the literature on childhood functioning does not take into account the influence of sibling relationships. The focus has been on normative development, natural stresses, pathology, traumatic events, dysruptions and, more recently, on positive coping patterns and resiliency. A brief review of these areas will illustrate some of the major conceptual issues embedded in this literature.

Normative Development/Natural Stresses

Most of the literature on normative experiences has been influenced by developmental and personality theories. These theories and concepts emphasize the importance of early primary relationships and the connections between developmental tasks at each stage. For instance, Bowlby (1977) describes attachment as "a way of conceptualizing the propensity of human beings to make strong affectional bonds to particular others" (p. 201). The benefits of attachment for children include validation and support, nurturing, socialization, role modeling, and the development of relational skills. Freudian theory indicates that attachment occurs both from child to parent(s) and from parent(s) to child. Parental attachment comes from being needed and a sense of kinship, while the child's attachment evolves from the parents' authority and their positive and nurturing responses in meeting the child's essential needs (Strean, 1986).

An underlying assumption is that mostly positive experiences with early parent-child attachment result in strong bonding. Such experiences enhance childhood, adolescent, and adult functioning by helping the individual to develop a capacity for "good" bonding in other relationships. Initially, good bonding occurs when the individual feels close to and is valued by parents and yet, by a particular stage of early development, is able to separate **physically** from the parents with minimum anxiety (Bowlby, 1977). The individual only develops that ability, however, after building a gradual tolerance for and way of coping with natural separations. Examples of early separations involve the parent leaving the room temporarily or the child being left with other caretakers for brief periods.

The ability to separate physically from primary attachment figures has implications for on-going individuation. Individuation is the ability to understand the self as an **emotionally** separate individual who has, nevertheless, an ongoing and positive connection with loved ones (Bowlby, 1977). In an expansion of attachment theory, siblings may be viewed as important persons with whom the child learns to "share" parental attention and love. They also can be a source of secondary bonding by meeting other essential needs such as acceptance in what are usually the individual's first experiences with parallel relationships.

In addition to these concepts from Bowlby (1977) and Freudian (Strean, 1986) theory, other relevant theories focus on normative development and stresses. They address cognitive development (Piaget, 1952), the interaction of family life cycle stages and individual development (Rhodes, 1980), or the conflicting developmental tasks and themes for each stage (Erikson, 1985).

For instance, Erikson's (1985) stage of industry versus inferiority emphasizes the development of competence. This stage involves the school age child being able "to comprehend the tool world of his culture . . . and receive systematic instruction of some kind . . . " If competence does not occur, the danger is in the child "developing a sense of inadequacy and despair about his skill or his status among his tool partners" . . . and being "discouraged from further learning" (p. 39). A child's first tool partners tend to be siblings or peers in the immediate neighborhood. Thus, this socially decisive stage lays the foundation for a hierarchy of future learning experiences. Here again, the early and significant role of siblings in normative development is apparent in terms of Erikson's (1985) theory and those of other developmental theorists.

Pathology, Traumatic Events, and Dysruptions

Against this backdrop of normative development, some other researchers and authors have described the general functioning of children under stressful family and environmental conditions. This literature is useful because it attempts to explain factors that interfere with normative development during childhood. Unfortunately, much of this literature has been characterized by an emphasis on problems alone, without a focus on the positive aspects of adaptation. It utilizes mostly negative concepts and theories to explain the conditions involved. Brett (1988) indicates that the "psychopathology assumption implicit in the crisis/stress paradigm means that the focus of most of the studies in this category ... is on ... maladjustment rather than adjustment" (p. 45).

Many of those authors assume that childrens' maladjustments begin as early efforts to cope adaptively with the stresses of daily living. One example of this type of stress is a failed early attachment experience between the child and the parent(s). Thus, Bowlby's (1977) attachment theory summarized in the previous section has been applied also to understanding the effects of stressful family conditions. This author assumes there are "many forms of emotional distress and personality disturbances, including anxiety, anger, depression, and emotional detachment, to which unwilling separation and loss give rise" (p. 201). In such circumstances, children often struggle to please parents in ways that conflict with their needs in order to seek approval, maintain attachment, and manage rejection anxiety. For example, some become parentified children who perform required adult tasks in a family, such as caretaking of younger children, prior to a point when they are able to manage such tasks emotionally.

In addition to failed bonding experiences and premature role transitions, this literature identifies a number of other traumatic events and dysruptions that can have negative consequences for children. Examples include a parental psychosis or other mental disability, death or chronic illness of a parent or sibling, emotional abuse, family violence, out of home placements, and parental separation and divorce (Balk, 1990; Kritsberg, 1986; Hegar, 1988) (see Chapter 1 for a discussion of a conceptual framework on sibling relationships from a systems perspective involving these types of family life events). Balk (1990) states that parental figures in these situations may not be predictable in nurturing a child or in meeting his or her basic needs. Such experiences may teach children that their needs are of a lesser priority within the family unit.

As a result, many youngsters in these situations can develop adaptive coping mechanisms that help them to negotiate and survive their stressful family system. These ways of coping often become maladaptive when children generalize them to other systems such as the school or neighborhood (Freeman and Dyer, in press). For instance, some authors have indicated that family violence may lead a child to adopt aggressive behavior towards others that is consistent with family patterns. But those responses are generally labeled as acting out behaviors and barriers to a positive school adjustment (Freeman and Pennekamp, 1988).

Two other types of family dysruptions cited in this literature are receiving increased attention currently due to their negative impact on childhood functioning and development. The sexual abuse literature draws upon family systems theory to clarify how the developmental task of individuation is discouraged in these families in order to initiate the abuse and maintain the "family secret." In these circumstances, not only are the child's basic needs not attended to (e.g., the need for safety and the need for trusting parental relationships), but the child is also exploited sexually and emotionally. These family patterns are highlighted in the literature without equal focus on the sources and types of positive coping patterns that allow children to survive such experiences (Finkelhor, 1984).

A similar emphasis in the literature on parental alcoholism is reflected in Wegscheider's (1981) conclusion that "every alcoholic family is in severe stress... they evidence all the characteristics of the unhealthy family" (p. 55). Furthermore, Black (1981) labels as dysfunctional those roles that children develop to cope with the alcoholic's family rules of "don't talk, don't feel, don't trust." For example, the role of family hero means pretending to outsiders that the family is functional, excelling in school to mask the pain, and not asking for support from others (Black, 1981). However, the possibility that these adaptations have positive functions as well as negative ones has seldom been explored (Kritsberg, 1986).

In addition to its emphasis on the negative consequences of family dysruptions, this literature contains many examples of linear thinking and cause and effect analyses. A systemic explanation is more useful for understanding the family and sibling process in these troubled circumstances. This perspective helps to clarify how each factor influences and is influenced by others. Moreover, the process by which complementary and noncomplementary family roles are assumed by siblings and the occurence of other sibling dynamics has not been explored sufficiently in this literature (Freeman, 1989). It is not clear whether these roles and dynamics are expressions of individual personality and ability in children and/or part of a collaborative effort within the sibling subsystem (Goetting, 1986) (see Chapter 1 on a conceptual framework for sibling and other family relationships).

Coping and Resiliency in Childhood

In contrast to the above literature on family dysruptions, much of the literature on coping and resiliency is more recent. This literature was written in the last ten to fifteen years based on longitudinal adaptation and risk research. Such research focuses on children who survive the most adverse conditions while also developing positive coping abilities. Although the coping literature uses some of the same concepts as the literature in the previous section, it differs in two important ways. First, the coping literature developed when researchers shifted their attention to findings that were **not** consistent with a pathology perspective. They began to explore unanticipated subsamples of invulnerable children (6 to 12%) in retrospective and prospective studies involving children of parents with psychoses and other mental disorders.

Secondly, new and more positive concepts were developed by those researchers to describe the lack of clinical vulnerability in these children (Anthony, 1987; Cowen, 1988; & Flach, 1988). The concepts of invulnerability, coping, adaptation, competence, and resiliency have been used interchangeably by many researchers to describe the common characteristics in resilient children and some interesting variations. These concepts are drawn from ego psychology, and cognitive, stress, and psychoanalytic theories.

Common Characteristics of Resilient Children. Anthony (1987) noted that "the resilient child is characterized by sound normal defenses, a wide range of coping skills, many available competencies, constructive and even creative capacities that provide imaginative ways of dealing with frightening realities—and an inherent robustness that enables him to generate psychoimmunity" (p. 148). This "innoculation" effect develops when these children become "habituated to repeated threats" (Anthony, 1987, p. 148). As a result of this effect, they are good in coping and they manifest a high degree of competence in problem solving.

Some of their common characteristics include an ability to recover from transient setbacks and the availability of adult models of resilience who can provide a strong support system. When under stress, for example, these children are prepared to retreat for awhile to safety and to take time out to recuperate. They use a combination of self-comforting and self-soothing devices to "ride out" traumatic experiences, and often use fantasy to tolerate and filter out some of the family dysruptions described in the previous section (Cowen, 1988; Murphy & Moriarty, 1976; Taylor,

1983). The results include, according to Murphy & Moriarty (1976), good feelings about themselves (a healthy narcissism) and good insights into interpersonal situations. They also tend to be flexible in regard to the means and ends of problem-solving, can translate ideas into action, and can be original and creative in their resistance to the negative effects of stress.

Variations in the Patterns of Resilient Children. While these similarities in coping do exist, the patterns of coping and the types of competence developed by resilient children vary widely. The literature makes distinctions between survivors and thrivers among resilient children. Anthony (1987) indicates that constructive competence is used by "survivors" to do practical and concrete problem-solving. A down-to-earth approach is used to accomplish tasks which leads to a sense of efficacy and self-confidence. These children are able to organize, actively plan, and persist in efforts to bring a situation to a successful resolution. On the other hand, some children develop creative competence which allows them to "thrive" or to go beyond the situation or methods at hand (Anthony, 1987). These children are able to move from the practical to the abstract in order to solve problems inside their heads. This ability broadens their tools for reducing the threat of a situation and either avoiding the tension or developing alternative ways to cope with it.

Anthony (1987) has also developed a typology to clarify differences among resilient and invulnerable children who fit the following categories:

1. **Invulncrable/Sociopathic:** Often they are uninvolved with the world, their estrangement means the element of intimacy is missing.

2. **Invulnerable/Charmed Life:** They are unchallenged by the realities of life due to the parents' overprotectiveness (often the mother).

3. **Pseudoinvulnerable:** These children are prone to endless risk taking (and accidents) that usually occur in the presence of an audience.

4. **True Invulnerable:** They perform better than ever when the going "gets rough"; their object relationships are enduring and they use a wide range of competencies.

5. **Persistent/Invulnerable:** Those who begin life as frail and weak, but who "bounce back" by continuing to rebound from high risks and vulnerabilities leading to an implacable resolve "not to be broken."

The literature on invulnerable children is filling a major gap by providing a focus on strengths and positive coping patterns. As can be seen from Anthony's (1987) typology above, this literature is generalizable to children and adults who have been exposed to a variety of risks and vulnerabilities. It is also useful for understanding the unique nature of sibling relationships in childhood, to which it has not been applied until recently.

Current Assumptions About Sibling Relationships During Childhood

Research involving siblings during childhood has tended to focus on the following issues: (1) birth order, (2) sibling rivalry, and (3) sibling solidarity. These three categories of research have been useful in providing explanations about sibling relationships and their structure and functions in the lives of children. Interestingly, the recentness of this literature has made it possible for researchers to integrate information about resiliency and coping into some areas, mostly in research in the last category just noted. Since these positive concepts have seldom been integrated into literature in the other two categories, recommendations about how the concepts can be applied to sibling relationships are made in the following discussion.

Research on Sibling Birth Order

The concept of birth order is an umbrella term for research on a range of sibling status or family structure variables. These interacting variables include family position, gender, the spacing between siblings, and the number of siblings in a family. These childhood variables have been found to "influence an individual's interests, preferences, style of thinking, self-esteem, conformity, and eminence and achievement as an adult" (Dunn, 1983, p. 788). Scarr and Grajek (1982) indicate that many of these studies have focused primarily on the behavior of preschool children toward a younger child in the families. Most studies have failed to explore the quality of interaction between older, middle, and younger siblings or what factors other than status variables might affect that quality (Pollak and Hundermar, 1984).

Instead, many of these studies have focused on interpersonal characteristics. For instance, Perlin and Grater (1984) found that birth order predicted that older siblings would be more dominant than middle and younger children, while younger siblings were more submissive than older siblings. However, Pulakos (1987) noted that siblings assume family roles which they perceive to be consistent with their birth order. The eldest child is perceived typically in the responsible role, the middle child in the popular role, and the youngest in the spoiled role. In a different type of research, Powell and Steelman (1990) used two national longitudinal studies of adolescents to test the effects of sibship size (number of children), spacing, and gender on educational outcomes. They concluded that close spacing between siblings had a more detrimental effect on grade point average (GPA), test performance, and degree of parental involvement in reading to children than did wide spacing. Their findings imply indirectly that parental support may be a factor in siblings' educational achievement, but this and other environmental factors are seldom addressed directly in these studies.

Clearly, sibling status variables alone do not explain the nature and magnitude of differences in the characteristics and roles of siblings in these studies. Some researchers argue that environmental differences, rather than birth order, account for variations in personality, psychopathology, and cognitive abilities (Plomin and Daniels, 1987). Moreover, this research on birth order has been criticized for its' significant methodological shortcomings. For example, a common practice has been for researchers to use secondary analysis procedures on data sets that were collected for other purposes and which involve missing data (Heer, 1986; Scarr and Grajek, 1982).

The focus of future research should be modified to address some of these problems, including the need to explore more positive aspects of sibling relationships. Studies utilizing primary analysis of data and which account for missing data are needed as well as those focused on the influence of important sibship and environmental variables. Those variables include, for example, the degree of value consensus among siblings and their social support network activities along with role modeling by adult family members (see Table 1.1 in Chapter 1). Exploring the nature of the sibling support network could clarify variations in the subsystem's resiliency: the types of "normal" conditions and family dysruptions in which different categories of Anthony's (1987) typology of resiliency can be observed.

Then too, there should be an emphasis on exploring the quality and nature of sibling relationships including the following: (1) what older, middle, and younger siblings communicate or what activities they engage in separately and together; and (2) how sibship size, spacing, and gender composition affect resource pooling or acceptance/validation among the members. These recommendations imply that studying the one-to-one effects of status variables on sibling roles is too simplistic. Instead, the emphasis should be on exploring the circular and dynamic influence among a range of variables on the quality of sibling interactions to determine childhood coping patterns, resiliency, and other positive aspects of functioning (Freeman and Palmer, 1989).

Studies on Sibling Rivalry

Unlike the above research on sibling status variables, research on sibling rivalry has been grounded in particular theoretical orientations. For instance, much of the latter research has been focused on Freudian and neo-Freudian theory. Heer (1986) conducted an extensive review of this literature and found that although Freud described other aspects of sibling relationships, the overwhelming emphasis in the psychoanalytic literature has been on sibling rivalry. Similarly, much attention has been paid to the detrimental effects of the following life events and behaviors from a pathological perspective (Abend, 1984; Bryant and Crockenberg, 1980; Schacter and Stone, 1987; Perlin and Grater, 1984; Schacter, 1985):

1. The birth of a sibling.
2. Sex play between siblings.
3. Mutual seduction between siblings.
4. Antisocial play behaviors toward siblings.
5. Siblings' roles in symptom formation.
6. Sibling deidentification or the development of different identities to mitigate on-going competition.

Heer (1986) stresses that seldom has research focused on the above examples explored positive issues. This type of research has typically ignored areas such as constructive roles of siblings, their enjoyment from playing together, or the closeness of siblings as children and later as adults. These authors and others note that the negative research indicated above has limited the ability of practitioners to emphasize prevention of sibling problems through education about natural sibling interactions (Schacter and Stone, 1987).

Research is needed to clarify the natural interactions and issues between siblings and the critical periods in the life cycle when those interactions typically occur (See Figure 1.2 in Chapter 1 on the natural history of sibling relationships and issues addressed in those relationships). This type of naturalistic research could provide a more informative context for later research focused on sibling interactions that involve extreme competition and rivalry and the circumstances in which those interactions develop. In other words, knowledge about the natural history of sibling relationships is necessary for helping researchers to effectively formulate and interpret research on problem areas such as sibling rivalry (Freeman and Palmer, 1989).

Sibling Solidarity Research

The literature in this area, unlike literature in the previous two areas, has integrated the positive concepts of coping and resiliency. The focus has been on the sibling bond and attachment, the sibling social network, and the notion of sisterhood-brotherhood. Bank and Kahn (1975) note that most of the major family theories have as their cornerstone the assumption that transmission within families is from the parents to the children downward or the reverse. Thus, these theories may have restricted attention that should have been directed toward the intragenerational or sibling relationship.

According to Bank and Kahn (1975), while parents supervise and monitor sibling relationships, there is a limit to their influence over the sibling subsystem. "Siblings live in their subsystem according to specific subsystem rules just as other subsystems do" (Bank and Kahn, 1975, p. 319). Such rules govern a range of positive functions that siblings serve for each other unrelated to parental monitoring. In this regard, siblings perform the following functions (Bank & Kahn, 1975; Dunn, 1983; Minuchin, 1974):

1. Serve as a source of mutual identification **and** differentiation (separateness).
2. Provide mutual regulation in terms of new ideas and roles.
3. Serve as brokers of services within and outside the family.
4. Provide individuals with their first experiences in direct reciprocal relationships and loyalty bonds.
5. Develop coalitions for handling the power of parents.

These positive functions of sibling relationships are not performed consistently across the life span. They may be influenced by the developmental stages of the individuals and by the issues that are addressed periodically in sibling and other relationships (Mosatche, Brady, and Noberini, 1983; Dunn, 1983). These functions are important sources of early socialization. In addition, as reflections of the sibling bond and solidarity, they are models for other relationships across the lifespan as well as adult sibling relationships (Freeman, 1989).

In summary, research on the sibling bond and solidarity is an exception in terms of the focus on positive adaptations. Clearly, this research has benefitted from the studies on normative childhood functioning and family dysruptions that were described in a previous section. However, not enough research has been conducted on the positive areas of functioning between siblings in contrast to the stronger emphasis on pathological functioning. Furthermore, much of the existing literature documents the need to explore with children and youth **their** perceptions about sibling relationships. Both prospective and retrospective studies are needed to compare individuals' current and after-the-fact perspectives about those relationships. This author's retrospective study of resiliency in children's and youths' sibling relationships was an effort to address some of these gaps in the research literature.

An Ethnographic Study of Sibling Relationships in Childhood and Adolescence

Study Methodology

An exploratory retrospective study was undertaken by this author to examine primarily sibling relationships in childhood and adolescence. A secondary focus on sibling relationships in adulthood is the subject of Chapter 3. The study methodology involved qualitative, ethnographic techniques which help to encourage subjects to tell their stories in their own words. These techniques lessen the possibility that a researcher's preconceived assumptions about the phenomenon under study will delimit the process of data gathering or bias the outcomes in this type of community-based research. The approach can range from completely unstructured interviews and observations based on a set of general topic areas developed by the researcher to semistructured interviews involving a small number of stimulus questions about the phenomenon under study. In either case, the researcher allows the subjects and their ideas/thoughts to guide the interview process and determine the sequence, tempo, content, and meaning.

Spradley (1979) supports the efficacy of this approach in exploring "the acquired knowledge that people use in order to interpret their experiences and generate social behavior" (p. 5). Spradley's (1979) underlying premise is that individuals act and react toward other people and events on the basis of the meaning they attribute to those people and events. Although his focus was on the use of ethnography to describe cultures, Spradley's (1979) assumptions can be generalized to families since each family develops unique patterns of relationships, interactions, language, values, and customs that govern the life of the members. This idea of the family as a culture helped in the planning of the study methodology in terms of the research questions, the subjects, the research instruments and interview process, and the data analysis.

The Research Questions. This author developed a set of research questions as the focus for this exploratory study. The goal was to explore what was unique about each family in terms of sibling and other relationships, while also identifying common experiences and events in the culture of the families. The following questions are focused on childhood and adolescence, the topic of this chapter, while the research questions from the study pertaining to adult sibling relationships are identified in Chapter 3:

1. What is the range of sibling relationships and roles that occur during childhood and adolescence?
2. What environmental factors internal and external to the family and its' culture influence the quality of relationships and roles between siblings?
3. To what extent do sibling's activities, repetitive games, mutual or diverse coping patterns, and identification of the most significant sibling reflect the developmental themes of childhood and adolescence?
4. In what ways can the characteristics of resiliency from the literature be applied to individual children, the sibling subculture, or the family culture of the subjects?

The Subjects and Setting. To be included in the study, the following criteria had to be met by the subjects: 25 to 60 years of age, native-born American, family of one or more siblings, and at least one of the natural parents must have lived in the same household during childhood and adolescence. The study included a purposeful sample of thirty-seven subjects. Of that number, 87% were European-American (32), 10% were African-American (4), and 3% were Hispanic (1) (see Table 2.1). The number of participants in each of the four age groups ranged from 22 to 30%, with the ends of the range representing the youngest and oldest groups respectively. Approximately 54% of them were females while 46% were males. In terms of marital status, the largest percentage of subjects were either married (43%) or single (never married) (27%).

Table 2.1. Characteristics of the Study Sample (N = 37).

Variable	Frequency	Percentage
Age:		
25–30 years	11	30%
31–40 years	9	24%
41–50 years	9	24%
51–60 years	8	22%
Gender:		
Females	20	54%
Males	17	46%
Race/Ethnicity:		
European-Americans	32	87%
African-Americans	4	10%
Hispanics or Latinos	1	3%
Marital Status:		
Married	16	43%
Single (never married)	10	27%
Divorced	7	19%
Widowed	3	8%
Separated	1	3%
Income:		
Less than $15,000 per year	4	11%
$15,000–$30,000 per year	9	25%
$31,000–$50,000 per year	20	53%
$51,000 and over per year	4	11%

The subjects came from a variety of socio-economic backgrounds: 11% had incomes of less than $15,000 per year (4), 25% were in the $15,000 to $30,000 range (9), 53% had incomes in the $31,000 to $50,000 range (20), and the remaining 11% earned incomes of $51,000 and over per year (4). The lowest educational attainment in the group was the 11th grade while the highest was completion of graduate school (55% had some college). Their occupations ranged from unskilled and semi skilled (clerk and factory worker) to self-employed (small business owner) to professional (psychologist and social worker).

The majority of the interviews were conducted in the homes of these subjects, reflecting an assumption that the subjects would be more comfortable in their own environments. Convenience and privacy were other factors that influenced the choice of home visits for most of the interviews. Other interviews were conducted in the author's office whenever that site was preferred by a subject.

The Instruments/Interview Process. The instruments used for the study included a semi-structured interview guide and a data coding and analysis form. The interview guide consisted of a set of stimulus questions designed to initiate the interview and focus it if and when subjects had difficulty talking during the process. These stimulus questions reflected the general focus of the research questions identified in a previous section, but interviews were not limited to those areas. The stimulus questions were open-ended to allow the subjects as much latitude as possible in "telling their stories." For example, questions were included that asked subjects to describe the family they grew up in; issues that developed in the family from time to time that were important to the subjects; what their relationships with their siblings were like; what types of recurring games were played with siblings in childhood and adolescence; and how they and their siblings coped with particular issues, events, and relationships in the family at various times. Participation in the study was voluntary; subjects were recruited by advertising and through a snowball technique by having participants identify other potential subjects.

The interviews ranged from 2 to 2½ hours in length. The process was often intense as subjects recalled relationships and events very vividly. In some instances, those recollections involved expressions of anger, sadness (crying), and joy. When it seemed appropriate based on these types of reactions and the content of interviews, recommendations were made for subjects to address unfinished issues with siblings and other individuals informally or by involving themselves in counseling. Each interview was audio-taped with the permission of the participant. Taping the interviews facilitated the data analysis portion of the study.

Data Analysis. The data coding and analysis form designed for this study was developed from listening to the audio-taped interviews in a preliminary way to determine patterns in the data. Once the coding and analysis form was developed based on those patterns, the tapes were systematically reviewed to collect and record more detailed information from each interview (a content analysis). The benefits of the ethnographic approach were evident as the data analysis was conducted: important unanticipated areas related to sibling relationships were discussed in the interviews and became part of the findings for this study.

Study Findings and Discussion

The study findings are discussed in the following section based on the research questions identified in the previous section on methodology. Those questions focus on the internal sibling subsystem interactions as well as family and other environmental factors that may influence or be influenced by those interactions. The focus is on findings that clarify the positive and negative functions that the subjects identified as part of their sibling relationships.

Sibling Roles and Relationships

The participants responded to a number of questions about the nature and quality of their roles/relationships with their siblings during childhood and adolescence. Their comments about relationships with siblings included comments that indicated close nurturing relationships as well as distant and rivalrous relationships. For instance, some noted that they played well with their siblings, had common interests, could depend on their siblings to understand when they had problems, and liked some aspect of a sibling's behavior or attitude such as losing gracefully in a game or being accepting of a sibling's faults. These types of comments reflected a strong sibling bond and solidarity along with documentation of the important aspects of the sibling social support network (Bank and Kahn, 1975; Allan, 1977; Pollak and Hundermar, 1984).

Other subjects indicated they did not interact much with siblings until they were older due to age differences or conflicts. Those responses tended to indicate neutral relationships or ones with little emotional connection during particular developmental periods. Other responses indicated a lack of or conflicted affect as noted by Dunn (1983). For instance, a few participants admitted not liking a brother or sister, pointing out that they probably would not have interacted or played with him or her if it had not been for the parents' mediation. Often, mediation was accomplished by other siblings or by an extended family member such as a cousin or grandparent.

Along with these responses about sibling relationships during childhood and adolescence, the subjects' responses about roles during those periods were equally enlightening. Pollak's and Hundermar's (1984) and Freeman's (1989) categories of sibling roles were useful criteria for analyzing the subjects' responses in this area. The findings included examples of each of the roles below (see Chapter 9 for an application of these roles to a case study on sibling relationships):

1. The quasi-parental role: adoption of parental concerns by one or more siblings in regard to other siblings (e.g., a teenage brother tried to get his younger sister to follow the parents' rules about curfew).
2. The quasi-therapeutic role: provision of support to one another and being an ally in the developmental struggle of individuation and separation (e.g., a young adult encouraged her younger brother to stay with her whenever he felt like running away and to enter the military as a way of getting away from the parents' physical violence and inability to let him make some decisions).
3. The gang formation role: strengthening of familial ties among siblings and resulting from a degree of closeness that has been lost in the parent/child relationship (e.g., two young siblings placed in separate foster care homes wrote letters to each other and continuously requested to be placed together until one foster parent agreed to have both of them placed in her home).
4. The counter role: acting opposite from a sibling's role to influence the family toward positive change and help siblings cope with family dysruptions (e.g., one 12 year old acted out in school and began experimenting with alcohol which called attention to the parents' neglect and alcoholism while another sibling assumed a parental caretaking role).
5. The positive risk-taking role: modeling by one sibling how the others can be different in a positive manner in families where there are strong rules for compliance (e.g., an older adolescent utilized a grandparent to discuss his grief over the death of a sibling several years prior in a family where his parents and siblings followed the family rule of "feelings aren't important").
6. The neutral/waiting role: provision of covert support and coaching to siblings who take positive risks and learning by observation due to negative family rules and sanctions against change (e.g., a ten year old observed how an older sister used educational achieve-

ment to bolster her self-esteem in a family where the rule was that "education was unimportant"; he helped by playing quietly when she tried to study or getting the parents focused on him).

It is interesting to note that many of these roles are consistent with the positive functions of siblings that were discussed previously in this chapter. For instance, the quasi-therapeutic role is closely related to siblings serving as a source for emotional closeness and individuation during various developmental stages. On the other hand, the gang formation role could facilitate the provision of social network supports by siblings to each other, particularly during crises and other transitions (Freeman, 1989).

Family Culture and Environmental Influences

Many of the examples of sibling roles including those identified in the previous sections were influenced by factors internal and external to the sibling subsystem. The subjects indicated these influences included the following:

1. Individual temperament, personality, coping patterns, abilities, and attitudes.
2. The emotional connection between the members of the sibling subsystem, whether they liked each other or felt some attachment/common experience.
3. The parent's views about how siblings should get along together or be different, as well as how they demonstrated ways to get along in their own relationships, especially with their siblings (often covert rather than overt).
4. The availability and quality of peer relationships.
5. Relationships within the extended family (e.g., grandmothers often provided nurturance and acceptance along with how to problem-solve/cope with problems).
6. Key persons in other systems often helped with sibling solidarity indirectly by helping individuals to be different from siblings in acceptable ways, e.g., teachers or bosses at work.

Culture seemed to be a major influence whether in the broader or more narrow sense. For example, the case studies described in Chapters 5 through 11 clarify many aspects of each family's internal culture that influenced the roles and relationships of siblings. Family rules, patterns of communicating, role proscriptions, coalitions, problematic dysruptions, and the "normal" developmental milieu of childhood are part of this type of culture. Participants mentioned examples of these factors such as rules against sharing family secrets, parents communicating with the children through one identified sibling, one sibling being designated in the scapegoat role, unusual closeness between the parent and an older sibling, parental alcoholism and violence, and learning to handle their own conflicts within the sibling subsystem.

Then too, the family's ethnicity as part of culture in the more narrow sense was often identified as an influence on sibling roles and relationships by subjects. One subject indicated that "In Italian families, brothers and sisters remain close for life; they are expected to do things to help each other whenever there is a need." Another noted that in African-American families, it is not uncommon for distantly related or unrelated children to be raised as natural siblings in a family.

Developmental Themes and Sibling Activities/Games

In addition to describing their roles and relationships with siblings in general, the study participants were asked to identify the sibling they felt influenced their lives the most significantly. Then they were asked to describe their activities, games, themes, and coping patterns in regard to that particular sibling. The majority of subjects identified a sibling of the same sex regardless of their gender when responding to these questions (59%) (see Table 2.2). Most chose the identified sibling for positive reasons, but even when the reason was negative, some of the subjects could point out some part of the experience that had strengthened them. Moreover, Table 2.3 indicates that the majority of the subjects came from families where they had from two to five siblings (67%).

Table 2.2. The Subjects' Identification of Their Most Significant Sibling Relationship (N = 37).

Subject/Most Significant Sibling Dyad in Terms of Gender	Frequency	Percentage
Female/Female	12	32%
Male/Male	10	27%
Female/Male	8	22%
Male/Female	7	19%

Note: N of 37 = 20 Females
          17 Males

Table 2.3. Number of Siblings in The Subjects' Families of Origin (N = 37).

Number of Siblings	Frequency	Percentage
One	2	3%
Two to three	13	35%
Four to five	12	32%
Six to eight	8	23%
Over nine	2	5%

When asked why they selected the identified sibling, many of the reasons given were related to developmental themes. The themes included (in order of their frequency): separation and individuation, identity, trust/loyalty, career choice and planning, and socialization to play or peer groups (see Figure 3.2 in Chapter 3 for other findings on the most important themes during these phases). Separation and individuation was often related to the theme of trust and loyalty among siblings. For instance, some of the participants said the identified sibling helped with individuation by accepting them as they were, or he or she facilitated separation within the sibling subsystem in order to enhance the process with the parents. In one case, this was accomplished by a role shift from the quasi-parental to quasi-therapeutic role (from reminders to do better in school to supporting the sibling's decision to select a career and life style the parents were not likely to agree with).

Responses to questions about the participants' activities and "games" together were not as informative. Games were defined by the researcher as repetitive interactions (verbal or nonverbal) and activities which the siblings involved themselves in over time. Most of the participants had difficulty recalling specific activities or interactions related to games with siblings except for card or table games which occurred often during younger years. When they talked about those interactions, they tended to focus on conflicts around siblings not playing fairly or being overly competitive.

It was clear that those interactions during structured games tended to reflect the feelings of rivalry and conflict that were a part of the natural interactions between siblings at other times. What was not clear from the findings, however, is whether these games served a positive function by allowing siblings to express those feelings during socially acceptable activities or a negative one by validating those feelings. Another question is what siblings learned from those experiences, and what individual, sibship, or family factors contributed to the learning whether it was positive or negative.

Resiliency Applied to the Individual/Sibling/Family Culture

Many examples of effective coping and resiliency were included in the findings from the study. Anthony's (1987) typology of resiliency was utilized in this study to analyze these findings related to resiliency. For expediency, one example of individual, sibling subsystem, and family resiliency has been included below. There is an emphasis on the cultural context in which the persons in those examples developed and thrived (Anthony, 1987):

1. Individual resiliency: A 12 year old girl lived in a family culture of violence. She was scapegoated through physical and emotional abuse by her mother and sexual abuse by her brother. She used school achievement to develop her identity and self-esteem after beginning life as a premature infant less than 2 lbs in weight. She now works as a child psychologist who treats abused children after living as an emancipated minor while finishing high school and later successfully completing treatment as an adult. All of her siblings have major addiction and family problems as adults. She fell into the "Persistent Invulnerable" category while each of her siblings were more in the "Pseudoinvulnerable" category during their childhood.
2. Sibling subsystem resiliency: Three African-American siblings from 5 to 7 years of age in a racially-mixed school involving racial stress and prejudices utilized their sibling support network to address sibling acculturation issues. They also used the extended family's strong emotional ties, ethnic identity, cultural stories about handling experiences involving oppression, and role modeling of positive sibling relationships to grow and thrive in their school environment. They exhibited the characteristics of the "True Invulnerable" category of resiliency.
3. Family resiliency: A family involving the mother, a 17 year old son, 15 year old son, and 13 year old daughter continued to run their farm after the death of the husband and father. The older son developed a chronic depression in reaction to the father's sudden death from cancer and a series of other losses including the death

of the younger sister and the mother developing a heart condition. They were able to ask for and use emotional and financial resources from their extended family and others to cope with survivor guilt related to the death of the sister, value conflicts, and a dramatic change in lifestyle and family identity. This family exemplified the category of "True Invulnerability."

To summarize, the findings from this study indicate that siblings assume a wide range of roles and relationships that are influenced over time by their developmental stage and a number of other environmental and cultural influences. In that sense, it is important to note that these roles should not be viewed in terms of right or wrong, but in terms of how consistent they are with the developmental and cultural needs. Role flexibility, rather than role proscriptions, is an important factor. Moreover, resiliency and coping are important aspects of sibling roles and relationships, although different levels of resiliency are possible. Therefore, resiliency during childhood may not result automatically in resiliency in adulthood, depending on the level of resiliency during earlier life and whether the individual can change in his or her ability to be more resilient as development tasks and other life events change. What then are the implications from this discussion for preventing problems and enhancing the sibling bond?

Implications for Prevention in Family Treatment

The importance of a broadly conceived field of family treatment is discussed in other chapters of this book. The implications that flow from the present chapter on sibling relationships in childhood and adolescence, however, actually relate to the area of prevention. This means that the function of family treatment is not only to help families handle problems once they have developed. Prevention of such problems must be a major priority as well. As implied by the analysis of the literature on childhood in general and specifically related to sibling relationships, along with findings from the author's study, problems in these areas may be preventable.

One implication is that parents may need to become more educated about sibling relationships in early life. Parents may be more knowledgeable about parent education in general as the range of structured programs has grown. While those programs are extremely useful, their focus tends to be on what Bank and Kahn (1975) describe as the parent downward to children communication pattern. Programs need to be developed to include educational material about how sibling relationships can be understood in the context of normal child development and family dysruptions, emphasizing the autonomous functions of the sibling subsystem (Bank and Kahn, 1975).

Because sibling relationships are an important influence throughout the developmental phases of childhood and adolescence, another implication is the need to organize this educational content to be consistent with those phases. Thus, it might be useful to present the content in staggered mini-packages over several years to fit the developmental needs of the children in families. The customary way of presenting parent education in one package over several consecutive weeks may be insufficient for adequate learning and application (Freeman and Pennekamp, 1988).

A third implication is related to the issue of resiliency. Helping professionals in public schools, day care centers, Headstart and other preschool programs have opportunities to study, teach, and support existing examples of resiliency (Anthony, 1987) at the individual, sibship, and family levels in informal and counseling contacts with young people. In addition, any parent education program focused on sibling relationships should integrate content that builds on and enhances the resiliency of children and youth if indeed this is possible.

Finally, more attention must be directed toward those factors that influence the nature and quality of sibling and other relationships in families. Prevention efforts require that the manner in which these factors influence the development of sibling rivalry in childhood, for example, be more clearly understood. Factors from childhood that help to maintain barriers to sibling solidarity into later years must be understood also. This information should be included in prevention programs for parents and helping professionals in order to reduce the likelihood of lifelong alienation that occurs in some sibships.

Conclusion

Childhood is a critical period because of its effects on growth and development during this early phase, but also in terms of the impact during adulthood. This fact is especially relevant to sibling relationships given the important functions and roles identified as part of childhood and adolescence. The author's research supports previous findings in the literature about the importance attached to common sibling experiences and relationships during the early years. Clearly, some of these experiences are normative while others are examples of more severe problems. However, both effective and ineffective patterns of coping with normative and problematic experiences may be useful in helping us to understand how to prevent lifelong conflicts in sibling relationships.

REFERENCES

Abend, S. (1984). Sibling love and object choice. *Psychoanalytic Quarterly, LIII*, 425–430.

Allan, G. (1977). Sibling solidarity. *Journal of Marriage and the Family, 39*, 177–184.

Anthony, E.J. (1987). Risk, vulnerability, and resilience: An overview. In E.J. Anthony and B.J. Cohler (Eds.), *The invulnerable child* (3–48). New York: Guilford Press.

Balk, D.E. (1990). The self-concepts of bereaved adolescents: Sibling death and its aftermath. *Journal of Adolescent Research, 5*, 112–132.

Bank, S. and Kahn, M.D. (1975). Sisterhood-brotherhood is powerful: Sibling subsystems and family therapy. *Family Process, 14*, 311–337.

Black, C. (1981). *It will never happen to me.* Denver, CO: M.A.C. Printing and Publications Division.

Bowlby, J. (1977). The making and breaking of affectual bonds. *British Journal of Psychiatry, 130*, 201–210.

Brett, K.M. (1988). Sibling response to chronic childhood disorders. *Issues in Comprehensive Pediatric Nursing, 11*, 43–57.

Bryant, B. and Crockenberg, S. (1980). Correlates and dimensions of prosocial behavior: A study of female siblings with their mothers. *Child Development, 51*, 529–544.

Cowen, E.L. (1988). Resilient children, psychological wellness, and primary prevention. *American Journal of Community Psychology, 16*, 591–607.

Dunn, J. (1983). Sibling relationships in early childhood. *Child Development, 54*, 787–811.

Erikson, E.H. (1985). Life cycle. In M. Bloom (Ed.), *Life span development: Bases for preventive and interventive helping: Second edition* (35–43). New York: Macmillan.

Finkelhor, D. (1984). *Child sexual abuse-new theory and research.* New York: Free Press.

Flach, F. (1988). *Resilience: Discovering a new strength at times of stress.* New York: Fawcett Columbine.

Freeman, E.M. (1989). Adult children of alcoholics: Study of parental, sibling, and work relationships. Paper presented at the 34th Institute on the Prevention and Treatment of Alcoholism. Pontault-Combault, France: International Council on Alcohol and Addictions.

Freeman, E.M. and Dyer, L. (In press). High risk children and adolescents: Clarifying their family and community environments. *Social Casework*.

Freeman, E.M. and Palmer, N. (1989). Reconceptualizing dynamics in the alcoholic family: A secondary study in sibling relationships. Research report. Lawrence, KS.: University of Kansas School of Social Welfare.

Freeman, E.M. and Pennekamp, M. (1988). *Social work practice: Toward a child, family, school, community perspective.* Springfield, IL: Charles C Thomas.

Goetting, A. (1986). The developmental tasks of siblingships over the life cycle. *Journal of Marriage and the Family, 48,* 703–714.

Heer, D.M. (1986). Effect of number, order, and spacing of siblings on child and adult outcomes: An overview of current research. *Social Biology, 33,* 1–4.

Hegar, R.L. (1988). Legal and social work approaches to sibling separation in foster care. *Child Welfare, 67,* 113–121.

Kritsberg, W. (1986). *The adult children of alcoholics syndrome: From discovery to recovery.* Pompano Beach, FL: Health Communications, Inc.

Minuchin, S. (1974). *Families and family therapy.* Boston: Harvard University Press.

Mosatche, H., Brady, E., and Noberini, M.R. (1983). A retrospective life span study of the closest sibling relationship. *The Journal of Psychology, 113,* 237–243.

Murphy, L.B. and Moriarty, A.E. (1976). *Vulnerability, coping, and growth: From infancy to adolescence.* London: Yale University Press.

Perlin, M. and Grater, H. (1984). The relationship between birth order and reported interpersonal behavior. *Individual Psychology Journal of Adlerian Theory, Research, and Practice, 40,* 22–28.

Piaget, J. (1952). *The origin of intelligence in children.* New York: International Universities Press.

Plomin, R. and Daniels, D. (1987). Why are children in the same family so different from one another? *Behavioral and Brain Sciences, 10,* 1–16.

Pollak, O. and Hundermar, D. (1984). Some unexplored aspects of the sibling experience. *Adolescence, 76,* 869–874.

Powell, B. and Steelman, L.C. (1990). Beyond sibship size: Sibling density, sex composition, and educational outcomes. *Social Forces, 69,* 181–206.

Pulakos, J. (1987). The effects of birth order on perceived family roles. *Individual Psychology Journal of Adlerian Theory, Research, and Practice, 43,* 319–328.

Rhodes, S.L. (1980). A developmental approach to the life cycle of the family. In M. Bloom (Ed.), *Life span development: Bases for preventive and interventive helping* (30–39). New York: Macmillan.

Scarr, S. and Grajek, S. (1982). Similarities and differences among siblings. In M.E. Lamb and B. Sutton-Smith (Eds.), *Siblings relationships: Their nature and significance across the lifespan* (223–241). Hillsdale, NJ: Erlbaum.

Schacter, F. (1985). Sibling deidentification in the clinic: Devil versus angel. *Family Process, 24,* 415–427.

Schacter, F.F. and Stone, R.K. (1987). Comparing and contrasting siblings: Defining the self. *Journal of Children in Contemporary Society, 19,* 55–75.

Spradley, J. (1979). *The ethnographic interview.* New York: Holt, Rinehart, and Winston.

Strean, H.S. (1986). Psychoanalytic theory. In F.J. Turner (Ed.), *Social work treatment: Interlocking theoretical approaches* (19–45). New York: Free Press.

Taylor, S.E. (1983). Adjustment to threatening events: A theory of cognitive adaptation. *American Psychologist, 78,* 1161–1173.

Wegscheider, S. (1981). *Another chance: Hope and health for the alcoholic family.* Palo Alto, CA: Science and Behavior Books.

Chapter 3

THE SIBLING BOND IN ADULTHOOD: LIFELONG ADAPTATIONS IN CLOSE, TENUOUS, AND ALIENATED RELATIONSHIPS

Sibling relationships in adulthood may range from the intimate and satisfactory to the barely tolerated to those involving painful emotional and physical cut-offs. As discussed in Chapter 2, the quality of these relationships is dependent on the extent to which unfinished business from earlier periods has been resolved successfully between siblings. Furthermore, some of the typical adult developmental tasks may "trigger" these unresolved issues or give rise to new ones that need to be addressed (Freeman, 1984; Krout, 1988). For instance, the transition into the caretaking role for elderly parents often requires siblings to plan as a co-equal caretaking unit for the safety, health, and financial needs of their parents. According to Goetting (1986), unresolved sibling rivalry from childhood or rigid proscribed roles based on birth order may be revived by the intensity of the task and become the basis for their interactions within the adult sibling caretaking unit.

In those situations, the elderly parents' current needs and the collaboration required to meet those needs may become secondary to the siblings' prior unresolved relationship issues. If siblings are aware of the barriers created by those issues, the planning for parents can provide an opportunity to resolve the old issues as well as grow closer through achieving mutual tasks (Goetting, 1986; Ross and Milgram, 1982). Some individuals, however, may be unable to use these situations for growth. They may refuse to be involved in the planning or they may disrupt the situation to the extent that the parents are harmed either emotionally (from stress) or physically (by neglect).

In other situations, new issues may emerge as individuals attempt to master some of the adult developmental tasks. Siblings may place new demands on each other which may not be met during developmental transitions (Leigh, 1982), for example, as when one sibling becomes divorced. Other siblings may not provide the amount or type of support requested by the divorced sibling or for the period of time he or she feels it is needed. Or they might maintain a cordial relationship with the divorced in-law in spite of their sibling's wish or demand that they end the relationship. Such experiences can create rifts in heretofore close relationships that may then require concentrated efforts to mend.

There is a need to distinguish between these typical sibling relationships in which issues develop and are experienced as transitional problems from relationships in which the problems are of a more severe, chronic nature. Such distinctions are useful for educating the general public about the predictable joys and stresses of sibling relationships and when such relationships should be addressed directly or indirectly through formal treatment. Consequently, this chapter summarizes literature on the nature of adult sibling relationships. A section is included on recurring and new developmental themes in adulthood that influence and are influenced by sibling relationships. The author's retrospective research on adult sibling relationships is described along with findings about how those relationships can impact adult relationships with parents, peers, spouses/companions, and coworkers. The implications for family treatment and self-help activities are addressed as well.

Sibling Relationships Across the Adult Lifespan

The literature on sibling relationships in adulthood falls generally into three major categories: (1) kinship relationships in the elderly including sibling relationships, (2) developmental tasks/themes in sibling relationships throughout the (adult) lifespan, and (3) interactional patterns in adult sibling relationships (e.g., sibling solidarity and sibling deidentification). This literature is useful for clarifying how the nature of sibling relationships vary over time in a number of important ways based on the following: the stage of adult development, gender, the presence and quality of other supports including children, the type of community (urban or rural), the opportunities for and frequency of contact, physical proximity, external events, and the quality of the relationship previously. Although some authors assume that only one (or two) of these factors are responsible for changes in the nature of sibling relationships, it is more likely that a combination of such factors influence the changes.

Kinship Relationships in the Elderly

This specialized subsection of the literature is based on the assumption that resources in the elderly, including support networks and social activities with kin, are less available during this period of development. Often, however, the research findings have documented a larger number of contacts than were expected among elderly siblings and high levels of satisfaction with sibling and other relationships even when contacts occur infrequently (Lamb, 1982). Thus, the focus of this literature has been broadened to explore, in a more detailed way, other factors in addition to the number of contacts.

For instance, Dorfman and Mertens (1990) conceptualized the quality of sibling and other kinship relationships in rural and urban elderly based not only on the frequency of contact, but also on proximity, the type and frequency of aid, affectional closeness, value consensus, and overall satisfaction with family life. These authors studied a cohort of 252 retired men and 199 retired women in two midwestern rural communities. Their findings indicate that proximity, contact, affectional closeness, and value consensus were high for their subjects in terms of the child seen most frequently and the sibling closest in age. The type of aid was most often advice on decisions, help when sick or moving, gifts, and transportation rather than financial assistance.

Dorfman's and Mertens' (1990) findings also show how gender differences influenced their subject's sibling relationships. Females had significantly more contact of all kinds with siblings than the males, and they exchanged more phone calls with children than did males in the study. In addition, the females received aid from kin more frequently than the males, while also rating affectional closeness and value consensus with kin higher than males. These researchers concluded that females (particularly those from rural areas) "... are both recipients of aid from kin and 'kinkeepers' more frequently than their male counterparts" (Dorfman and Mertens, 1990, p. 171).

Other authors have attempted to explore additional factors that could influence the amount and type of aid and other social supports available to the elderly. In contrast to the above findings by Dorfman and Mertens (1990) which identified gender as a determinant of aid, Kivett (1985) concluded that the amount of aid from siblings was negatively related to the number of children available to assist older adults who live in rural areas. Similarly, other researchers have examined the type of relationship as a factor in the provision of aid to nonrural elderly. Many indicate that elderly individuals in urban and suburban areas most frequently receive aid from spouses, children, grandchildren, and siblings in that order (Bengston, Cutler, Mangen, and Marshall, 1985; Coward, 1987).

Lee and Ihinger-Tallman (1980) noted that the provision of aid from these various relatives and the frequency of contact are contingent on the siblings' physical proximity. Scott (1983) studied a group of urban elderly aged 65 to 90 years of age; he found that almost ½ in his sample had a sibling living less than 60 minutes away. Again with respect to siblings, Bultena (1969) proved that as many rural elderly as urban elderly had siblings in the same community or county (37%). However, in spite of these findings, other authors emphasize that, for both urban and rural elderly, contact with siblings is less frequent than is contact with children (Leigh, 1982; Powers, Keith, and Goudy, 1981; Scott, 1983).

Some studies have compared the nature of sibling relationships in the elderly with such relationships in individuals in earlier developmental stages. For example, Ross and Milgram (1982) concluded that contact with siblings is more valued among older than among younger adults, while Suggs and Kivett (1986–87) noted that value consensus among elderly siblings 65 years and above is perceived as higher than in any other age group (78%). Finally, Leigh (1982) indicated that contact with siblings is associated with affectional closeness, enjoyment, and exchange of aid in many urban elderly. These patterns in sibling relationships in the elderly are no doubt a reflection of the developmental themes and tasks which must be addressed in this and in other stages of the life cycle.

Siblings' Lifespan Development: Tasks and Themes

Research in this section of the literature is very limited according to Goetting (1986). The lifespan perspective presumes there are critical developmental periods which affect the nature and course of siblings' lives and relationships throughout adulthood. The lifespan perspective is counter to an earlier pattern in the literature which limited the scope primarily to child development and psychological issues (Goetting, 1986). Mosatche, Brady, and Noberini (1983) used this perspective to study how 35 women and 12 men (mean age 59.3 years) perceived/remembered their relationships with their closest sibling during various periods of the life cycle. Those authors identified seven life periods representing either a significant portion of the life cycle or a critical event: elementary school, high school, just before leaving home, beginning of the subject's marriage, birth of the subject's first child, when the subject's children left home, and the death of a parent. Their study provides an overview of adult developmental themes and tasks related to sibling relationships, after which each stage of adult development is addressed separately in this section.

Overview of Adult Developmental Themes/Tasks. Mosatche et al. (1983) found that the developmental tasks/themes, and thus the quality of sibling relationships, shifted over time. Figure 3.1 illustrates some of the patterns in their subjects' shifting relationships. For example, it is evident from Figure 3.1 that reciprocity is more important during crises, differentiation is the main focus during childhood and adolescence, and compatibility is very important in the early adult years based on Mostache et al.'s (1983) research. In comparison, sibling relationships did not seem to be as salient while the subjects' children were still at home. These authors believe siblings may provide instrumental and expressive support not readily available at particular times from other relatives for the following reasons:

1. Durability of the relationship.
2. Accessibility.
3. Blood ties.
4. Similarities in siblings' backgrounds and experiences.
5. Social expectations of the role.

Lamb (1982) drew a similar conclusion, indicating that although sibling interaction rates are relatively low during adulthood, the capacity for the relationship to fulfill vital functions in terms of key developmental tasks may still prevail. Cicirelli (1982) indicates that sibling relationships may be important during significant periods of adult development because they are "highly equalitarian" (p. 268). This quality of sibling relationships is particularly significant in the young adult stage of development.

Young Adulthood. Related to the above assumption about the equalitarian nature of sibling relationships, Cicirelli (1980) notes whether young adults seek out siblings as a confidant, rather than another family member, is dependent upon whether the topic is more or less peer-oriented. That author concluded that young college age women perceived as much emotional support from the sibling they rated themselves closest to as they did from their mother. The subjects' actual use of their siblings for help and guidance overall, however, was less than their use of

Critical Life Events	Reciprocity ("There when I needed him")	Positive Affect ("Warm feeling for her")	Negative Affect ("Resented him for not calling")	Similarity ("Similar interests")	Differentiation ("She had her friends—I had mine")	Compatibility ("We had fun with each other")	Activity ("We went shopping together")
Elementary School					+		
High School					+	+	
Just Before Leaving Home	+	+					
Beginning of Subject's Marriage	+	+		+			
Birth of Subject's First Child						+	
When Subject's Children Left Home						+	+
Death of a Parent	+	+		+			+

Figure 3.1. Mosatche's et al.'s (1983) Study Findings on the Closest Sibling Relationship Over the Lifespan (N = 47)

the mother or father for those purposes. Bossard and Ball (1956) found young adults who recently had left the family of origin often provide economic aid and other forms of support to siblings still at home and to those in school.

The Interim Family-of-Procreation Years. In the years between young adulthood and middle age, adult sibling relationships have been characterized as "... high in perseverance but low in intensity" (Cicirelli, 1982, p. 275). The relationship is mediated by marriage, parenthood, and economic tasks along with frequent geographical distance. Siblings' previous developmental tasks/themes of nurturance, caretaking, and teaching each other are transformed into tasks related to becoming a spouse, parent, and the child of aging parents (Goetting, 1982). Although it is more dependent on voluntary contact for the first time, the sibling support system may continue with the ties becoming more loose and diffuse during these interim years. The exception during this and subsequent periods may be within particular ethnic groups where the pattern in both childhood and adult sibling relationships may be very different. Cicirelli (1980) indicates that in Italian-American families "frequent contact after marriage sets a lifelong pattern of sociability and mutual aid" among siblings (p. 164). Shorkey and Rosen (1993) indicate a similar pattern in African-American and Hispanic families. Additional research is needed to explore further the effects of ethnicity on the pattern of sibling relationships during early adulthood.

Middle Adulthood. A different picture emerges in the developmental themes and tasks for siblings during the middle adult years. Except for the developmental tasks of companionship and socio-emotional support, the most commonly cited tasks of this period for siblings are "... cooperation in the care of elderly parents and later in the dismantling of the parental home" (Bank and Kahn, 1982, p. 16). According to some authors, separated and divorced middle aged adults depend more on siblings in their provision of aid to elderly parents, indicating that during such developmental transitions, the sibling relationship serves a compensatory function (Cicirelli, 1984; Rosenberg and Anspach, 1972). Although initially reactivated to manage these developmental tasks related to parents, the sibling bond may continue to serve a socio-emotional function for siblings beyond the process of parental decline and death as noted by Mosatche et al. (1983).

Old Age. This stage involves the final years from the point of retirement to death. Geographical distance may continue to mediate the quality of the sibling relationship, but work and other roles external to the family are determinants to a much lesser extent. The elderly disengage from their roles outside the family, but generally continue their family involvements. "As their worlds shrink, their kinship networks, including their siblings, become more important to them" (Goetting, 1986, p. 710). In circumstances involving divorce or widowhood, there is a higher frequency of sibling interaction (Rosenberg and Anspach, 1973), although the existence of adult children may be a mediating factor (Scott, 1983; Farber and Smith, 1985). Siblings can provide help with the central developmental tasks of reminiscence and perceptual validation as documented by Cicirelli's (1985) study which identified these as common topics in discussions with elderly siblings in comparison to discussions with adult children. Aid and direct services may be provided as well by siblings: help with transportation, financial support, or homemaking.

The resolution of sibling rivalry is another important task of this stage, if it has not been resolved during prior developmental stages. Ross and Milgram (1980) indicate that sibling rivalry persists into old age for some individuals, whether it develops during childhood or later and whether it is initiated by the siblings or someone else. The developmental task of shared reminiscence may provide the means for resolving sibling rivalry, but the latter may also become a barrier to this task if it is too intense and intractible (Ross, 1982).

Some authors have noted that the gender composition of the sibling dyad is a factor in the quality of such relationships during old age. Research demonstrates the sister-sister relationship bond is stronger generally than other combinations during this developmental stage (Goetting, 1986; Dorfman and Mertens, 1990). This finding is supported by other kinship studies on the role of females as "kinkeepers" (Mosatche et al., 1983). In addition to gender as a developmental factor in elderly sibling relationships and the other factors summarized in this section, a number of concepts help to explain the interactional patterns of siblings in adulthood.

Adult Siblings' Interactional Patterns

The concepts of sibling solidarity and deidentification refer to each end of a sibling relationship continuum involving similarities and differences. Sibling rivalry (competition) and cooperation are two of the terms used to describe diverse reactions to perceived differences and/or similarities. Although the consequences for these two types of reactions are very different throughout the lifespan, they both result from the process of siblings making comparisons related to the perceived similarities and differences. The reactions are based on the siblings' subjective perceptions, whether or not those perceptions can be documented by objective facts.

Sibling Solidarity. Very little empirical research has been conducted to explore sibling solidarity as a quality of sibling interactions. Many authors have had difficulty in defining and operationalizing the concept as a result. For instance, Allan (1977) notes that simply quantifying the contacts and interactions between siblings as the only criterion of solidarity is inadequate, given the many forms those contacts and interactions can take. It may be more useful to conceptualize sibling solidarity as a range within the solidarity and deidentification continuum as follows:

SIBLING SOLIDARITY (Perceived similarities and and toleration of differences are the determinants of interactions)		SIBLING DEIDENTIFICATION (Perceived differences are viewed as the only determinants of interactions)	
X	X	X	X
Making a Personal Choice	Maintaining Contact	Maintaining Distance	Coping with Sibling Rivalry

Solidarity ranges on this continuum from relationships between siblings who have a perceived sense of compatibility and liking for each other to relationships in which contacts are used to maintain and reinforce the kinship network. Both types of sibling relationships operationalize the concept of sibling solidarity. The two types of solidarity **are** different in a number of significant ways. The "maintaining contact" end is characterized by diffuse and limited direct involvement between siblings.

However, those contacts are maintained for two reasons: (1) parents and sometimes older siblings (especially after the parents' death) mediate sibling solidarity by sharing information about a sibling the individual is not directly involved with or by arranging mutual visits to the parents' home, and (2) social norms require only limited interaction in adult sibling relationships (Allan, 1977). At that end of the continuum, these direct contacts between siblings often can involve very modest activities (visits to each other homes, discussions about areas of mutual interest). There is, nevertheless, a sense of maintaining and expressing sibling solidarity through these direct **and** indirect contacts.

On the other hand, sibling solidarity can be operationalized at the left end of the continuum based on a sibling relationship in adulthood that involves a high degree of compatibility and positive affection. At this end of the continuum, interaction is based on personal choice as well as kinship norms, perhaps strengthening the sibling bond in those relationships (Cicirelli, 1980). This degree of sibling solidarity may enable individuals to maintain a relatively close relationship with parents and other siblings even during periods when there are conflicts in those relationships.

These assumptions about solidarity in adult sibling relationships are supported by Mostache's et al. (1983) research on developmental themes and tasks in adulthood. Those authors found that sibling solidarity (most likely operationalized by the dimensions of similarity and compatibility in that study) has the greatest salience in young adulthood and old age. On the other hand, those two dimensions were less frequently used to describe sibling relationships during childhood and middle adulthood. Particularly in regard to childhood and adolescence, differentiation was most frequently identified as a characteristic of sibling relationships during those periods (See Figure 2.1 in Chapter 2). The assumption is that "normal" issues of differentiation between siblings have been resolved by most individuals by adulthood unless there is a high degree of sibling rivalry that has not been addressed adequately. These findings provide some useful comparisons between the concepts of sibling solidarity and sibling deidentification.

Sibling Deidentification. This aspect of sibling interaction has not been researched sufficiently. Deidentification, the process of judging a sibling to be significantly or entirely different from the self, may be an extreme mechanism for coping with sibling rivalry or maintaining a distance (Schacter, Shore, Feldman-Rotman, Marquis, and Campbell, 1976). Often, the process has involved a parallel child-parent identification, with each sibling being described as similar to one of the parents (Sutton-Smith and Rosenberg, 1970). Schachter's et al. (1976) retrospective research involved 383 young adults including first, second, and "jump" pairs. These researchers' findings indicate that deidentification is most likely to be present between same-sex than opposite-sex siblings, is not related to the number of years between siblings, and is not associated with birth order (and power differentials).

Further study is needed for determining whether deidentification is a factor in underachieving youngest children who have high achieving siblings or in delinquents who have more conventional siblings (Schachter et al., 1976; Cicirelli, 1982). This review of literature about influences on adult sibling relationships has provided some useful guidelines for the author's retrospective study which is discussed in the following section.

An Exploratory Retrospective Study on Sibling Relationships in Adulthood

Study Methodology

The pilot study described in Chapter 2 is also the focus of this chapter, with special attention to those aspects of the study related to adult sibling relationships. Based on the literature review summarized in the previous section on such relationships, this part of the study was designed to replicate **and** expand Mosatche's et al. (1983) research on lifespan development by exploring the following questions:

1. How do proximity and the frequency of contact affect the type, quantity, and timing of aid provided by adult siblings to each other?
2. What is the relationship between the developmental tasks/themes which confront adult siblings throughout their life span and the quality of their relationships with each other?
3. To what extent does the quality of siblings' relationships in childhood and adolescence affect their relationships in adulthood?
4. What is the connection between the quality of adults' sibling relationships and their relationships with other significant persons: their parents, spouse/companions, peers and coworkers?

Questions 1 and 2 above are similar to the focus of Mostache's et al. (1983) study on developmental themes and tasks. Questions 3 and 4 were added by the present author since those areas on adult sibling relationships have seldom been researched if at all. These questions were explored through an ethnographic retrospective study involving 37 subjects ranging from 25 to 60 years of age with a mean age of 36. The majority of the subjects were European-American (10% were African-American and 3% were Hispanic). Many had incomes of less than $50,000 per year (36%), their educational levels ranged from the 11th grade to graduate school, and their occupations included unskilled, semi-skilled, self-employed, and professional.

The two hour plus semi-structured interviews were conducted mostly in the subjects' homes and were audio-taped and then analyzed through a content analysis completed with a data coding form. Subjects were recruited through advertising and the use of a snowball technique. A full description of the study methodology is included in Chapter 2.

The Findings

The study findings have been summarized in the following section based on the research questions listed above. Some common findings across subjects are reported, although the advantage of the ethnographic study method in highlighting what is unique about each life experience is illustrated through the use of brief examples and vignettes.

Sibling Proximity/Frequency of Contact/Quality of the Relationship. The present study differed from that of Mostache et al. (1983) in that subjects were asked to identify the sibling who has had the most significant impact on their lives rather than the sibling they feel closest to. Fifty-five percent selected a younger sibling (20) while 41% selected a sibling of the opposite sex (15). In all but five situations, siblings were chosen for positive reasons (for example, "he made me feel safe", or "I knew I could depend on her when no one else would be there for me").

Among these other five situations, three subjects' siblings were identified as significant for clearly negative reasons: involving a female victim of incest which was committed over several years by an older brother, lifelong power and control conflicts between a male subject and his older brother who was also a business partner, and rivalry or deidentification between a female subject and her older sister. Two siblings were selected for neutral or mixed reasons. In one situation a male subject chose a sister who was thirteen years older than him because "she was like a third parent," and in another a female subject chose a younger brother who " . . . is avant garde and fun to be around, but I know he uses people."

In terms of proximity, the subjects were almost evenly distributed in the geographic distance between them and the chosen sibling: less than 50 miles, between 50 and 250 miles, between 251 and 500 miles, between 501 and 1000 miles, or over 1000 miles. The subjects were asked how often they had contact with their chosen sibling and how they would characterize the current relationship on the basis of those contacts. In this way, it was possible to explore the relationship between proximity, frequency of contact, and the quality of the sibling relationship. Mostache et al. (1983), Goetting (1986) and others warn against using only the geographic proximity and frequency of contact as a descriptor of sibling relationships.

Among the fifteen subjects who lived 500 miles or less from their siblings, eleven had a variety of weekly or monthly contacts with their siblings. They described their relationships as warm, close, or friendly (indicating the "making a personal choice" type of sibling solidarity). The other four subjects described their relationships with their sibling as "ok," "so-so," "tolerable," "we only see each other when we have to." Those subjects indicated their contacts (the maintenance type of solidarity) were mainly during family celebrations once every few months. Those contacts are usually initiated by parents or other relatives. Two of them reported they or their sibling do initiate contact once or twice per year (a telephone call, letter, or birthday card), while the other two said they never initiate contacts with their sibling. Clearly, among those subjects who live reasonably close to their siblings, the majority have frequent contact and feel they are close. Those who have negative or neutral feelings toward their sibling, not surprisingly, have fewer or no self-initiated contacts. In those situations, parents or other relatives serve the type of mediating function described by Schacter et al. (1976).

In comparison, those individuals who live more than 500 miles from their siblings reported a different pattern in frequency of contact but were similar in how they described the quality of their sibling relationships. Of those 22 subjects, fourteen indicated they have monthly contact, six have contact once or twice per year, and two have little or no contact. Among the fourteen who have monthly contact, they describe their sibling relationships as close and supportive as do four of the six who have contact once or twice per year due to family gatherings.

The four remaining subjects (two with contacts once or twice per year and two with little or no contact), described their relationships as "just family," "close but not real close," "we're not angry; we just don't have anything in common," and "we have a lot of resentment towards each other." These comments about the quality of the subjects' sibling relationships reflect both past and current perspectives, but do not reveal the patterns in their relationships over time. A focus on findings related to developmental themes made it possible to explore such changes over time.

Developmental Tasks/Themes and Quality of Siblings' Relationships.

The findings in regard to lifespan development and siblings relationships were similar to those of Mostache et al. (1983) in some ways but were different in other ways. A comparison of data in Figure 3.1 on those researchers' findings and Figure 3.2 which contains data from the current author's study summarizes those similarities and differences. As in Mostache et al.'s (1983) findings, subjects in the author's study experienced positive affect and reciprocity more frequently just before leaving home, at the subjects' marriage, and at the death of a parent, than at other periods. Also, findings in the two studies related to shared activities, compatibility, similarity, and differentiation are similar during some periods.

However, unlike Mostache et al. study (1983), the current research documented instances of reciprocity, positive affect, and negative affect prior to the stage of leaving home. The quotes included under each category of themes/tasks in Figure 3.2 provide examples of some of those instances. Moreover, in this study the activity category was salient during the period before leaving home, at the beginning of marriage, and at the death of a parent. Mostache et al. (1983) found the activity category significant only during the latter two periods.

Two more significant differences in the two studies involves the last two categories of developmental themes/tasks included in Figure 3.2. Mostache et al. (1983) indicated that future research should focus on identifying additional domains or categories related to sibling relationships such as role modeling. In the present study, it was possible to identify two additional categories: role modeling (education) and collaboration (pooling resources). The findings indicate that role modeling often involves the chosen sibling modeling how to be different in the family in a positive manner, particularly in families where there are strong rules about being compliant and loyal. One example was a younger sister who often pointed out evidence of the father's alcoholism and the consequences through the use of humor and contrary to the unspoken family rule about not discussing the subject. This was an example of positive-risk taking which was good for that sibling's mental health. The experience demonstrated to the sister how to oppose family rules about secrecy, how to be an individual in a fused/enmeshed family.

The collaboration category is a second additional dimension of the quality of sibling relationships found in this study that changes over the lifespan. The findings indicate that this dimension is most salient during the periods of elementary school, just before leaving home (the

Life Cycle Stage or Critical Event	Reciprocity ("Sometimes I'd help him, other times he'd take the blame")	Positive Affect ("I like her")	Negative Affect ("I hated him, he was always interfering")	Similarity ("We have the same values")	Differentiation ("We have nothing in common, we could never stand each other's friends")	Compatibility ("We enjoyed each other's company")	Activity ("We still play cards when we get together")	Role Modeling ("I learned a lot from him")	Collaboration ("It was better when we talked things out, we were a better team than individuals")
Elementary School	+	+	+						
High School	+	+			+	+		+	+
Just Before Leaving Home	+	+			+	+	+	+	+
Beginning of Subject's Marriage	+	+		+		+	+		
Birth of Subject's First Child									
When Subject's Children left Home							+		
Death of a Parent	+	+		+					+

Key: + = periods when each developmental theme was most salient or important

Figure 3.2. Freeman's (1989) Study Findings on the Most Significant Sibling Relationship: Developmental Themes Over the Life Span (N = 37)

family of origin), and at the death of a parent (see Figure 3.2). However, the quality of the sibling relationship in regard to collaboration is different during these periods. The subjects' description of this dimension during the elementary school period indicates it is often impulsive and reactive to some external threat such as stress related to the parental relationship or peer conflict. One example involved physical child abuse by the mother which resulted in an older brother and the subject spontaneously hiding from and/or helping to distract her when she was drinking and abusive.

In the periods of leaving home and the death of a parent, the sibling collaboration seems to have a more planned, proactive, or sibling unit-initiated quality. In one situation, the chosen sibling (an older brother) and the subject decided to become roommates and developed a six month plan to save money so that they could move out of the parents' home together. Previous efforts by each of them to move alone had resulted in the parents' covert sabotaging of their plans by using money as an inducement for them to remain dependent. Although the qualitative aspects of the collaboration task/theme shifts over the developmental cycle, a common result is the strengthening of the sibling bond (or solidarity). This process is similar to Pollak and Hundermar's (1984) description of gang formation within the sibling unit as a result of parental neglect or rejection.

Influence of Earlier Sibling Relationships on Adult Sibling Relationships. Many of the childhood and adolescent sibling relationships described previously seem to have influenced the subjects' current relationships with their siblings in adulthood. Some of those unchanging relationships were reported as positive while others were reported as increasingly distant and hostile. In one family, for example, the subject and his siblings were rivals for the parents' affection and often took sides when the parents were in conflict based on which parent was in control of a particular situation. The father and his parents and siblings were in business together, and disagreements between them and between the subject's parents over finances and who had the power to make business decisions were constant. The subject and his siblings scapegoated each other and took turns in the victim role in their continuing efforts to top one another throughout their young years.

The subject related a story during the interview that typifies his current distant and hostile relationship with the identified sibling, an older brother. He had become a partner in a business with this brother.

They fought for several years and then the brother succeeded in ousting the subject from the business. The subject received a lot of support from one sister at the time, but very little from other family members. The subject then refused to be present at the parents' home whenever the older brother and "nonsupportive" siblings were present. Several years later when the parents purchased a house for this sister and her family, the older brother called her to suggest that her husband should get a better job so he could buy his own house instead of allowing his in-laws to do so. When the sister told the subject about the phone call, he called his former business partner and "told him off" for interfering in the sister's family life. This sibling triangle of victim (scapegoat), perpetrator (bad guy), and rescuer (good guy) simply mirrors their childhood sibling relationships and the relationships between the subject's father and his siblings ("maintaining distance").

Although some negative sibling relationships from childhood did not become positive in adulthood, they did improve and did not involve cut-offs such as in the example above. In one situation, the older sister was described as the family hero in childhood: she was a high achiever and was distant and often angry with her younger sister and parents. In contrast, the subject described herself as the exact opposite of the older sister as part of a process of deidentification. The subject acted out in school, used drugs beginning at age 13, and did poorly academically. She felt her efforts to gain acceptance from her older sibling and the parents were always rebuffed, so eventually she decided she would get even by causing problems.

When she was 16, she joined Youth for Christ and stopped using drugs, encouraging her sister to join the organization where they experienced mutual participation in the same activity for the first time in years. This alliance or collaboration helped them to handle conflicts with their parents about curfew and choice of friends. It also brought them close together emotionally for a period (the "making a personal choice" type of sibling solidarity). In adulthood, they have become distant from one another again, but without the previous hostility. They generally only have contact through the parents' inviting them to the same family functions (the "maintaining contact" type of solidarity). They tolerate each other simply because they are related, see themselves as very different in values and interests, and often only communicate through the mother primarily as they did when they were children.

Other subjects had positive relationships with siblings which have continued throughout their adult years. One male subject who is gay remembers his older brother as being supportive when he told the parents about his sexual preference at 25. The brother refused to boycott family events as requested by the parents when the subject brought his partner with him. The brother was also understanding during a period when the subject was a drug abuser **and** during several periods of treatment and relapse. The subject describes their current relationship as close even though there has been some friction about differences in their lifestyles: what they spend their money on and the older sibling's "swinging" nonmonogamous marriage.

Impact of Adult Sibling Relationships on Other Significant Relationships. The findings indicate that the subjects often developed relationships with significant others that in some ways reflected resolved and unresolved issues from their relationships with the identified sibling. In some circumstances, the subjects seemed completely unaware of those dynamics, some even denied them as a possibility when the question was raised during the interview based on information they had shared. In the example mentioned previously about sibling incest, the subject had been married to a man who, in a similar manner, sexually and physically abused her. And like her brother, this woman's husband had been an alcoholic during their marriage.

This woman could describe the violation of trust that occurred when her brother abused rather than protected her as "an older brother is supposed to do," and her unresolved anger because he has continued to deny that the incest occurred even when she has confronted him several times in adulthood. She remains distant from the brother and rebuffs his attempts to maintain contact and the appearance of a close sibling relationship.

McCollum (1990) notes that "Not maintaining contact with an abusive sibling in adulthood may be an act of self-preservation, not an emotional failure" (p. 94). This subject's denial that her husband was similar to her brother or that the marriage could be a repetition of the loss of trust that she experienced with her brother may be part of her current efforts to cope with the abusive sibling relationship. She may not be ready at this time to examine how that relationship might have influenced her other relationships with men. Although some research has been conducted on the impact of sibling relationships on the choice of love partners, the findings have been inconclusive generally (Greenfield and Weatherly, 1986; Abend, 1984). Therefore, additional research is needed in this area.

In other situations, subjects indicated an awareness of the connections between their siblings and other relationships. One subject reported that her work relationships were characterized by the same interpersonal issues that were of concern in the sibling relationship: overfunctioning and boundary infringements. She felt she recreated family and sibling dynamics in each of her work experiences by focusing on those issues. She would seek out relationships with coworkers in which her privacy, individuality, and personal identity would be subsumed. This type of work relationship created stress and caused her to make frequent job changes. What she experienced as unresolved overprotection by an older sibling encouraged her to recreate similar self-defeating work relationships until she was able to recognize this pattern. She is now able to identify when she is close to repeating the pattern and to resist getting involved or "hooked" into the same type of dysfunctional work relationships. She has also decided she is not likely to ever have the type of equal relationship she desires with that particular sibling.

Similarly, the findings indicate that some subjects' adult choices of friends may be influenced by dynamics in their sibling relationships. A number of subjects concluded that they are more demanding of themselves and their friends in adulthood in an effort to keep from repeating some of the mistakes they have made in their sibling relationships. Those subjects stressed being open and sharing how they actually feel about interactions with friends along with the need to point out when things are not going well. One subject said her tendency to "hide" how she feels from her sister has made her more aware of how she did the same thing with friends for a period of time. The sister was a very argumentative during childhood and, similarly, in their adult relationship is often angry and controlling. The subject's response has been to become "cut-off" from her sister periodically when hiding her feelings does not work. Another subject commented that his brother had rejected him and chosen to be closer to friends all of their lives. Consequently, the subject feels he now finds it hard to trust and maintain friendships as an adult.

In contrast, many of the subjects who described their adult sibling relationships as close indicated that this has helped them to recognize when particular friendships are dysfunctional. Others noted that they view their siblings as close friends in adulthood. That experience has made them more tolerant of their friends' flaws but also more willing to work at maintaining difficult friendships over time. Research in this area has not documented if and how sibling relationships influence adult friendships (Leventhal, 1970; Greenfield and Weatherley, 1986). But some of the descriptive literature suggests that when sibling relationships do not work well, friends sometimes provide the sense of connection that may be missing between siblings (McCollum, 1990).

Sibling relationships seemed to influence many subjects' adult relationships with their parents as well. Allan's (1977) concept of parents in the role of mediators when siblings simply tolerate each other was evident in some of the descriptions of family dynamics by subjects. The parents in those situations often provided indirect information about other siblings to the subjects. One young adult subject stated this parental role made him feel closer to the parents, but he also felt the role gave them more control over his life than they should have at his age.

Watzlawick, Weakland, and Fisch's (1974) description of system dynamics related to maintenance of a family's emotional distance was illustrated by some subjects' sibling/parental relationships. This concept means that relationships may change in a family, but the overall balance of emotional distance in the system remains the same, thus maintaining the status quo. In one subject's family as the emotional distance between her and a younger brother increased, it was counterbalanced by their mother becoming more distant from the subject and closer to the brother. When the subjects' job and the retired father's volunteer activities in the same field brought them closer and gave them something in common, the mother became even more distant and uninvolved with the subject. These and other relationship dynamics related to siblings have implications for formal and informal treatment.

Implications for Treatment

The findings from the author's retrospective study of sibling relationships and the previous review of the literature in that area may be useful to helping professionals in a number of ways. The conclusions suggest that social workers, psychologists, family therapists, child guidance and family service practitioners, addiction counselors, and mental health therapists can apply this knowledge in their work with individuals and families across the lifespan. The focus of therapeutic efforts on sibling relationships is important in both formal and informal helping situations.

Formal Treatment and Prevention

Helping professionals may be able to provide more effective services to families and to individuals who want to work on sibling issues in their formal treatment sessions. This can be accomplished by integrating the focus on sibling relationships and how they influence other childhood and adult relationships with traditional family assessment and treatment activities. The genogram and ecomap (Hartman, 1984), as well as the practitioner's application of systems theory, could be expanded to include questions about the nature of sibling relationships in the client's current situation and in the family's generational history (See Chapter 4 for a detailed discussion on this topic).

More efforts could be made to involve children and adolescents in family treatment, not only to impact the parent/child relationship problems in the family, but to increase sibling solidarity and other sibling supports as well (a combined form of prevention and treatment). The practitioner may need to be creative in providing different forms of sibling treatment in dyads, triads, sibling groups, or other combinations in order to address what Bank and Kahn (1975) call the autonomous functions or dysfunctions in sibling relationships. Family network therapy may need to be focused more on sibling relationships in some situations than it has been in the past. Often such sessions include extended family members and nonrelated support persons without particular attention to important strengths or conflicts that exist in natural sibling relationships or networks. McCollum (1990) noted that while siblings may drift apart at particular points in the life cycle their bond may remain strong. During crises, developmental transitions or other key times, having a shared task in treatment may help to address the immediate situation and reactivate the sibling bond.

In individual work, homework assignments may be useful when siblings and other family members are unavailable to be involved in treatment for many reasons. Homework can take the form of telephone contacts, letters, or visits during family celebrations or transitions to handle unresolved sibling issues (Hartman and Laird, 1983). In-session tasks can include the Gestalt "hot seat" technique of talking to siblings as though they are present to resolve issues (Blugerman, 1986).

Family education about sibling relationships may be useful as a preventive strategy. Family sessions involving children and adolescents can be used to normalize some sibling interactions and to allay parental concerns and their sense of obligation to intervene in what may be autonomous sibling functions. Family life education programs can provide information for the general public about sibling relationships that clarifies and normalizes expected behavior in the area of sibling relationships. Problematic sibling relationships in which one or more siblings may be in pain may need to be the focus of treatment in order to address deidentification, rivalry, scapegoating, or parental triangulation of a child, all factors that negatively affect sibling relationships.

Self-Help Activities

In addition to these formal treatment and prevention services, helping professionals may be able to provide informal consultation or to facilitate education and support groups focused on sibling relationships. Victim support groups and 12 step programs are examples of services in which the focus could include the loss of a sibling or other relative to violence or on how to cope with the addiction of such relatives (Freeman, 1992). Practitioners could encourage natural sibling subsystems to form their own informal support groups during times of crisis or other transitions: when an aging parent or one of the sibling's children dies, when siblings' children have left home, when one sibling gets a divorce or is critically ill, or at the point of retirement. These types of self-help activities help to strengthen the sibling bond and can contribute to the overall growth and development of individuals across the lifespan.

Conclusion

It is clear from the foregoing discussion that sibling relationships are an important part of childhood and adult development. They influence and are influenced by other primary relationships across the life span, including those with parents, coworkers, love partners, and friends. Additional influences on sibling and other relationships include changing developmental tasks and themes which are common to all individuals and the family system dynamics that may vary from family to family. While family systems approaches and techniques such as the genogram and ecomap help to clarify the effects of sibling relationships, these approaches and techniques are too limited in their current applications. Failure to include siblings in treatment in relation to their importance may be due to practitioners' own sibling and other relationship experiences. Additional research and improved education of practitioners in this area can enhance the quality of prevention and treatment services to families and individuals. Such efforts also can help to strengthen the sibling bond and other resources that siblings can provide in their self-help activities with each other.

REFERENCES

Abend, S. (1984). Sibling love and object choice. *Psychoanalytic Quarterly, LIII,* 425–436.

Allan, G. (1977). Sibling solidarity. *Journal of Marriage and Family, 39,* 177–184.

Bank, S. and Kahn, M.D. (1982). *The sibling bond.* New York: Basic Books.

Bank, S. and Kahn, M.D. (1975). Sisterhood-brotherhood is powerful: Sibling subsystems and family therapy. *Family Process, 14,* 311–337.

Bengston, V.L., Cutler, N.E., Mangen, D.J., and Marshall, V.W. (1985). Generations, cohorts, and relations between age groups. In R.A. Binstock and E. Shanas (Eds.), *Handbook of aging and the social sciences* (Second Edition) (304–338). New York: Van Nostrand Reinhold.

Blugerman, M. (1986). Contributions of gestalt theory to social work treatment. In F.J. Turner (Ed.), *Social work treatment: Interlocking theoretical approaches* (69–90). New York: Free Press.

Bossard, J.H.S. and Ball, E.S. (1956). *The large family system.* Philadelphia: University of Pennsylvania Press.

Bultena, G.L. (1969). Rural-urban differences in the familial interaction of the aged. *Rural Sociology, 34,* 5–15.

Cicirelli, V.G. (1985). Sibling relationships throughout the life cycle. In Lucian L'Abate (Ed.), *The handbook of psychology and therapy* (177–214). Homewood, IL: Dorsey Press.

Cicirelli, V.G. (1984). Marital disruption and adult children's perception of their siblings' help to elderly parents. *Family Relations, 33,* 613–621.

Cicirelli, V.G. (1982). Sibling influence throughout the lifespan. In M.E. Lamb and B. Sutton-Smith (Eds.), *Sibling relationships: Their nature and significance across the life span* (267–284). Hillsdale, NJ: Erlbaum.

Cicirelli, V.G. (1980). Sibling relationships in adulthood: A lifespan perspective. In L.W. Poon (Ed.), *Aging in the 1980's* (455–462). Washington, DC: American Psychological Association.

Coward, R.T. (1987). Factors associated with the configuration of the helping networks of noninstitutionalized elders. *Journal of Gerontological Social Work, 10,* 113–132.

Dorfman, L.T. and Mertens, C.E. (1990). Kinship relations in retired rural men and women. *Family Relations, 39,* 166–173.

Freeman, E.M. (In press). Substance abuse treatment: Continuum of care in services to families. In E.M. Freeman (Ed.), *Substance abuse treatment: A family systems perspective.* Newbury Park, CA: Sage.

Freeman, E.M. (1984). Multiple losses in the elderly: An ecological perspective. *Social Casework, 65,* 287–296.

Goetting, A. (1986). The developmental tasks of siblingship over the life cycle. *Journal of Marriage and the Family, 48,* 703–714.

Greenfield, G. and Weatherley, D. (1986). Sex-of-sibling effects on opposite and same-sex friendships. *Psychological Reports, 59,* 67–70.

Hartman, A. (1984). Diagrammatic assessment of family relationships. In B. Compton and B. Galaway, *Social work processes* (52–59). Homewood, IL: Dorsey.

Hartman, A. and Laird, J. (1983). *Family-centered social work practice.* New York: Free Press.

Kivett, V.R. (1985). Consanguinity and kin level: Their importance to the helping networks of older adults. *Journal of Gerontology, 40,* 228–234.

Krout, J.A. (1988). Rural versus urban differences in elderly parents' contact with their children. *The Gerontologist, 28,* 198–203.

Lamb, M.E. (1982). Sibling relationships across the lifespan: An overview and introduction. In M.E. Lamb and B. Sutton-Smith (Eds.), *Sibling relationships: Their nature and significance across the lifespan* (1–27). Hillsdale, NJ: Erlbaum.

Lee, G.R. and Ihinger-Tallman, M. (1980). Sibling interaction and morale. *Research on Aging, 2,* 367–391.

Leigh, G.K. (1982). Kinship interaction over the family life span. *Journal of Marriage and the Family, 44,* 197–208.

Leventhal, G. (1970). Influence of brothers and sisters on sex-role behavior. *Journal of Personality and Social Psychology, 16,* 542–465.

McCollum, E.E. (1990). Our brothers' and sisters' keepers: Rediscovering the bonds. *New Choices,* 92–94.

Mosatche, H.S., Brady, E.M., and Noberini, M.R. (1983). A retrospective lifespan study of the closest sibling relationship. *The Journal of Psychology, 113,* 237–243.

Pollak, O. and Hundermar, D. (1984). Some unexplored aspects of the sibling experience. *Adolescence, 76,* 869–874.

Powers, E.A., Keith, P.M., and Goudy, W.J. (1981). Family networks of the rural aged. In R.T. Coward and W.M. Smith, Jr. (Eds.), *The family in rural society* (199–217). Boulder, CO: Westview Press.

Rosenberg, G.S. and Anspach, D.F. (1973). Sibling solidarity in the working class. *Journal of Marriage and the Family, 35,* 108–113.

Rosenberg, G.S. and Anspach, D.F. (1972). Working-class matricentricity. *Journal of Marriage and the Family, 34,* 437–507.

Ross, H. and Milgram, J. (1982). Important variables in adult sibling relationships: A qualitative analysis. In M.E. Lamb and B. Sutton-Smith (Eds.), *Sibling relationships: Their nature and significance across the lifespan* (225–249). Hillsdale, NJ: Erlbaum.

Ross, H.G. and Milgram, J.I. (1980). Rivalry in adult sibling relationships: Its antecedents and dynamics. Paper presented at the Annual Meeting of the American Psychological Association, Montreal, Canada, September 3.

Schacter, F.F., Shore, E., Feldman-Rotman, S., Marquis, R.E., and Campbell, S. (1976). Sibling deidentification. *Developmental Psychology, 12,* 418–427.

Scott, J.P. (1983). Siblings and other kin. In T.H. Brubaker (Ed.), *Family relationships in later life* (47–62). Beverly Hills, CA: Sage.

Shorkey, C.T. and Rosen, W. (In press). Alcohol addiction and co-dependency: Facilitating movement toward autonomous family relationships. In E.M. Freeman (Ed.), *Substance abuse treatment: A family systems perspective.* Newbury Park, CA: Sage.

Suggs, P.K. and Kivett, V.R. (1986–87). Rural/urban elderly and siblings: Their value consensus. *International Journal of Aging and Human Development, 24,* 149–159.

Sutton-Smith, B. and Rosenberg, B.G. (1970). *The sibling.* New York: Holt, Rhinehart, and Winston.

Watzlawich, P., Weakland, J.H., and Fisch, R. (1974). *Change: Principles of problem formation and problem resolution.* New York: W. W. Norton.

Chapter 4

SIBLINGS AND FAMILY THERAPY: AN HISTORICAL PERSPECTIVE

Although siblings bring many strengths to their relationships, they may experience a number of problems unique to sibships during various points in the lifespan for which family therapy may be the appropriate treatment. In some circumstances, sibling issues may **directly** affect the individual, the sibship (the sibling subsystem), and/or the family's functioning in a negative manner. Examples include physical fights among young siblings, their collusion in avoiding household and other family responsibilities, grief due to an involuntary separation from siblings in childhood or adulthood, or adult siblings who are overinvolved in each other's lives to the point of impeding the growth of one or more of them (Timberlake and Hamlin, 1982; Bennett, 1990; Klein, Alexander, and Parsons, 1977). Here, the sibling issues are often the direct and central focus of the treatment sessions, depending on the presenting problem.

In other situations, the central issues might involve individual internal factors (low self-esteem) or other interpersonal relationships and areas of functioning (conflicts with coworkers) that are being affected **indirectly** by sibling relationships (Freeman, 1989). The indirect effects may stem from unresolved sibling issues during childhood (such as sibling rivalry) or ineffective coping patterns that have been generalized from sibling relationships to other relationships and areas of functioning. In those situations, the sibling issues may be barriers to the resolution of the central problems. The sibling issues may need to be addressed in treatment as related factors or as potential resources for initiating changes in the central problem or in sibling relationships (Kahn and Bank, 1981).

In spite of differences in this range of problems, until recently family therapy would have been used to address them in a number of effective ways. Using family systems theory as a guide, practitioners have often assumed that only the total family unit should be seen in sessions and that sibling issues should be addressed in relation to the total family (Hamlin and Timberlake, 1981; Miller and Cantwell, 1976). Other practitioners in similar cases recommend individual treatment based on the assumption that the sibling issues are a reflection of individual problems, particularly in adults (Bowen, 1974). Another approach has been to view the sibling issues of children as a function of problems in the marital dyad, leading to a decision to provide family and couples therapy either simultaneously or sequentially (Minuchin, 1974). Adjunct treatment might be provided to the children in these circumstances, but mostly as a supportive strategy while the primary work takes place in family and couples therapy.

Many skilled practitioners have provided treatment to sibships in full acknowledgement of the subsystem's autonomous functions and influence on individual members. They have begun the type of paradigm shift that is needed in family therapy as a whole. New knowledge about sibling relationships is emerging to indicate that family therapy can enhance its' prior effectiveness in serving families. This knowledge requires a new look at these relationships and family dynamics.

The treatment strategies above and prior knowledge tend to imply that sibships are benign subsystems within families that are subject to the system's unidirectional influences. Bank and Kahn (1976) indicate this view implies that sibling relationships are the "... products of the interaction between each child and the parents rather than among the children themselves" (p. 312). It is clear from the discussion in Chapters 2 and 3, however, that sibships are important in their own right and that addressing sibling issues at that level can be a significant and powerful form of treatment. The treatment of choice **and** the primary service, therefore, may be sessions for siblings without other family members being present or groups for siblings from several different families. An added incentive for providing primary treatment to siblings as needed is the opportunity to enhance the overall functioning of the family unit.

Given these assumptions, the following question must be raised: To what extent has the family therapy field shifted its' focus to address sibling issues directly over the years, considering the important autonomous functions that sibships perform within families? This chapter provides an historical perspective of the family therapy field in terms of its' response to sibling issues. On the basis of the field's failure to fully explore and address sibling relationships, functions, and treatment, recommendations are made for broadening the current structure of family therapy to a family treatment field. Such a step can redirect attention to this neglected area and to an emphasis on the strengths and other resources that siblings can provide to each other. The responsibility of social workers and other helping professionals to assume a leadership role in these efforts to broaden the scope of family therapy is discussed as well.

Family Therapy and Sibling Relationships: An Historical Review of the Literature

Family therapy emerged as a recognizable mode of treatment during the 1950's when the focus was on treating the family as a unit (Janzen and Harris, 1986). Consequently, the literature on family therapy prior to the 1970's contains very little information about the treatment of siblings except as members of the total family unit that is the focus of therapy. For example, in terms of substance abuse problems, Glynn (1981) summarized articles written on drugs and family therapy and found that even during the period between 1970 and 1981 only four of 117 articles included any specific mention of siblings. The literature also contains almost no research on sibling issues or interactions until recently (Riskin and Faunce, 1972). In the twenty years or so since the 1970's, there has been a gradual shift in the focus of this literature to include sibling interactions, issues, and treatment. For clarity, three distinct periods have been identified in terms of important shifts in the focus of this literature.

The Period From 1970 to 1979

This initial period in which the literature began to focus more on treatment directed toward sibling relationships coincided with the growing awareness by researchers and practitioners that sibling interaction and relationships are overlooked as important areas of family functioning. Bank and Kahn (1976) summarized some of the advantages of providing treatment to siblings in terms of family functioning:

> Understanding of sibling subsystem structure and dynamics can lead to more flexible therapeutic interventions. Direct work with siblings provides the therapist with more options and greater leverage in producing change for all siblings, as well as for other family members (p. 494).

The literature during this early period was focused on theories about sibling relationships in addition to some of the other benefits of sibling treatment. Acceptance of particular theoretical assumptions helped to shift the scope of treatment to include sibling issues, but often in restrictive ways. For instance, the theories of Adler (1959) and Bowen (1972) were popular during this period; these authors assumed sibling rivalry is a result of sibling sex status, birth order, and family size. Bank and Kahn (1976) note that such theories shifted attention to sibling relationships in individual treatment sessions, but practitioners continued to exclude all but cursory discussion of those relationships in family therapy. Furthermore, seldom were the siblings of referred clients included in sessions focused on sibling issues, thus preventing the practitioner from gaining "...a more balanced view of the child in his natural sibling ecology..." (Bank and Kahn, 1976, p. 499). Similarly, Bowen's (1972) theory of differentiation of self does not typically require siblings to be present in individual treatment sessions for adult clients. However, those individual sessions include attention to how to differentiate from the sibling subsystem while maintaining a personal relationship with siblings.

Another theory featured prominantly in the family therapy literature during this period was Caplow's (1968) theory of power relationships and sibling coalitions within families. This theory assumes that when the father and mother are nearly equal in power but do not have a strong parental coalition, sibling rivalry will become intense as siblings compete for the coalition opportunities provided by the weak parental alliance. It is not surprising that this theory emphasized strengthening parental solidarity through couples or family therapy, assuming this step would lead to a reduction in the intensity of sibling rivalry and cross generational coalitions.

The family therapy literature during this period also described modalities and strategies that are beneficial in the treatment of siblings, and for the most part, focused on children under 12 years of age. One thrust was the use of siblings as "therapeutic agents" and consultants in family therapy, in contrast to the usual strategy of teaching behavior modification and structural family therapy techniques to parents only. Miller and Cantwell (1976) found that both positive changes and problems result when siblings are involved actively in a few family therapy sessions. In their study, siblings eliminated interactions that reinforced problem behaviors in the target child **and** generalized their learning to other target behaviors, but they were uncomfortable in revealing family secrets during sessions about the parents' reactions to target siblings. Minuchin's (1974) structural family therapy involves separate sessions with the consulting sibling and the identified patient, not in the presence of parents, perhaps to address this problem. In general, the movement to provide behaviorally-oriented and structural family therapy in the natural environment of the home rather than in the practitioner's office might have provided opportunities not previously available for focusing on sibling interactions as a special aspect of the family assessment and intervention process (Miller and Miller, 1977; Patterson, 1971).

This literature also includes descriptions of appropriate goals for sibling therapy. A basic assumption in this early literature is that substitute parental relationships may be established within the sibling subsystem (Anthony, 1970). Ranieri and Pratt (1978) indicate that for this reason, it may be necessary to treat the sibling subsystem in order " . . . to intervene in the dysfunction of a particular child . . . and facilitate change eventually in the entire family." (p. 418). Moreover, a focus on sibling relationships in treatment has been found to serve as a model for improving peer relationships in general, increasing expressions of positive feelings between siblings, decreasing sibling sexual fantasies about each other, and decreasing recidivism in delinquents while preventing delinquency in their siblings (Ranieri and Pratt, 1978; Pfouts, 1976; Mordock, 1974; Klein, Alexander, and Parsons, 1977).

The related intervention strategies described in much of this literature help to clarify how these goals are accomplished through the following activities (Bank and Kahn, 1976; Minuchin, 1974; Klein et al., 1977; Mordock, 1974):

1. Teach siblings to communicate more effectively and educably with each other in order to strengthen the sibling subsystem.
2. Use homework assignments to reduce the power and influence of parental siblings as a way to increase the power of the parents and improve their relationship to identified patient.
3. Use sibling concepts to relabel and normalize family problems to remove parents from issues related to the sibling subsystem (e.g., allowing siblings to establish their own ways of resolving conflict).
4. Rehearse behaviors with brothers and sisters insession that the client will try out later on parents and others to improve those relationships based on feedback from the siblings.
5. Use a sibling "rally" to help siblings to express and resolve resent-

ments when an impasse is reached in the sibling subsystem, thus encouraging the use of on-going rallies outside treatment sessions for addressing mutual subsystem issues.

The Period From 1980 to 1985

After the 1970's, the emphasis on sibling issues and relationships in treatment increased. Moreover, there was a greater emphasis placed on addressing those issues through primary treatment to siblings from the same family (sibships) without the presence of the parents and to siblings from different families in small groups. Another important shift in the family therapy literature during this period is the new focus on sibling issues as the presenting or primary problem rather than only as a secondary problem or as a treatment resource for resolving problems related to parents or to the individual client. For instance, Timberlake and Hamlin (1982) discuss the impact of separation on siblings placed in different foster homes related to child development and the development of natural support systems. Those authors utilized sibling treatment groups for helping children to address separation and loss issues that arise from the break-up of natural sibling groups. Their decision to utilize sibling treatment groups was the result of a study on foster care: while 93% of 187 children in placement had at least one sibling, three-fourths of those children were **not** placed with their siblings (Timberlake, Cutler, and Strobino, 1980).

Such losses can precipitate a grief and mourning process that involves withdrawal of emotional connections with the absent sibling and a failure to reinvest in new relationships. For these reasons, Timberlake and Hamblin (1982) recommend the use of the sibling treatment group prior to and after placement if possible. One finding is that these groups must help the members to recognize and label the feelings they are experiencing related to the loss, examine the roles assumed previously by siblings and the impact of lost roles, as well as develop plans for members to visit and communicate with each other.

Other authors have utilized sibling therapy groups as the primary treatment or in combination with other modalities to resolve losses that occur when a sibling becomes emancipated or departs from the family of origin, when the divorce and remarriage of a parent requires an adjustment to new stepsiblings, and when the referring person for the identified patient is a sibling (Hamlin and Timberlake, 1981; Rosenberg, 1980; Palazzoli, 1985). More specifically, Rosenberg (1980) indicates that sibling therapy is appropriate and effective for helping blended or "reorganizing families" to cope with the demands of new relationships. This author, like many authors in the literature of this period, encourages family therapists to re-examine and de-emphasize assumptions about the competitive nature of the sibling bond that have made practitioners reluctant to work with the sibling group. Rosenberg (1980) concluded that sibling therapy is beneficial where a sibling relationship is impeding appropriate development of an individual and the presence of parents is a barrier to the resolution of a problem. It may be indicated also when parents are unavailable or have inadequate parenting skills and siblings have the capacity to provide a natural (nurturing) support system to each other.

While the literature described above addresses the use of sibling and family therapy when sibling issues are the primary problem, other literature during this period is focused on the use of sibling therapy as a resource for helping individuals to cope with parental problems or with their siblings' special needs. Rosenberg (1980) recommends the use of combined sibling and family therapy for helping young siblings adjust to parental divorce. In a similar vein, Kahn and Bank (1981) conclude that individual and sibling therapy can be used to develop sibling alliances to help resolve dysfunctional relationships between adult clients and their parents. Such an approach is assumed to produce a greater change in the parent-adult child relationship than involving the parents directly in treatment, while the approach strengthens also the adult sibling support network and enhances the growth of individual siblings.

Family therapy was used in combination with other modalities during this period to help children meet the special needs of physically and mentally challenged siblings and those with a chronic illness. For example, Cunningham and Betsa (1981) utilized family therapy along with short term educational groups for siblings from different families to help the latter cope with sisters and brothers who had cancer. In addition, sibling dyads have been used by other researchers to train children to help their autistic siblings learn cognitive tasks such as telling time (Schreibman, O'Neill, and Koegel, 1983). Powell, Salzberg, Rule, Levy, and Itzkowitz (1983) trained "normal" children to help their mentally retarded siblings to develop reciprocal social interactions in a child- and parent-trainer family therapy program.

The Period From 1986 to the Present

Building on the knowledge about sibling relationships and family therapy that developed during the two preceding periods, the current period witnessed a broadening of the range of problems being addressed in the literature. Those sibling-related problems included death, alcohol and other drug abuse, eating disorders, chronic illnesses, physical rehabilitation after trauma, family violence, sibling conflicts, developmental disabilities, identity development, and parental divorce (Koch-Hattem, 1986; Dunn and Munn, 1986; Brody, Stoneman, and Burke, 1987; Huberty and Huberty, 1986; Bendor, 1990; Rosenberg, 1980; Schibuk, 1989; Schacter and Stone, 1987; Powell et al., 1983).

A second way in which the literature of this period is different from previous periods is that there was more attention to helping sisters and brothers perform their natural developmental and social support roles for each other. Powell et al. (1983) found sibling therapy was more effective than family therapy with parents in helping children and youth from 4 to 17 years of age to facilitate increased independence in their siblings who had cerebal palsy. The areas of independence included activities of daily living and range of motion exercises. Training of the "normal" youngsters helped them to assume the natural roles of teachers, role models, and agents of change with their brothers and sisters.

A third shift in the literature of this period involved an effort to address some of the more subtle aspects of sibling problems and relationships. In regard to eating disorders, Lewis (1987) indicates that, "While family therapy focuses on triadic and whole family relationship patterns, the sibling groups' impact on bulimia has been virtually overlooked" (p. 641). The symptom of bulimia may communicate five different categories of messages from the identified patient to one or more siblings that may change over time. The five categories of messages include the following (Lewis, 1987, p. 641):

1. Connecting message: "I'll bring us together" (even if it is through fighting about the bulimia).
2. Equalizing message: "See I too have a problem, we are not so very different."
3. Deflecting message: "I will protect you" (by deflecting the parents' attention away from other siblings).
4. Peacemaking message: "I will make you important and give you a

role in the family (e.g., as a support to the parents in their attempts to cope with the bulimia).
5. Dirty-fighting message: "Got-cha!" (a covert way to steal parental attention from siblings or to repay a childhood debt related to power).

If and when bulimics change their roles with parents **and** siblings in the family and eliminate the bulimia, this change may be the result of resolving some of the sibling issues underlying one or more of the messages described above. In conjunction with the role changes that occur in the identified patient through sibling and family therapy, the roles of other siblings change as well (Lewis, 1987). These outcomes are in contrast to the focus during the previous periods where the emphasis was on changing the triad only (the parents and the identified patient).

In another example of the shift in this literature to more subtle analyses of sibling issues and a stronger emphasis on providing direct sibling treatment is the work of Huberty and Huberty (1986) on complementary roles. Those authors note that among siblings "competition between two members of the family is always expressed through differences in character, temperament, interests, and ability. Conversely, the similarity of characteristics among siblings always indicates alliances" (p. 36). Therefore, where one sibling succeeds (in becoming the family hero for example), the others often give up on attaining that role. On the other hand, if one sibling shows weaknesses or deficiencies (in the scapegoat or lost child role), another steps in to assume a special or more competent role. Role assumption may occur not just based on birth order as indicated by earlier research, but also based on an interaction between this and other factors (e.g., age groupings, gender issues, and stages of personal development among siblings) (Huberty and Huberty, 1986).

These complex role dynamics are important in determining appropriate treatment for siblings. An individual who assumes any of the family roles (scapegoat, lost child, mascot, or hero) can sabotage the treatment of another sibling. Huberty and Huberty (1986) and Freeman (1989) indicate that in drug dependent adolescents in particular, if siblings and other family members refuse to change and remold their complementary roles, they may fail to allow the recoverying adolescent (who may have been the family scapegoat) a new identity or role in the family. An older sibling in the superior and powerful hero role, for example, may sabotage the individuality and self-worth that a younger drug dependent sibling needs to individuate from parents and the older sibling hero. The hero can do this by simply holding onto his or her powerful role. Sibling and/or family therapy may be needed to accomplish the following interventions (Huberty and Huberty, 1986):

1. Help the hero painfully examine attitudes of superiority ("I'm better, nicer, more successful"), both for personal growth reasons and to improve the sibling relationship.
2. Encourage the two siblings to let go of the inappropriate (and complementary) substitute parent-child roles that they have assumed with each other.
3. Help the parents recognize and confront the sabotaging role with the older sibling who is the family hero.
4. Support the parents in encouraging the older sibling (often in his or her early twenties) to move out on his or her own.

Although this review of the literature on family therapy and sibling relationships has documented a gradually increasing emphasis on this area of practice, there remain aspects of the topic that have not been addressed. Thus, while the family therapy field has become more responsive to addressing this area, the amount of attention continues to be inadequate given the importance of sibling relationships. A broadening of the focus of conventional family therapy to encompass a family treatment field may make it more likely that sibling relationships will receive sufficient attention in the practice and research literature in the future. That step can provide more direction and guidance for implementing and evaluating effective treatment for the range of sibling issues identified in this review.

A More Inclusive Family Treatment Field

The previous literature review reflects the polarized views that have developed in the family therapy field about sibling relationships. Over the years those views have ranged from paying no attention to such relationships at all to focusing on them only in relation to the family to emphasizing primary treatment of sibships within the context of other relevant family issues. The latter position highlights the sibling subsystem as a major and unique component of the family system that carries out some of the family functions, but possesses some unique autonomous functions of its own that are not the direct result of family or parent/child interactions (Kahn and Bank, 1981).

Janzen and Harris (1986) indicate this duality allows the sibling subsystem "... to act in concert and independently in and out of the parental presence" (pp. 16–17). According to these authors, the sibling boundary, like the spouse and parental subsystem boundaries "... symbolizes the right of the ... subsystem to engage in its own internal processes without interference from outside its boundary" (p. 11). As it is presently conceived, even with the emerging perspectives noted in the literature review, family therapy is just beginning the paradigm shift necessary for considering and providing adequate treatment to the sibling subsystem. Treatment is being provided for that subsystem alone in some instances, while in other circumstances, it is being provided in combination with family therapy and other forms of intervention. A new concept or approach is needed to encompass the broad range of appropriate interventions that are needed, including family therapy. That approach must include a sound theoretical base and have clear operational guidelines for both the assessment and treatment process.

Theoretical Underpinnings

Freeman (1993) has noted that family systems theories include a range of bridging theories that help to explain system dynamics and strengths along with effective methods for changing dysfunctional family interactions. Those theories include behavioral, communications, structural, psychoanalytic, problem-solving, strategic, and intergenerational family systems approaches. Family and general systems theories can be expanded beyond their current use in family therapy to include the different approaches and modalities identified under family treatment in Table 4.1 (Freeman, 1993). Within this broader framework of treatment, the possible options for addressing sibling issues has been increased. While some attention to those issues is possible within any of the components of family treatment, sibling therapy, multiple sibling groups, and sibling-oriented individual treatment offer the most concentrated focus for those issues (see Figure 4.1).

Table 4.1 illustrates additional underlying theories for each of the modalities included (e.g., mediation, task centered, and role theories) as well as the composition, main focus, and treatment procedures for each. The composition for each modality has been likewise expanded beyond conventional family therapy to include alternate family structures (e.g.,

Table 4.1. Components of Family Treatment as a Theoretical Approach.

Components	Modalities and Composition	Examples of Applicable Theories
Family-Oriented Individual Treatment for Siblings and/or Family Issues	Individual sessions/modality: an individiual from one sibship or family unit.	Role theory Structural family theory Intergenerational family theory Task Centered family theory
Couples Therapy/ Multiple Couples Therapy	Couple or Group Modality: married couples, cohabitating couples, divorced and divorcing couples, same sex couples (one or more couples).	Structural family theory Intergenerational family theory Small group theory
Sibling Therapy	Sibship Modality: sibling dyads, coalitions, subsystems from one family unit.	Role theory Structural family theory Task Centered family theory Intergenerational family theory
Multiple Sibling Groups	Group Modality: several sibling subsystems from different families.	Small group theory (e.g., mediation theory) Task centered family theory Problem-Solving family theory
Family Therapy	Family Modality: one family unit such as a nuclear family, blended family, or non blood-related family ("fictive kin").	The range of family theories including strategic, communications, intergenerational, structural, behavioral.
Family Network Therapy	Family and/or Social Network Modality: one nuclear family unit with extended intergenerational family members and/or non blood-related members ("fictive kin").	Intergenerational family theory Problem-solving family theory
Multiple Family Group Therapy	Group Modality: several different family units formed under social agency auspices or naturally based on a common perceived need.	Small group theory Community development theory General systems theory

same sex couples) and kinship relationships unique to some ethnic minority groups (e.g., "fictive kin" for nonblood kinship networks in

```
                                        As a Primary or Supplementary
                                        Component of Family Treatment

                                          ┌─────────────────┐
                                          │ Sibling Therapy │
                   ┌──────────────┐      └─────────────────┘
Most Common        │Family Therapy│ ──▶       ▲  │
Modalities in      │  Modality    │           │  ▼
Which the          └──────────────┘      ┌─────────────────────┐
Treatment of                             │Multiple Sibling Groups│
Sibling                                  └─────────────────────┘
Issues                                         ▲  │
Occurs                                         │  ▼
                   ┌──────────────┐      ┌─────────────────────┐
                   │  Individual  │ ──▶  │  Sibling-Oriented   │
                   │   Modality   │      │ Individual Treatment│
                   └──────────────┘      └─────────────────────┘
```

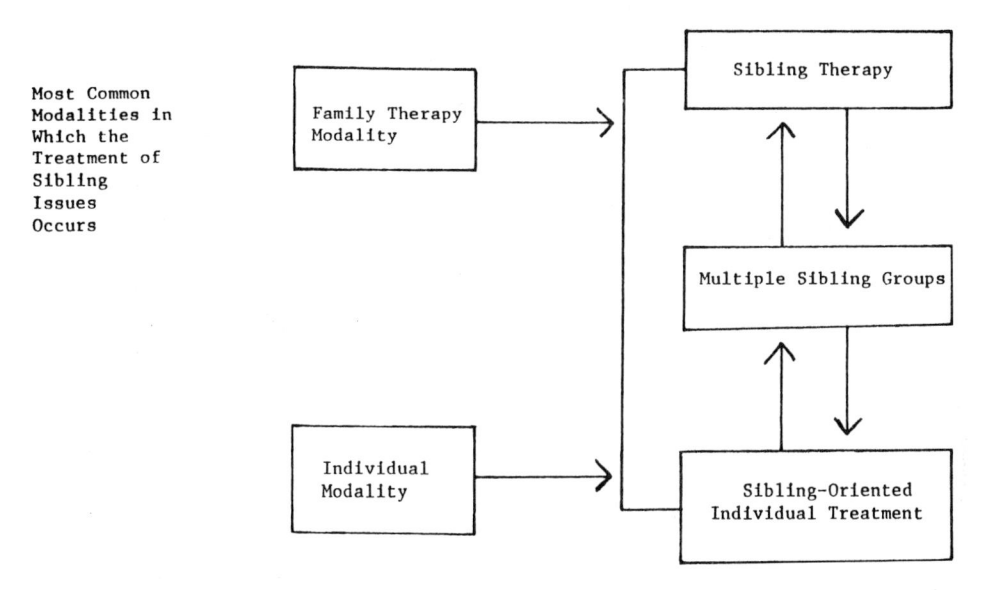

Figure 4.1. Components of Family Treatment Most Directly Focused on Sibling Relationships and Issues.

African-American families). Although some particular family therapy schools and individual practitioners have been providing treatment to these alternative family structures, the field as a whole has not done so. The term family therapy has been used in the literature to designate both a specific modality (therapy with one family) and a theoretical approach (family systems theory applied in any modality such as couple therapy). In Table 4.1, family therapy refers to one modality because family treatment is being used there to designate the overall family treatment approach.

An increasing number of practitioners and authors are now defining family therapy as a theoretical approach that can be applied to any single or combined set of modalities (i.e., family treatment) in order to broaden the number of theoretical applications that are possible (Hartman & Laird, 1983; Laird & Allen, 1983; Rhodes, 1986; Janzen and Harris, 1986). For instance, Rhodes (1986) notes that in family treatment, "The family may be treated as a whole or as smaller subgroups (subsystems) with or without extended family. At times, grandparents or sibling systems are targeted in a designated phase of treatment. As well, individual family members may be the focal point of a family-oriented treatment as the reciprocal and interactive effect family members have on one another is addressed" (p. 433). The determination of the focal point of family-oriented treatment should be made as part of the initial and on-going assessment process.

The Assessment Process

The genogram, a time-oriented cognitive map, has been utilized as the main procedure for assessing and monitoring changes in regard to family strengths and problems across all family systems approaches (McGoldrick and Gerson, 1985; Hartman, 1979; Hartman and Laird, 1983). It can illustrate very graphically intergenerational effects on the family as a whole and on the parental, marital, and child subsystems. While the current use of the genogram often touches on sibling relationships, in terms of their complementary or conflicting roles for example, this procedure could be used even more effectively in assessing that subsystem. And whenever possible, the entire sibship and other significant individuals or subsystems should be included in assessment and treatment sessions according to Lewis (1987), Huberty and Huberty (1986), Bank and Kahn (1976), and other authors.

Some potential areas of assessment in regard to the genogram and other tools include the following (for situations in which the presenting problem or subsequent information involve sibling issues either directly or indirectly):

1. Genogram: models for sibling relationships; ghosts (two people occupying the same emotional position in the family or in their respective sibships); or similar nicknames, labels, or sibling roles in the child, parent, or grandparent generations (Hartman and Laird, 1983; Logan, Freeman, and McRoy, 1987).
2. Social network analyses: quality of sibling relationships for the individual, sibship, or family involved in treatment (Tracy and Whittaker, 1990; Freeman, 1991).
3. Ecomap, timeline, or life history grid: changes in the siblings' relationships over time in terms of the developmental cycle and tasks (e.g., construct an ecomap for each developmental stage to reflect the relationship between sibling issues at the time and the tasks needing to be addressed, an ecological spatial assessment) (Hartman, 1979; Brown and Anderson, 1980).

4. Cultural ecomap: changes in sibling relationships and ethnic/racial identity within sibships of ethnic minority members in terms of the developmental cycle, related tasks, and supports/barriers related to the family, cultural group, or larger environment (Freeman and Landesman, 1992).

The above examples of assessment instruments for identifying and clarifying how sibling issues may be affecting a problem situation can be used alone or in combination as the need indicates. Some situations may require more specialized assessment procedures. Violence and other traumatic events involving siblings could be assessed with symptom check lists. For instance, the lists could include symptoms of loss and grief often experienced by siblings placed in separate foster homes or symptoms of post traumatic stress disorder for siblings who are victims of family violence or incest (Freeman, 1984; Pilat and Boomhower-Kresser, 1992; Hahn and West, 1985-86).

In a similar manner, the effects of living in a family in which a parent is an alcoholic could be assessed with inventories such as the children of alcoholics screening test (CAST) (Pilat and Jones, 1985). In all of these examples, the results from each sibling's assessment could be analyzed and compared to identify important influences among the siblings related to the problem and their respective strengths. The use of these instruments, along with an on-going observation and analysis of the sibling interactional process that occurs in session, can increase the quality of information available for determining an appropriate treatment strategy.

The Treatment Process

The issues identified during the assessment process will indicate who needs to be involved in the treatment sessions focused on sibling issues. As noted previously in Figure 4.1, the modalities of sibling therapy, multiple sibling groups, and sibling-oriented individual sessions offer the best opportunities to address sibling issues directly. Where sibling issues affect a problem situation indirectly (when an individual generalizes ineffective coping patterns from sibling experiences to new family relationships for instance), family or couples therapy may be more appropriate. However, other creative forms and combinations of treatment may be utilized in each situation.

In one example of individual treatment, a 35 year old client revealed during a session that she had been a victim of incest (her maternal grandfather was the perpetrator). Initially, her strong negative feelings about the grandfather had surfaced during assessment with the genogram. A later homework assignment involved having her make a visit to the parental home during a holiday celebration where, in sharing her secret, she learned that her mother had also been a victim. Hartman and Laird (1983) identify this powerful treatment strategy as "going home again" physically and psychologically in order to spread the problem (p. 237). Karpel (1980) supports the use of this strategy by cautioning practitioners against helping clients to keep family secrets that are barriers to their recovery and growth.

The revelation between mother and daughter freed the mother to explore with other family members whether any of them had been victims (she had never revealed her secret to any one before). The mother learned that two of her siblings and several of their children had been victimized by her father. She suspected that a third sister had been victimized, while the client believed **her** sister had been a victim too (both denied that they were victims or that they had been aware of the incest that had happened to their siblings). Perhaps the catalyst for the other family members' acknowledgements that the incest had occurred was the death of the grandmother during this period. The client felt that the intergenerational secret had been kept so long because the grandfather had always warned that if anyone told about what had happened the shock would kill the grandmother.

The client's mother and her two siblings initiated treatment in their home state in order to obtain help in encouraging their other sister to acknowledge her victimization. In the process, they received help in coping with the effects on them from revealing the family secret and in identifying unfinished business within the sibship (e.g., the older sisters had not revealed the incest while it was occurring, believing this would protect the younger sister but they also resented her status in the family as the special sister or family hero). The treatment later involved several sessions with the younger sister who continued to deny being victimized even though admitting she had been aware of one sister's incest experience. That information allowed the sibship to address her guilt from keeping the family secret. Too, they examined the effects of her distant/superior role versus their roles on their sibling relationships over the years.

Treatment with the client's mother and aunts provided a powerful illustration of the sibling problems in their generation that were influencing the client's sibling relationships, while also modeling the process of working through some of those issues. The similarities included the client's resentment of her sister's role as the family hero (and the client's role as the scapegoat). The client's individual work and later sessions involving the sister benefitted from the results of her mother's sibling therapy.

One outcome involved the mother and the aunts telephoning the client to thank her for helping to reveal the intergenerational secret and starting the family healing process. Their gratitude about the results of their treatment and the significance of the joint telephone call shifted the status of the client from family scapegoat to a knowledgeable collaborator. Hartman and Laird (1983) note that telephone calls "... are strategic communication devices in ... initiating role changes ... " (p. 241). Then too, the telephone call strengthened the client's alliance with her sister. After resolving some of their issues, they were able to mutually plan how to reconnect with their brother who was cut-off from the entire family.

This case highlights some important aspects of sibling treatment that can serve as general guidelines for this process (Hartman and Laird, 1983; Lewis, 1987; Huberty and Huberty, 1986; Freeman, 1989):

1. Explore the intergenerational aspects of sibling relationships in a family related to hidden scripts for the sibship or for the individual client within the sibship.
2. Help the client(s) utilize creative strategies to resolve cut-offs, ghosts, and family secrets as part of the healing process and to initiate changes in dysfunctional and painful sibling and other family roles.
3. When trying to strengthen sibling alliances, the most powerful route may be an indirect one rather than a direct one (e.g., rather than initially attempting to change the current sibling relationships, focus on intergenerational or individual barriers such as the impact of the mother's sibling relationship in the above case or the client's inability to talk about the incest with her mother).
4. In utilizing role change strategies, attention should be directed toward the complementary nature of sibling roles that may also be painful. Treatment should provide support for the risks involved in using such strategies, for example choosing the right time, place, and person for initiating the change very carefully and

making the attempt to change roles the criteria for success rather than a particular outcome within family relationships.
5. Help the client(s) be prepared for the reverberations that occur within the family unit or sibship when such changes are attempted (by identifying alternative ways resolve these effects of change). Although those reverberations can push the system or subsystem beyond the changes that were anticipated, it is important to encourage siblings to discuss the series of potential changes and what can be done at each step in the process (in the above case, one potential outcome was the client being relegated even more into the scapegoat role because of powerful forces within the family and the two sibships for maintaining the family secret and the dysfunctional sibling relationships).

Hartman and Laird (1983) indicate that the selection of treatment strategies such as those above and others should be determined by what changes hold the greatest promise for the client's life goals. These guidelines should help practitioners to connect emotionally with the individual, sibship, or family unit, while using the broad perspective of family treatment to focus on real life sibling issues and relationships. This process requires an examination of the leadership roles which social workers and other helping professionals need to assume in order to facilitate the changes discussed in this section.

Leadership Roles for Helping Professionals

It is necessary for social workers, psychologists, psychiatrists, marriage and family therapists, and other practitioners to redefine their key roles in terms of the family treatment field. The assumption of new leadership roles will help to further delineate family treatment and build on the emerging sibling literature. Although many of these roles have been assumed effectively by helping professionals in other practice areas, the roles are just being anticipated in the family treatment area. Examples of leadership roles include the advocate, preventionist, researcher-practitioner, and multidisciplinary educator.

The Systems Advocate

In regard to social work in particular, but including the other "psychiatric cousins" as well, some authors have pointed out that with the advent of clinical work, "... many practitioners have abandoned their social responsibilities as professionals" (Nulman, 1983, p. 19). Moreover, Simon's (1970) early distinction between case and policy advocacy helps to explain how the social responsibilities of practitioners doing conventional family therapy can be expanded within the family treatment field. In case advocacy, the practitioner is an advocate for the client, sibship, family, and their welfare. Policy advocacy, on the other hand, involves more of a leadership, proactive, and disruptive role related to the tendency of institutions to "minimize change not directed toward their own expansion" (Terrell, 1974, p. 333). Here, the practitioner advocates for societal change or changes in agency or organizational policy.

Societal or organizational change may be needed in a variety of settings in which helping professionals practice family treatment. For instance, schools often perpetuate dysfunctional roles in children and youth that are initiated in the family. Within a sibship, one child may be supported by school staff as the family hero and another as the scapegoat. Family treatment can be provided to the individual child who has been referred (typically the acting out scapegoat or the withdrawn lost child) and to the family as a whole if indicated.

The school social worker, school psychologist, or mental health consultant may need to advocate, however, for sibling therapy that includes the family hero in order to change the sibling dynamics. Schools often protect the family hero by proclaiming his or her lack of need for treatment and the fear that the siblings will influence the hero to become dysfunctional. The practitioner will need to advocate for organizational changes in the attitudes and practices among school staff that perpetuate such complementary sibling roles and the other siblings' school problems. Consultation and education about sibling issues/relationships may be needed along with a strong ongoing advocacy role (Freeman and Pennekamp, 1988).

Advocacy at the societal level may be indicated in many other situations. Child welfare legislation needs to be changed to reflect the importance of natural sibling networks to the growth and development of children (Timberlake and Hamlin, 1982). One model for this type of legislation is the Indian Child Welfare Act which reflects the importance of culture by requiring that Indian children be placed in Indian homes (Freeman and Pennekamp, 1988). Legislative changes at the national level may be the only way to force local agencies to change their policies about separating sibling groups for foster home placements.

Individual practitioners and volunteer child welfare organizations could become advocates by documenting in writing the effects of separation among sibling on their growth and development and then by providing this important data to policymakers. This type of advocacy can be operationalized through the use of multiple strategies based on systems theory: providing expert testimony to congress, writing position papers that are made available to legislators and their aides, organizing public forums for siblings and other family members to discuss the issues in the presence of the media, or holding public demonstrations in the Congress (Freeman and Pennekamp, 1988).

A Prevention Role

In addition to these advocacy strategies, practitioners can take a leadership role in family treatment by trying to prevent the development of problems among siblings and other family members. For instance, information about sibling issues and the related dynamics at various life cycle stages could be integrated into current family life and education courses and workshops being provided in schools and in the community. In this way, children and youth can be educated about sibling issues in courses that are part of their everyday school curriculum and in workshops provided for families in churches, community centers, cultural organizations, and boys and girls clubs. This knowledge can help young people and their parents to develop more functional sibling and family relationships. It can help practitioners and family members to normalize behaviors that are a natural part of autonomous sibling relationships and prescribe non-interference by parents when siblings need to work on their issues independently (Lewis, 1987; Huberty and Huberty, 1986; Dunn and Munn, 1986; Rosenberg, 1980).

The Researcher-Practitioner Role

Although some research exists in the area of family treatment related to sibling issues, additional research and evaluation are needed. Appropriate methodologies range on a continuum from case studies to single system research to evaluations of family treatment programs (Freeman and Pennekamp, 1988). These methodologies can be used most effectively through a combined researcher-practitioner role as prescribed by a number of authors (Bloom and Fischer, 1982; Patton, 1982; Allen-Meares and Lane, 1990). Such a role requires the helping professional to not only become a consumer of relevant research about families and the sibling subsystem, but to raise appropriate research questions that are generated by everyday practice issues and to conduct research along the continuum identified above. Some of the sibling literature now addresses this type of combined role in relation to family treatment for substance abuse (Freeman, 1993), emotional disorders (Clark, Cunningham, and Cunningham, 1989); and delinquency (Kline et al., 1977).

The Multidisciplinary Educator Role

The findings resulting from the researcher-practitioner role in family treatment and from other sources can be used to educate helping professionals from a wide range of disciplines. Although the format and content of such educational sessions will need to be varied depending on the needs and current roles of the participants, many of the topics discussed in this chapter may be very relevant (e.g., functions of the sibling subsystem and the relationship to the family, sibling dynamics in childhood and adulthood, the influence of the practitioner's sibling experiences on the work, and effective treatment strategies). The education role is particularly important for professionals in settings where family and sibling issues affect the services being provided across the life span. Examples include public school staff (administrators, teachers, social workers, guidance counselors, nurses, and psychologists); child protection workers; addiction counselors; psychiatric hospital staff; mental health therapists; marriage and family therapists; and counselors in retirement and nursing homes.

Practitioners who develop knowledge and skills related to sibling issues and family treatment can take a leadership role in providing inservice education to these other professionals. This process can enhance the professional growth and development of the participants as well as the practitioners who provide the educational services. Freeman and Pennekamp (1988) have conceptualized a continuum of professional development for practitioners. This continuum indicates that providing inservice education for other professionals is an effective formal mechanism for "Rethinking old assumptions and developing new ones about practice" (p. 281). The continuum emphasizes the role of practitioners as both learners **and** educators (Freeman and Pennekamp, 1988), an assumption that readily applies to practitioners in the area of sibling and family treatment.

Conclusion

This historical discussion about siblings and family therapy indicates the field has moved to address those issues increasingly in the past. But by using the same framework of family therapy as a modality, sibling issues have been conceptualized and treated in a manner that does not fully appreciate the power and influence of that subsystem over the life span. What is needed is a paradigm shift which some authors and researchers have anticipated by defining family therapy as a theoretical approach that can be applied in any combination of modalities.

Sibling issues that have both direct and indirect effects on the presenting problem many need to be addressed in terms of the new paradigm: family treatment as a theoretical approach. Leadership roles need to be generalized by practitioners from other practice areas as the main supports for this paradigm shift, including the important roles of advocate, preventionist, researcher-practitioner, and multidisciplinary educator. These proactive roles can place helping professionals in the forefront of change. They provide opportunities to build on the influence and strengths of the sibling subsystem.

REFERENCES

Adler, A. (1959). *Understanding human nature.* New York: Premier.

Allen-Meares, P. and Lane, B.A. (1990). Social work practice: Integrating qualitative and quantitative data collection techniques. *Social Work, 35,* 452–458.

Anthony, E.J. (1970). The behavior disorders of childhood. In P.H. Mann (Ed.), *Carmichael's manual of child psychology* (667–764). New York: John Wiley.

Bank, S. and Kahn, M.D. (1976). Sisterhood-brotherhood is powerful: Sibling subsystems and family therapy. *Annual Progress in Child Psychiatry and Child Development, 75,* 493–510.

Bendor, S.J. (1990). Anxiety and isolation in siblings of pediatric cancer patients: The need for prevention. *Social Work in Health Care, 14,* 17–35.

Bennett, J.C. (1990). Nonintervention into siblings' fighting as a catalyst for learned helplessness. *Psychological Reports, 66,* 139–145.

Bloom, M. and Fischer, J. (1982). *Evaluating practice: Guidelines for the accountable professional.* Englewood Cliffs, NJ: Prentice-Hall.

Bowen, M. (1972). Toward the differentiation of self in one's own family. In J. Frank (Ed.), *Family interaction: A dialogue between therapists and researchers* (111–174). New York: Springer.

Brody, G.H., Stoneman, Z., and Burke, M. (1987). Child temperaments, maternal differential behavior, and sibling relationships. *Developmental Psychology, 23,* 354–362.

Brown, R.A. and Anderson, D. (1980). Life history grid for adolescents. *Social Work,* 25, 321–322.

Caplow, T. (1968). *Two against one: Coalition in triads.* Englewood Cliffs, NJ: Prentice-Hall.

Clark, M.L., Cunningham, L.J., and Cunningham, C.E. (1989). Improving the social behavior of siblings of autistic children using a group problem solving approach. *Child and Family Behavior Therapy,* 11, 19–33.

Cunningham, C. and Betsa, N. (1981). Sibling groups interaction with siblings of oncology patients. *Journal of Pediatric Hematology Oncology,* 3, 135–139.

Dunn, J. and Munn, P. (1986). Sibling quarrels and maternal intervention: Individual differences in understanding and aggression. *Journal of Child Psychology and Psychiatry,* 27, 583–595.

Freeman, E.M. (1993). Substance abuse treatment: Continuum of care in services to families. In E.M. Freeman (Ed.), *Substance abuse treatment: A family systems perspective.* Newbury Park, CA: Sage.

Freeman, E.M. (1991). Teaching high risk adolescents how to assess their social networks and communities. Paper presented at the First Annual Conference on African-American Men, National Council of African-American Men, Kansas City, Missouri.

Freeman, E.M. (1989). Adult children of alcoholics: Study of parental, sibling, and work relationships. Paper presented at the 34th Institute on the Prevention and Treatment of Alcoholism. Pontault-Combault, France: International Council on Alcohol and Addictions.

Freeman, E.M. (1984). Multiple losses in the elderly. *Social Casework,* 65, 287–296.

Freeman, E.M. and Landesman, T. (1992). Differential diagnosis and the least restrictive treatment. In E.M. Freeman (Ed.), *The addiction process: Effective social work approaches* (27–42). White Plains, NY: Longman.

Freeman, E.M. and Pennekamp, M. (1988). *Social work practice: Toward a child, family, school, community perspective.* Springfield, IL.: Charles C Thomas.

Glynn, T.J. (1981). *Drugs and the family.* Rockville, MA: NIDA.

Hahn, L. and West, C. (1985–86). The violent deaths of adult children: Strategies for working with prolonged grief in black mothers. *Journal of Minority Aging,* 10, 1–15.

Hamlin, E.R. and Timberlake, E.M. (1981). Sibling group treatment. *Clinical Social Work Journal,* 9, 101–110.

Hartman, A. (1979). The extended family as a resource for change: An ecological approach to family-centered practice. In C.B. Germain (Ed.), *Social work practice: People and environments* (239–266). New York: Columbia University Press.

Hartman, A. and Laird, J. (1983). *Family-centered social work practice.* New York: Free Press.

Huberty, D.J. and Huberty, C.E. (1986). Sabotaging siblings: An overlooked aspect of family therapy with drug dependent adolescents. *Journal of Psychoactive Drugs,* 18, 31–41.

Janzen, C. and Harris, O. (1986). *Family treatment in social work practice.* Itasca, IL: Peacock.

Kahn, M.D. and Bank, S. (1981). In pursuit of sisterhood: Adult siblings as a resource for combined individual and family therapy. *The Family Process, 20,* 85–95.

Karpel, M.A. (1980). Family secrets: I. Conceptual and ethical issues in the relational context: II. Ethical and practical considerations in therapeutic management. *Family Process, 19,* 295–306.

Klein, N.C., Alexander, J.F., and Parsons, B.V. (1977). Impact of family systems intervention on recidivism and sibling delinquency: A model of primary prevention and program evaluation. *Journal of Consulting and Clinical Psychology, 45,* 469–474.

Koch-Hattem, A. (1986). Siblings experience of pediatric cancer: Interviews with children. *Health and Social Work, 11,* 23–31.

Laird, J. and Allen, J.A. (1983). Family theory and practice. In D. Waldfogel and A. Rosenblatt (Eds.), *Handbook of clinical social work* (174–209). San Francisco: Jossey-Bass.

Lewis, K.G. (1987). Bulimia as a communication to siblings. *Psychotherapy, 24,* 640–645.

Logan, S.L., Freeman, E.M., and McRoy, R.G. (1987). Racial identity problems of bi-racial clients: Implications for social work practice. *The Journal of Intergroup Relations, 15,* 11–24.

McGoldrick, M. and Gerson, R. (1985). *Genograms in family assessment.* New York: W.W. Norton.

Miller, N.B. and Cantwell, D.P. (1976). Siblings as therapists: A behavioral approach. *American Journal of Psychiatry, 133,* 447–450.

Miller, N.B. and Miller, H. (1977). Training siblings as change agents. In J. Krumboltz and C. Thoresen (Eds.), *Behavioral counseling methods* (223–245). New York: Holt, Rinehart, and Winston.

Minuchin, S. (1974). *Families and family therapy.* Cambridge, MA: Harvard University Press.

Mordock, J.B. (1974). Sibling sexual fantasies in family therapy: A case report. *Journal of Family Counseling, 2,* 60–65.

Nulman, E. (1983). Family therapy and advocacy: Directions for the future. *Social Work, 28,* 19–23.

Palazzoli, M.S. (1985). The problem of the sibling as the referring person. *Journal of Marital and Family Therapy, 11,* 21–34.

Patterson, G. (1971). Behavioral intervention procedures in the classroom and in the home. In A.E. Bergin and S.L. Garfield (Eds.), *Handbook of psychotherapy and behavior change* (751–777). New York: John Wiley.

Patton, M.Q. (1980). *Qualitative evaluation methods.* Beverly Hills: Sage.

Pfouts, J.H. (1976). The sibling relationship: A forgotten dimension. *Social Work, 21,* 220–224.

Pilat, J.M. and Boomhower-Kresser, S. (1992). Dynamics of alcoholism and child sexual abuse: Implications for interdisciplinary practice. In E.M. Freeman (Ed.), *The addiction process: Effective social work approaches* (65–78). White Plains, NY: Longman.

Pilat, J.M. and Jones, J.W. (1985). A comprehensive treatment program for children of alcoholics. In E.M. Freeman (Ed.), *Social work practice with clients who have alcohol problems* (141–159). Springfield, IL: Charles C Thomas.

Powell, T.H., Salzberg, C.L., Rule, S., Levy, S., and Itzkowitz, J.S. (1983). Teaching mentally retarded children to play with their siblings using parents as trainers. *Education and Treatment of Children, 6,* 343–362.

Ranieri, R.F. and Pratt, T.C. (1978). Sibling therapy. *Social Work, 23,* 418–419.

Rhodes, S. (1986). Family treatment. In F.J. Turner (Ed.), *Social work treatment: Interlocking theoretical approaches* (432–453). New York: Free Press.

Riskin, J.M. and Faunce, E.E. (1972). An evaluative review of family interaction research. *Family Process, 11,* 365–455.

Rosenberg, E. (1980). Therapy with siblings in reorganizing families. *International Journal of Family Therapy, 2,* 139–158.

Schacter, F.F. and Stone, R.K. (1987). Comparing and contrasting siblings: Defining the self. *Journal of Children in Contemporary Society, 19,* 55–75.

Schibuk, M. (1989). Treating the sibling subsystem: An adjunct of divorce therapy. *American Journal of Orthopsychiatry, 59,* 226–237.

Schreibman, L., O'Neill, R.E., and Koegel, R.L. (1983). Behavioral training for siblings of autistic children. *Journal of Applied Behavior Analysis, 16,* 129–138.

Simon, B.K. (1970). Social casework theory: An overview. In R.W. Roberts and R.H. Nee (Eds.), *Theories of social casework* (390–391). Chicago: University of Chicago Press.

Terrell, P. (1974). The social worker as radical: Roles of advocacy. In P. Weinberger (Ed.), *Perspectives on social welfare: An introductory anthology* (333–356). New York: Macmillan.

Timberlake, E., Cutler, P., and Strobino, J. (1980). *A study of the children in foster care in one county department of social services.* Washington, DC: The National Catholic School of Social Service.

Timberlake, E.M. and Hamlin, E.R. (1982). The sibling group: A neglected dimension of placement. *Child Welfare, 61,* 545–552.

Tracy, E.M. and Whittaker, J. (1990). The social network map: Assessing social support in clinical practice. *Families in society, 71,* 461–466.

PART II

APPROACHES TO FAMILY TREATMENT FOR RESOLVING SIBLING AND OTHER RELATIONSHIP ISSUES

Each chapter in this section of the book addresses some of the common and unique developmental themes of sibling relationships identified in Part I, illustrating how the same themes manifest themselves in various phases of the life span. These themes are addressed through one or more family treatment approaches in the chapters based on the different developmental transitions or problem situations involved. The overlap and connections between the range of family treatment approaches applied in these chapters are reflected in the matrix included in Table 1.1, Chapter 1.

These approaches are applied through the use of separate and detailed case studies summarized from the author's research on sibling relationships. The case studies and the discussions are organized to focus on family treatment of sibling issues across the life span, progressing from early childhood (Chapter 5) to old age (Chapter 11). In some of these chapters, the sibling relationship is identified as the presenting problem or direct focus of treatment (Chapters 6, 7, and 11). In other chapters, this relationship is a background issue that is affecting the presenting problem (Chapters 5, 8, 9, and 10).

The emphasis is on normative development as a process in which relationship problems can occur, but where coping skills are being continuously refined through the resources of sibling and other interpersonal relationships. Thus, the opportunities present for growth, enhancement of strengths, prevention, and family treatment in each case study are made explicit as the treatment approaches are applied. In the discussions on family treatment in these seven chapters, evaluation and practice are presented in an integrated manner along with practical examples of evaluation tools.

The selection of evaluation tools and the treatment approaches is related to the developmental tasks and sibling issues addressed by the different chapters. Chapter 5 is focused on identity and the sibling acculturation process, utilizing a case study of an African-American family with young children. In Chapter 6, individuation is addressed along with sibling coalitions, support networks, and resiliency in the face of family violence and incest. Chapter 7 involves the task of value consolidation during adolescence and issues of sibling loyalty in a Mexican-American family, while Chapter 9 focuses on the task of establishing a separate household and sibling control issues in a family with an alcoholic father.

The issue of sibling rivalry and the task of consolidating lifestyle choices are addressed in Chapter 9 within the context of the culture of the South. Chapter 10 includes a discussion about sibling role proscriptions and the task of generativity in an intergenerational farming family. In Chapter 11, the focus is on the final resolution of sibling solidarity and the task of accepting one's own mortality in the young and middle elderly stage, along with issues of homophobia.

Chapter 12 contains the Epilogue, a response to the question of why practitioners should evaluate family treatment. The chapter describes selected examples of how the complex social environment is affecting practice, including the caretaking of siblings who are HIV positive. Some principles are included for integrating evaluation and family treatment in order to achieve quality practice while impacting this changing environmental context and social policies.

Chapter 5

FAMILY NETWORK THERAPY TO ENHANCE YOUNG SIBLINGS' STRATEGIES FOR COPING WITH RACIAL STRESS

> How do I identify myself racially? That's hard to say, I don't see differences. I don't really think race matters. Now if you ask my sister, well, you'd definitely get a different answer because she's always had real strong feelings about race.
>
> —Ann

Ann's comment about her sister's level of acculturation is a reminder that ethnic and racial identity develop very early, often being readdressed in later stages of development across the lifespan. In childhood, two dominant identity themes involve the dilemma of being emotionally connected while also developing some emotional separateness or boundaries. It is important to develop a sense of belonging and acceptance by identifying with one's sibship, family, and ethnic group. At the same time, there is a need to be viewed and to perceive oneself as a separate being with an individual identity.

Dunn's (1983) assumption that the relationship between young siblings is of developmental importance can be applied to these two ethnic and personal identity themes. In essence, "... siblings may, by their behavior toward each other, create very different environments for one another within the family" (Dunn, 1983, p. 787). These environments are shaped by reciprocal and complementary interactions between brothers and sisters which greatly influence their developing identities.

For children in ethnic minority groups, siblings may provide added opportunities for working on the identity themes of being connected (acceptance) and differentiation as noted above. They can help each other through modeling and mutual problem-solving, for example, to "develop positive images of themselves in several areas including their racial heritage" (McRoy and Freeman, 1986, p. 166). The extended family may be another resource by providing intergenerational resources for learning to cope with racial stress. The latter is an on-going reality that requires cultural competence. Too, racial stress influences the individual's and family's ethnic identity (Chestang, 1979; Manns, 1981; Hill, 1972).

These issues of ethnic identity and coping with racial stress by young African-American children are the focus of the present chapter, although some of this discussion can be generalized to families of other ethnic groups. The use of reciprocal and complementary interactions between siblings for facilitating the development of a positive ethnic and personal identity is summarized briefly. These social support network activities can strengthen the sibling bond and the process of sibling acculturation. Then the case study of Ann is included to clarify how sibling, parental, and extended family dynamics can affect this process of identity development. A culture-specific family treatment and evaluation approach is discussed involving the use of sibling, family, and network therapy to illustrate how identity conflicts and ineffective coping can be resolved.

Ethnic Identity and Sibling Acculturation

Ethnic Identity Development

McRoy and Freeman (1986) emphasize that "The preschool and early elementary-school years (ages 3–7 approximately) are recognized as a crucial period in the growth and differentiation of the child's feelings about self and about others who are ethnically different" (p. 165). At this developmental stage, children learn first to make racial distinctions at a conceptual level, and then, to evaluate their membership in a racial group. This sequence of learning-from recognizing racial differences to making social distinctions-parallels the identity development sequence from clarifying "who I am" to assessing "the value of who I am" (Logan, 1981; McRoy and Freeman, 1986). There are several possible acculturation outcomes to this ethnic and personal identity dilemma (Phinney, Lochner, and Murphy, 1990; Berry and Kim, 1988; Berry, Kim, Minde, and Mok, 1987):

1. Denial of the importance of race and culture to the individual's self-perception and identity (the color blind perspective evident in Ann's comments about her views at the beginning of this chapter).
2. Devaluation by the individual of his or her racial/ethnic heritage and identification with the dominant culture's view and values including its' negative perceptions of the individual's racial/ethnic group (the assimilation or "melting pot" perspective).

3. Acceptance of the negative images presented about his or her racial/ethnic group by society, alienation from his or her own culture, and failure to adapt to the majority culture (the marginalization perspective).
4. Total immersion in and identification with the person's own ethnic group; this perspective usually involves rejection of the dominant culture's perceptions of the individual's ethnic group (the cultural immersion or separatist perspective).
5. Development of biculturalism or the ability to function effectively in the dominant culture as needed and in the individual's ethnic group, while identifying with and accepting the values of the latter (the dual perspective).

These acculturation outcomes indicate that ethnic identity development is a dynamic and changing process over each person's life span. Changes occur due to developmental and external influences. Important in this process is the conscious and unconscious assessment by the individual of the advantages and disadvantages of each level of acculturation. Although there are commonalities in the dilemmas at each level, there are important differences in the sources and types of stress experienced. The social supports available for coping with the stress are often different as well. Levels 1 through 3, for example, involve stress from the loss of ethnic values, traditions, and pride along with a lack of support from members of the ethnic group for handling this stress. The color blind perspective may hinder the person's social sensitivity for identifying and coping effectively with negative messages about his or her ethnic group. On the other hand, denial of how ethnic differences are perceived and acted upon in society may lead the person to believe racism does not exist, temporarily reducing the racial stress he or she might experience.

Sibling and Family Influences

It is clear from the discussion above that individuals can differ in this on-going process of ethnic identity development. Moreover, the consequences of the process may be different related to the individual's level of acculturation at various periods. Within the context of the family, the whole range of acculturation outcomes and ethnic identities may be present in different members (see Table 1.1 on sibling acculturation). Dunn's (1983) concepts of reciprocity and complementarity are useful for clarifying these differences and how siblings and other members influence each other's level of acculturation.

Reciprocity applies to parallel relationships or those more equal in power and status. It means siblings often recognize and share each other's interests, have an emotionally intense relationship, and are involved in the same behaviors and roles with one another (Dunn, 1983). Complementarity involves both equal and unequal relationships. It refers to behaviors between siblings or between parent and child that are different but that complement each other. Dunn (1983) notes that complementarity is often based on differences in age and ability levels, while reciprocity is based on similarities in characteristics and experiences.

In terms of reciprocity, siblings may influence each other's self-perceptions about ethnic values and traditions, and thus each other's ethnic identity through their play and actual experiences with racial/ethnic issues. Research has shown that in general siblings' reciprocal interactions involve: (1) imitation, (2) co-action sequences (performing the same action simultaneously), (3) warmth and matched positive affect (equal friendliness toward one another), and (4) a sense of attachment and acceptance that provides a secure base (Dunn, 1983; Pepler, Corter, and Abramovitch, 1982; Dunn and Kendrick, 1982).

In contrast, complementarity involves parents' and siblings' directly or indirectly influencing the child through education or role modeling in specific areas related to identity formation and the level of acculturation. Examples of complementary behaviors and roles include the following: (1) caregiving or caretaking behaviors, (2) the teaching of certain skills, (3) demonstrating social sensitivity, and (4) cooperative helping acts (Light, 1979; Dunn, 1983; Weisner and Gallimore, 1977; Pepler, Corter, and Abramovitch, 1982). These behaviors are valuable in ethnic identity development. Caregiving may occur through the provision of social supports for coping with racial or ethnic stress. This type of stress may be experienced when individuals receive negative messages or observe discriminatory practices based on their ethnicity. Caregiving provides positive messages about ethnic identity and self-worth.

Parents often teach or model assertiveness skills for handling discrimination. Siblings may model role taking skills for reflecting a certain ethnic identity or for practicing appropriate actions during symbolic play. Social sensitivity for decoding ethnically-related messages from within or those directed at a group can be learned through teaching and modeling as well. These avenues for developing a positive ethnic identity and cultural competence are illustrated in the case study that follows.

Ann: A Case Study

Ann Riley is a 41 year old African-American woman who grew up in the East. She is the oldest of three children. As can be seen from her genogram, Ann is married to 45 year old James who lived in Barbados all of his life until they were married eight years ago. Ann is a training coordinator for a management consulting firm while James teaches at a university. For James, the most significant concern since moving to this country has been adjusting to racial barriers and clarifying his own ethnic identity. In her interview, Ann noted that in his country, people are identified with the country itself rather than with a particular racial group. Their ethnic connections are accepted as a given and are not emphasized. So when he moved to this country, James was overwhelmed by the subtle and open racial discrimination that he encountered. He had difficulties in discerning clues to that discrimination in social and work situations. Ann found his questions about those experiences difficult to answer because she does not believe discrimination is a major problem. She thought he was being a little oversensitive.

Ann's brother and sister believe strongly that discrimination should not be tolerated. Janine in particular is like their mother in her active involvement in civil rights organizations. She is an attorney who uses her knowledge of law when providing volunteer legal services to several of those organizations. She and Alford enjoy debating about antidiscrimination policies and strategies. Ann, on the other hand, believes that racial and ethnic differences are unimportant. She acknowledges that her parents and siblings have different views from hers and from each others'. Those differences have been a concern, but Ann is convinced that all of them are entitled to their views. Ann's and James's views, along with those of her siblings, represent different levels of acculturation. These acculturation issues are evident in the following case study. Only the early and middle childhood years have been included to illustrate this process during that developmental period.

The Early Childhood Period

Ann describes herself as quiet and easy to get along with from a very young age. She does note that she was also very strong willed and that her parents found it difficult to stop her from doing something if she was determined. She would often try new activities by herself even if her parents told her to wait until they could show her (e.g., learning to roller skate). Most of the time, though, she was obedient.

Her family was a close one. They had many gatherings during holidays and at other times, usually involving their large extended family (see Figure 5.1). Ann and her brother and sister got along well. Ann remembers looking through family albums as an adult and noting a sense of closeness among family members, especially between her siblings. There were many pictures of Ann holding her brother in candid shots and numerous photographs of the three siblings playing together. Because the three of them were close in age, they spent a lot of time together. Also both parents took college courses during this period. The children learned to entertain themselves while their parents were in class or studying at home.

Their large extended family on both sides involved different cultural traditions and celebrations. Ann's maternal grandmother was from Ireland and her grandfather was from Jamaica, although both grew up in Jamaica. In looking back, Ann realizes that many of the family traditions and values stemmed mostly from Carribean and African influences. Ann's mother, Claire, believed their African heritage should be emphasized and that working on civil rights causes was important. She was a teacher's aide who was active in the National Association for Colored People (NAACP) and the Urban League, two important civil rights organizations at the time. She frequently took the children with her to meetings and special projects that the members were involved in. Ann did not understand what these organizations were or the nature of their activities at the time. She noticed that people got excited during the meetings and there was always something different going on. Her father, Giles, was less involved in the various meetings but sometimes helped Claire with her projects at home. He worked at a furniture store as a refinisher and his long hours there and his night classes seemed to keep him busy.

The Middle Childhood Years

Ann recalls being very excited about starting kindergarden in the same building where her mother worked. Each evening she would teach Alford and Janine a part of what she had learned that day. She did well academically and socially during those first years. She made friends and felt accepted by her class mates although she was introverted. She felt it

Family Network Therapy

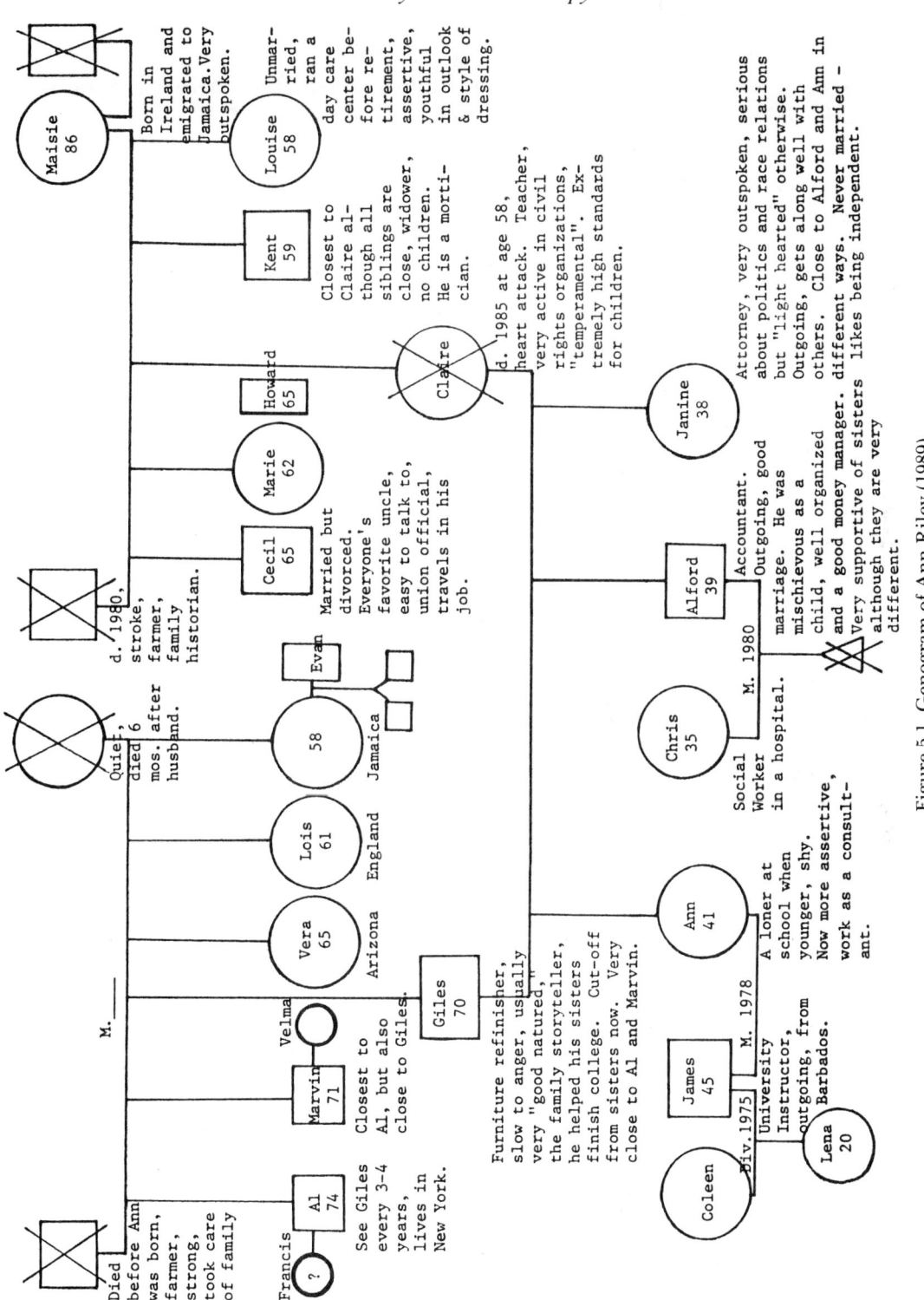

Figure 5.1. Genogram of Ann Riley (1989).

helped to know some of the students from previous contacts at church and in the neighborhood. When she entered the third grade, Alford was in the first grade, and Janine was in the kindergarden. That year they were bussed to an integrated school across town. Ann found it difficult to adjust to the new school and to her classmates. Most of the students were white with the next largest group being Hispanic. She felt alone in the school although there were other African-American students there, some of whom were friendly toward her. She also wanted to protect Alford and Janine from the racial name calling that was directed toward all of them by some of the white and Hispanic students. Ann missed being in the same school building with her mother.

During this same time, Ann's mother would read ethnic magazine articles on the achievements of various African-Americans and newspaper articles reporting on civil rights issues. She would then make up questions to ask Ann and Alford to test their growing knowledge about those issues. Sometimes when the three children played they would act out the interactions between members of the civil rights groups their mother would take them to. Or they would play the "teacher" game, instructing the class members on how they should play together without name calling. Using what their parents said to them as a model, Ann would often tell Alford not to worry if some of the children at school would not play with him: "you're as good as anyone else."

Alford was more aggressive than Ann in making friends and getting along with his classmates. If someone would not play with him he would find other classmates to play with, often including children from all three ethnic groups. He was playful in class and sometimes did not get all of his work done. Ann learned years later that during the first weeks of that year, his teacher recommended that Alford be placed in a special education class for those reasons. Claire's experience as a teacher's aide and her college courses in education were useful in helping the parents to resist the teacher's recommendation. They requested that Alford be given the chance to stay in the regular class the rest of that year. Then they tutored him at home and helped him to concentrate and be less playful while doing his school work.

Ann believes their parents did not see his sociability as a limitation in the same way the teacher did. Like Alford, Janine also seemed to adjust more readily and to relate well to the other students from different ethnic groups in her class. She did above average work academically from this first year and throughout her school years. Ann, on the other hand, felt the rejections more and would only play with a few of the African-American children in the school. Although she earned average grades, Ann always felt she could have done better if she had been treated more fairly by her teachers.

She remembers her third grade teacher in particular who told her that everyone is the same and that race does not matter. Ann saw that this teacher did little to address the name calling and unfair treatment of African-Americans and Hispanics by white students in the class. Ann did not know how to interpret the conflict between what the teacher said and how she reacted to the racism reflected in students' behavior. Ann recalled that her maternal grandmother, Maisie, also believed that color was not important and that everyone was the same. She is closer to Ann than to the other grandchildren and has always been nurturing and supportive of Ann.

One of the children's favorite times was on the weekend because their father would read them stories he had written about his childhood and his family. The stories included the period when his family lived on a farm in the South. They detailed some of the things he and his brothers and sisters did while growing up as well as some of their hardships. One story was very significant to Ann and her siblings:

> A white farmer had been trying to buy a large area of the family's land to add to his holdings. When they decided not to sell the land, he had the county assessor show the taxes had not been paid on the land for a sufficient period and therefore it could be sold through public auction. None of the family saw the notice in the newspaper so the land was purchased by the other farmer without their knowledge. During that period it was not possible to use legal channels to get their land back; the family had to accept what had happened. Giles's father decided that they would look for additional land elsewhere in the county but recognized that landowners raised their prices when the potential buyer was African-American. So he sent Giles and his two brothers out into the county to "scout" for potential land without asking questions about buying it. A white attorney whom they trusted negotiated the sale and got them a fair price. The land was recorded in the names of relatives who lived in another state. It was assumed throughout the county that Giles's family was working on that farm for the absentee owners.

Ann thinks this story appealed to them as children because it was adventurous and it taught them about a type of family unity (Freeman, 1992; Martin, 1987). After the children were sent to the integrated school, they sometimes called themselves the three scouts. In looking back, Ann thinks they tried to portray the three brothers during symbolic play (Dunn, 1983), acting out their frequent trips to find land. Their "teacher" game may have fulfilled a similar need of the siblings to simulate a more positive school environment (complementarity) and to reinforce a positive image or ethnic identity among themselves (reciprocity). In this way they were able to strengthen their mutual social support system in terms of sibling solidarity (Bank and Kahn, 1982; Cicirelli, 1985; Dunn and Kendrick, 1982). The symbolic play provided opportunities to practice interpreting subtle and overt messages from others about who they were and their value as African-American children.

Sometimes at their large family gatherings, the members would get into discussions about their current lives and how they were coping with racial barriers. They would get into heated arguments at times about how to respond to social interactions between people of different races and acts of discrimination. Most often, other family members would disagree with Ann's uncle Al. At the time Ann did not understand their disagreements, but she remembers uncle Al did not participate in as many of the gatherings as the other members. Later she learned he was considered too radical by the older members; he had lost several jobs for "speaking up" and resisting discrimination. The uncle's reactions and coping patterns are consistent with Phinney's et al. (1990) stage of ethnic identity search: the immersion stage where there is a heightened political and personal consciousness about one's ethnicity. Atkinson, Morton, and Sue (1983) describe this stage as "a growing awareness that not all cultural values of the dominant group are beneficial to him/her" (p. 37).

Also on her father's side, Giles and his brothers were cut-off from their sisters who did not visit or ever participate in family gatherings. The sisters all lived far away and would send cards on birthdays and holidays, their only contacts (See Figure 5.1). Giles worked and helped the three sisters financially so they could attend college or vocational school. Education was important in their family as it is in many minority families (Freeman, 1990). It was only after the sisters had completed their education that he then began taking courses himself. Ann does not believe there was any type of disagreement or argument, but that they simply "drifted apart." When the family would tell stories during their gatherings about the different members' successes and struggles to get ahead economically, they would frequently include the struggles of the three sisters.

A Culture-Specific Family Network Treatment Approach

The ethnic identity and acculturation issues reflected above in Ann's family relationships require a treatment approach that addresses those important issues. Such an approach involves sensitive work with the sibling subsystem and the family network involving both nuclear and extended family members. Helping professionals in public and private schools, mental health centers, and child guidance/child welfare agencies are in a position to identify ethnic minority students in the middle to late childhood period who, like Ann and her siblings, are addressing ethnic identity issues. This normative and developmental work can be enhanced through an assessment and treatment approach that is respectful of the cultural strengths in the family network (Manns, 1981) and sensitive to the role of the sibling subsystem in the identity/acculturation process.

Culturally-Oriented Assessments

Because ethnic identity development is a normative process, children might not be referred for counseling except in extreme situations. This probability indicates a need for active case finding by practitioners and the provision of prevention as well as intervention services. Practitioners in schools, churches, community organizations, and the other settings noted above can identify children who might benefit from such services by observing them in their daily activities. Practitioners' assessments can be based on these informal observations of children during class, recess, in the lunchroom and the halls of schools for example (Freeman and Pennekamp, 1989). These informal observations of the interactions, relationships, activities, concerns, and strengths of children from different ethnic groups can be helpful in determining what prevention services may be needed. In Ann's situation, similar observations at her school and church might have revealed how different her behavior and self-perceptions were in the two settings. In addition, those observations could have identified environmental factors that were influencing the acculturation process of Ann and her siblings.

As needs are identified through observations, practitioners can utilize informal discussions and interviews as well as formal assessment procedures and tools. Logan, Freeman, and McRoy (1987) have adapted the traditional genogram's and ecomap's cultural perspective to reflect an increased emphasis on ethnicity. It may be useful to have parents help in constructing the family genogram in the children's presence or for a sibling subsystem to be involved in sessions for this purpose. With younger children in Ann's age range, it is more appropriate for the parents to take the lead in this assessment process. In the case of older children and youth, having one sibling subsystem or a group of different sibships work on their genograms together might be very effective developmentally and in terms of sibling solidarity. Practitioners can pose questions that help in clarifying the ethnic identity development and levels of acculturation of various members, for instance (Logan, Freeman, and McRoy, 1987; Hartman, 1979):

1. The racial and ethnic backgrounds of siblings and parents.
2. Family members' attitudes towards racial and ethnic differences.
3. How the various members identify themselves in terms of ethnicity and race, particularly similarities and differences between siblings.
4. Descriptions of the members' lifestyles: where they work, go to church, purchase goods and services, spend their leisure time, and affiliate socially and organizationally.
5. The members' relationships with the extended family: the frequency and quality of contacts as well as the types of supports provided and received from this network.
6. The members' educational levels as well as the ethnic composition of institutions where they received their education across the lifespan.

The ecomap can be a culturally-relevant assessment tool in a similar manner. Individuals and organizations important to the individual, sibship, and family should be placed on the ecomap around the large central circle for the immediate household (Hartman, 1979). An effort should be made to clarify those persons and environmental factors that are affecting the members' levels of acculturation. Some examples of areas that can be explored by practitioners include the following: whether any cutoffs are related to ethnic identity issues, environmental supports or barriers to the desired level of acculturation, and the presence of role models in the environment that support a positive ethnic identity (Manns, 1981; Phinney et al., 1990).

This form of assessment could have been beneficial in working with the family of Ann. An ecomap assessment, based on her case study, probably would have revealed that the sibling bond was a strong factor in Ann's ability to cope with racial stress. It might have helped to sort out the different identity messages she was receiving from her parents, siblings, the teacher, and extended family members (e.g., from her grandmother, uncle Al, and the other members' reactions to his handling of discrimination experiences).

The assessment might have pointed out how the outcomes of the sibling acculturation process were different for Ann, Alford, and Janine.

It is important in assessing families to convey that a person's acculturation level is neither right nor wrong, and that the practitioner's role is to assist in clarifying the different levels, how each is related to ethnic identity, and the consequences of each level. For example, Ann's adoption of a color-blind perspective may have been a way of managing her hurt and anger about rejection, while also utilizing her caucasian grandmother and teacher as role models. Dunn's (1983) concept of complementarity helps to explain the impact of their role modeling on Ann's identity development. The influence of the sibling acculturation process, in terms of demonstrating acceptance and involvement in cooperative helping acts, was important as well.

Family Treatment, Prevention, and Evaluation

The above culture-specific assessment process provides a solid foundation for appropriate family treatment. Because the sibling subsystem is a natural social network within which ethnic identity and other aspects of development are addressed, sibling therapy is an ideal modality for prevention **and** treatment. Siblings can be provided age-appropriate information about ethnic identity and acculturation which they can then apply during problem-solving exercises. Practical applications might include how to respond when other children call the child racial names and how to identify adults who will intercede appropriately to make the environment more supportive of ethnic differences. This normalizes the hurt feelings that result from name calling and rejection, while also teaching children of all races about their own identity and how to interpret racial/ethnic differences from a positive perspective (Phinney and Rotheram, 1987; Berry, Kim, Minde, and Mok, 1987).

These problem-solving exercises can be used along with information from the ecomap assessment on positive role models to teach siblings how to cope with racial stress. Siblings can use the sessions to practice and give each other feedback about how to gain information from those role models about effective coping patterns. An alternative strategy is for those key persons to be invited to participate directly in a session. For younger children, it is important for practitioners to explore the parents' views about particular role models before using this strategy. Differentiation exercises can be valuable too for helping siblings to understand and value how they may be different in their ethnic identities and acculturation. For instance, having siblings draw their different feelings about interethnic social and school situations can help to clarify their differences in a neutral manner. Encouraging them to draw the different ways each of them responds to discrimination or prejudice is an additional way to enhance differentiation within the subsystem.

Often, sibling therapy may need to be augmented with a stronger environmental intervention. This may be the case where the extended family has a close relationship with the nuclear family and exhibits a range of acculturation levels that are useful for teaching children about ethnic identity. This type of family treatment may be appropriate also when identity issues have become a major problem beyond the normative sibling and parental differences (Hartman, 1979). In both instances, the practitioner's concerns about ethnic identity and the rationale for recommending family network therapy should be explained to the parents. The desire to utilize the strengths and close relationships with the extended family to enhance the natural social supports that they provide is an appropriate rationale.

A secondary benefit may be for extended family members who are still struggling with identity and acculturation issues: they can use the network as a resource for resolving the issues and serve as an intergenerational model for the children. The parents' ideas about the roles each member has played and can play in helping the young siblings with identity issues should be explored prior to involving the extended family. The number of sessions can range from 2–6, depending on the issues and the members' availability (see Table 4.1 on the use of family network therapy) (Attneave, 1977; Hartman and Laird, 1983; Watzlawick, Weakland, Fisch, 1974; McGoldrick, Pearce, and Giordano, 1982).

During these sessions, the extended family can be utilized as cultural consultants in identifying other issues that are of concern and how they can be coped with or resolved (Attneave, 1976; Martin and Martin, 1978). For instance, in Ann's family an unanticipated issue related to identity might have been how other members in the family felt about Maisie's ethnicity and their own bi-ethnic heritage. As consultants, the members are expected to illustrate their different ethnic identities in how they label or represent themselves and through information/advice about methods of coping with racial/ethnic stress.

The practitioner can help to "coach" members through this process of helping: they can ask the children questions, use storytelling to illustrate their experiences and specific coping patterns/problem-solving efforts, give direct advice, and model different levels of acculturation in their interactions with each other. The story of "the three scouts" in Ann's father's family is an example of the type of story that reconstructs the family's history, continuity, and ethnic identity for each child and the siblings as a unit. Such stories are relevant to the identity development of children in any ethnic and national group (Freeman, 1992; Briggs, 1977; Calvino, 1980; Greenbaum and Holmes, 1983). The stories emphasize the importance of interactions between extended family members in the same sibling subsystem as models of sibling acculturation for the children.

There may be instances when it is appropriate for the practitioner to address issues that surface within the family network. Examples can include unresolved sibling or intergenerational issues that are impeding the work or when members of the network directly request input from the practitioner (Manns, 1981; Freeman, 1990). In Ann's family, unresolved differences among the father's siblings may also have affected the sibling acculturation process for Ann, Alford, and Janine (e.g., the cut-offs from the three sisters and the rejection of his brother Al's views about identity and discrimination). Family network therapy might have been useful for helping the members to discuss what their differences were in terms of Al, how they have handled them, the effects on them and the current generation of sibships, and what is needed to change the situation. Also, the practitioner could have helped the brothers to explore whether to attempt to reconnect with their sisters and how that could be accomplished.

Evaluation of this culture-specific sibling and family network treatment approach could involve a number of informal and formal procedures. One strategy involves monitoring changes in the clients' responses to ethnic identity exercises. Gordon (in press) has identified a number of these practical exercises for clarifying identity. Changes in the responses of each member could be compared over time as well as differences between members of the sibling subsystem. An advantage of these exercises is that they focus on ethnic self-knowledge, -esteem, and -identity. An example of one exercise lists eight terms used to refer to African-descended individuals (e.g., Black, African-American, minority, slave). Then a list of questions are used to clarify the individual's identity related to those terms (e.g., "which of the above best describes who you are, what do you like most about being a person of African descent, name five African countries, and name three African-Americans whom you admire and explain why"?) (Gordon, in press).

In addition, changes in particular areas on the genogram and ecomap can be used to monitor whether the treatment is effective. For instance, it is possible to identify changes in the amount of information included on these maps: information the members have about their own ethnic identities and those of other family members, the family's patterns of handling racial stress effectively, the number of positive ethnic role models identified by a child in his or her environment, and the number of reciprocal and complementary behaviors children identify as evidence of sibling and extended family supports.

Finally, the children's art work designed for enhancing the sibling differentiation process is useful also for evaluation. Changes in the content of drawings over time and in how children describe and discuss their drawings can help to determine if the treatment is effective. The practitioner can do a content analysis of the drawings and discussions to identify the following: how do the children describe themselves ethnically (identity) at intake and at termination, how do they feel about themselves ethnically (self-esteem), how are sibling's identity and self-esteem an influence on the other members either positively or negatively, and what negative environmental factors have been reduced or positive factors enhanced by the siblings or family network.

Conclusion

Both the sibling subsystem and extended family network can be a positive or negative influence in ethnic identity development. This influence is accomplished primarily through role modeling, affection, cooperative helping acts, and representing the self directly through advice or indirectly through storytelling. Laird (1990) notes that stories or family narratives are extremely important mechanisms that carry powerful prescriptions for behavior and attitudes. They are important because they involve descriptions and interpretations of particular events and persons.

In essence, children learn how to view themselves and others who are like and unlike them ethnically through stories and other reciprocal and complementary family interactions. The sibling subsystem is important in this identity development process, because it provides yet another "looking glass" reflection of the self (Stone, 1981) **and** it provides a vehicle for acting out different acculturation dilemmas. The role of helping professionals is two fold: (1) to provide information to families that normalizes this identity process, and (2) to enhance the supports for resolving normative and more serious conflicts that are provided by the sibship, parents, and the extended family network.

REFERENCES

Atkinson, D., Morton, G., and Sue, D. (1983). *Counseling American minorities.* Dubuque, IA: William C. Brown.

Attneave, C.L. (1976). Therapy in tribal settings and urban network intervention. *Family Process, 15,* 56-65.

Bank, S. and Kahn, M. (1982). *The sibling bond.* New York: Basic Books.

Berry, J. and Kim, U. (1988). Acculturation and mental health. In P.R. Dasen, J.W. Berry, and N. Sartorius (Eds.), *Health and cross-cultural psychology:* Vol. 10 (23-45). Newbury Park, CA: Sage.

Berry, J., Kim, U., Minde, T., and Mok, D. (1987). Comparative studies of acculturative stress. *International Migration Review, 21,* 491-511.

Briggs, K. (1977). *British folktales.* New York: Bantam.

Calvino, I. (1980). *Italian folktales.* New York: Pantheon.

Chestang, L. (1979). Competencies and knowledge in clinical social work: A dual perspective. In P.L. Ewalt (Ed.), *Towards a definition of clinical social work* (8-16). Washington, DC: National Association of Social Workers.

Cicirelli, V.G. (1985). The role of siblings as family caregivers. In W.J. Sauer and R.T. Coward (Eds.), *Social support networks and care of the elderly* (93-107). New York: Springer.

Dunn, J. (1983). Sibling relationships in early childhood. *Child Development, 54,* 787-811.

Dunn, J. and Kendrick, C. (1982). *Siblings: Love, envy, and understanding.* Cambridge, MA: Harvard University Press.

Freeman, E.M. (1992). The use of storytelling techniques with young African-American males: Implications for substance abuse prevention. *Journal of Intergroup Relations, 29,* 53-72.

Freeman, E.M. (1990). The black family's life cycle: Operationalizing a strengths perspective. In S.L. Logan, E.M. Freeman, and R.G. McRoy (Eds.), *Social work practice with black families: A culturally specific perspective* (55-72). White Plains, NY: Longman.

Freeman, E.M. and Pennekamp, M. (1988). Joining children and adolescents: An under-utilized resource. *Social work practice: Toward a child, family, school, community perspective* (36-46). Springfield, IL: Charles C Thomas.

Gordon, J.U. (In press). A culturally-specific family systems approach to ethnic minority young adults with substance abuse problems. In E.M. Freeman (Ed.), *Substance abuse treatment: A family systems perspective.* Newbury Park, CA: Sage.

Greenbaum, L. and Holmes, I. (1983). The use of folktales in social work practice. *Social Casework, 64,* 414-418.

Hartman, A. (1979). The extended family as a resource for change: An ecological approach to family-centered practice. In C.B. Germain (Ed.), *Social work practice: People and environments* 239-266). New York: Columbia University Press.

Hartman, A. and Laird, J. (1983). *Family-centered social work practice.* New York: Free Press.

Hill, R. (1972). *The strengths of black families.* New York: Emerson Hall.

Laird, J. (1990). Women stories: Restorying as a tool for transformation in clinical practice. Paper presented at the Building on Women's Strengths Conference. Lawrence, KS.: University of Kansas School of Social Welfare.

Light, P. (1979). *The development of social sensitivity.* Cambridge: Cambridge University Press.

Logan, S.L. (1981). Race, identity, and black children: A developmental perspective. *Social Casework, 62,* 47–56.

Logan, S.L., Freeman, E.M., and McRoy, R.G. (1987). Racial identity problems of bi-racial clients: Implications for social work practice. *Journal of Intergroup Relations, 25,* 11–24.

Manns, W. (1981). Support systems of significant others on black families. In H.P. McAdoo (Ed.), *Black families* (238–251). Beverly Hills, CA: Sage.

Martin, R.R. (1987). Oral history in social work education: Chronicling the black experience. *Journal of Social Work Education, 23,* 5–10.

Martin, E.P. and Martin, J.M. (1978). *The black extended family.* Chicago: University of Chicago Press.

McGoldrick, M., Pearce, J.K., and Giordano, J. (1982). *Ethnicity and family therapy.* New York: Guilford.

McRoy, R.G. and Freeman, E.M. (1986). Racial-identity issues among mixed-race children. *Social Work in Education, 8,* 164–174.

Pepler, D., Corter, C., and Abramovitch, R. (1982). Social relationships among children: Siblings and peers. In K. Rubin and H. Ross (Eds.), *Peer relationships and social skills in childhood* (211–222). New York: Springer.

Phinney, J.S., Lochner, B.T., and Murphy, R. (1990). Ethnic identity development and psychological adjustment in adolescence. In A.R. Stiffman and L.E. Davis (Eds.), *Ethnic issues in adolescent mental health* (53–72). Newbury Park, CA: Sage.

Rotheram, M.J. and Phinney, J.S. (1987). Introduction: Definitions and perspectives in the study of children's ethnic socialization. In J. Phinney and M. Rotheram (Eds.), *Children's ethnic socialization* (1–14). Newbury Park, CA: Sage.

Stone, G. (1981). *Social psychology through symbolic interactionalism:* Second edition. New York: Prentice-Hall.

Watzlawick, P., Weakland, J.H., and Fisch, R. (1974). *Change: Principles of problem formation and problem resolution.* New York: W.W. Norton.

Weisner, T.S. and Gallimore, R. (1977). My brother's keeper: Child and sibling caretaking. *Current Anthropology, 18,* 169–190.

Chapter 6

COMBINING STRATEGIC FAMILY AND SIBLING THERAPY IN TREATMENT FOR BLENDED FAMILIES

> I felt scared, ugly, and worthless most of the time. Inside though, unconsciously, some part of me must have been hopeful... like a beautiful butterfly hidden away... waiting to be rescued from my parents' and brother's abuse.
>
> —Rosalind

The type of resiliency exhibited by some victims of emotional, physical, and sexual abuse has been called persistent invulnerability by some authors. Anthony (1987), for example, has characterized this category of resilient individuals as thrivers because, like Rosalind above, they have an implacable resolve "not to be broken" (p. 45). They do not simply survive extreme adversity, they are able to rebound and thrive inspite of the abuse and other traumatic family experiences. These individuals are able to wait out the storms of family life while coping creatively with their negative environments (Cowen, 1988).

Researchers have noted that it is not yet completely clear why some individual victims of family abuse are less vulnerable than others (Taylor, 1983; Cowen, 1988), particularly children living in similar family circumstances such as those in the same sibling subsystem (Finkelhor, 1984). In addition, the collective resources utilized when the sibling subsystem is also resilient need to be clarified. Little is known about how the subsystem draws upon its collective resources in coping with abusive parents. The effects of these experiences on siblings' lifelong relationships with each other require more study as well. Such information could enhance family treatment **and** prevention services related to parent-child and sibling abuse.

This chapter builds on the discussion about resiliency in Chapter 2 by illustrating some of the characteristics of resilient individuals and sibships in the case study of Rosalind who is from a blended family. A combined strategic family systems and cognitive-behavioral approach is described in relation to Rosalind's treatment for sexual abuse in family and sibling therapy. Trust, identity, loss, and differentiation from the sibling subsystem are focused on during the discussion of treatment and evaluation, along with the relationship dynamics that occur when an alternative sibling subsystem is developed.

Rosalind: Case Study and Analysis

Although Rosalind thought of herself as ugly and worthless most of her early life, she sensed something positive inside was being protected from the abuse that she experienced in her family. She now calls that something inside a vibrant butterfly that would eventually fly away from the family and the abuse. She was not aware that her siblings experienced similar trust, identity, and loss issues from their early family experiences, because typically, abused siblings are not able to talk openly about what is occurring or their reactions to it (Frey-Angel, 1989; Finkelhor, Gelles, Hotaling, & Strauss, 1983). This meant that each of Rosalind's sisters and brothers were somewhat isolated in their abuse experiences within the family. Sometimes they supported each other, but at other times their natural support network was inhibited by the family dynamics present during various developmental stages. The following background information provides a context for understanding how those stages were experienced by Rosalind and her siblings.

Background Information

Rosalind Bowers was a 38 year old caucasian woman and a child psychologist when she participated in the author's research on siblings. Her parents and their six children lived in Montana. As can be seen from Rosalind's genogram in Figure 6.1, the oldest and youngest children in this blended family were from another marriage of the father and mother respectively, while the four middle children were from the parents' marriage to each other. All of the siblings except Steve developed addictions in their adolescent or young adult years. Such addictions may be a result of the family projection process described by Bowen (1974), reflecting similar addiction patterns in the parent and grandparent generations of Rosalind's family (See Chapter 9 for a discussion on family patterns of addiction).

Rosalind is currently cut-off from her siblings except for Mae and Steve. Although she feels close to those two siblings she is pained by their

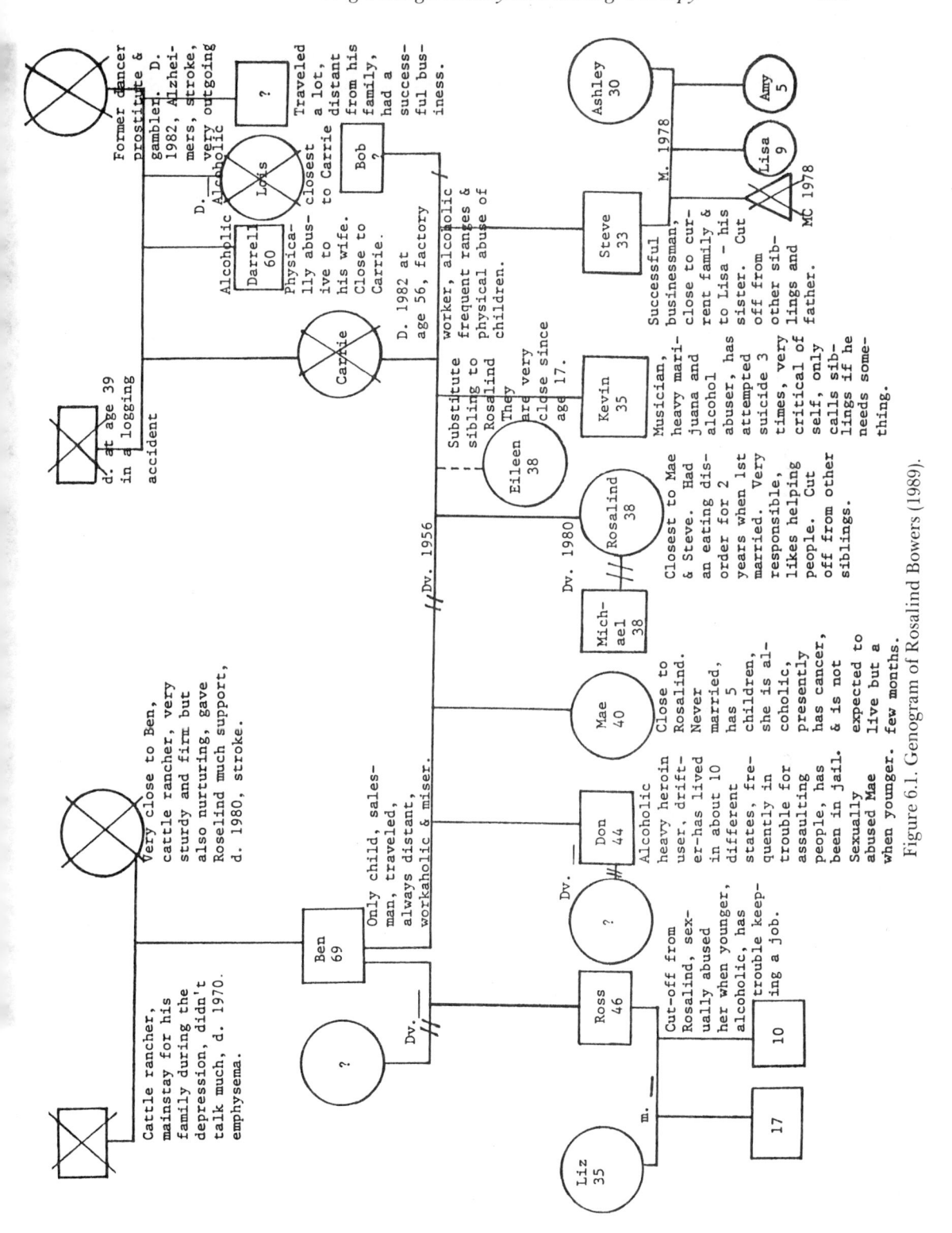

Combining Strategic Family and Sibling Therapy

Figure 6.1. Genogram of Rosalind Bowers (1989).

addictions and by Kevin's numerous suicide attempts. Rosalind's mother died of cirrhosis of the liver at age 54 due to alcoholism. Rosalind and Carrie were not able to resolve their relationship issues before the mother's death. The father lives in another state and Rosalind stays in contact with him by telephone, but it remains a distant relationship. Rosalind feels that although she is cut-off from Ross, she is still tied to him by her anger because he refuses to acknowledge that he sexually abused her. None of her siblings except Steve finished high school, and they have all experienced long periods of unemployment and underemployment.

Early, Middle, and Late Childhood

Rosalind was born prematurely, weighing less than two pounds. The doctors thought she would live only a few days and were surprised when she survived beyond that period. They kept her in the hospital for four months due to her low birth weight and numerous medical problems. Her paternal grandmother told Rosalind that Mae was only fifteen months old at the time and that she cried constantly. Much of the mother's energy was focused on Mae whom she abused physically. The grandmother went to visit the family on the day Rosalind was brought home from the hospital. She observed the mother, Carrie, throw Mae against a bed from across the room when she would not stop crying and then refuse to pick up Rosalind when she too began to cry. The grandmother decided to take Rosalind home with her for a several weeks because she feared Carrie would not provide the care that Rosalind needed. Rosalind believes this early six month separation prevented Carrie from bonding with her. Although Rosalind tried to establish an attachment between them for many years, she believes those efforts were never successful. And as Bowlby (1977) noted, such failed early attachment experiences can diminish the individual's capacity to establish strong affectional bonds with others during childhood, adolescence, and adulthood (see Figure 1.2, Chapter 1 related to sibling bonding).

Those early years were characterized by a great deal of physical violence by Carrie toward all of the children. She drank heavily, although until she was six, Rosalind did not know that Carrie drank. Nor did Rosalind understand how Carrie's drinking contributed to the abuse until family treatment provided her with that knowledge years later. Carrie would become angry and hit the children with anything she could find (for example, a belt, stick, bottle, iron, or pot). The source of the anger varied: it developed if they did not clean the house in the way she wanted it cleaned, if they did not get up in the morning when she thought they should (often before dawn), or if they tried to talk to her at the wrong time.

Carrie was a factory worker and would often stay away for long hours drinking with her friends after work. Ben Long, the father, was a salesman and was often away from home because his job required frequent travel for weeks at a time. Carrie would warn the children that they should not tell Ben anything that occurred in the family while he was away. Rosalind indicated there were very few instances when she was nurtured by her mother who was angry and abusive most of the time, or by her father who was emotionally distant even when he was at home. A few times Carrie would hold Rosalind in her arms. Rosalind remembers this cuddling was extremely comforting because her mother's arms and breasts were so large and warm. Ben would say something kind to Rosalind occasionally, but then would often turn his kindness into something painful (e.g., "This is a good report card. Don't get big headed about it though, anybody can get good grades").

As the oldest, Ross was always expected to take care of Rosalind and her siblings when the parents were gone. She recalls that he was almost like a second parent to the other children. However, when she was about four, Ross began to sexually abuse Rosalind. She is able to pinpoint when the abuse began because she remembers thinking that if she could go to school like Mae, the abuse would stop. Ross and Don were often kept home from school to babysit the younger children. Rosalind now sees a big contrast between the "good Ross" who was nurturing and protective and the "bad Ross" who was very cruel to her. The "bad Ross" would tie her up, sodomize her with kitchen utensils, call her stupid, and curse her. He also told her that because they had the same birthday, he was free to do whatever he wanted to her for the rest of their lives. Mae was sexually abused by Don, sometimes in the same room while Ross was abusing Rosalind.

In contrast to the pain he inflicted on Rosalind, Carrie's emotional and physical abuse of the children caused Ross to organize them into a sibling support network (Pollack and Hundermar, 1984; Bank and Kahn, 1982). The children learned to help each other by distracting Carrie when she was abusing one of them. They would sometimes hide from her as a group when she "went into one of her rages," and, too, they helped with each other's household responsibilities because Carrie was "such a perfectionist" about how things should be done. This resource pooling strategy was one of the strengths of their sibling subsystem and illustrates the type of subsystem resiliency that Anthony (1987) has described in terms of individuals. Their survival as a unit in this family depended totally on their ability to collaborate in avoiding the abuse and in foraging for food and other resources as they sometimes had to do.

While their successful collaboration was a strength, individually the family violence robbed them of their ability to be empathic with each other beyond concerns about immediate safety and survival. Frey-Angel (1989) notes that empathy is learned from adult role models and by experiencing pain and relating to someone else's feelings. In violent families, the parents do not model the empathy their children need for becoming socialized, so siblings do not learn how to identify with each other's pain. Thus, this assumption helps to explain how Ross could inflict abuse on Rosalind that was as painful and degrading as the parental abuse he had experienced. Moreover, if children like Ross from violent families do attempt to identify with the pain they witness or experience themselves, such identification may simply magnify their feelings of helplessness and inability to intervene. It is also difficult for them to identify with the anger and rage of the perpetrator, since his or her remorse is usually not apparent, or if it is displayed, it is short-lived (Frey-Angel, 1989). This assumption is consistent with the pattern in the Long family, from Rosalind's perspective, Carrie did not seem to be remorseful about her abuse of the children.

At the age of five, school provided Rosalind with an escape from some of the mother's and Ross's abuse. She soon learned how she could feel competent and valued in school through observing how well fellow students were treated by their peers and teachers when they excelled academically. So from her first year in school, doing well became important to Rosalind. She said it was the only way she could get "positive strokes." She felt good about herself only during report card time and at her various graduations, beginning with her kindergarden graduation.

Going to school did not stop the abuse as Rosalind expected. It continued, usually at night when both parents were away from home. When Rosalind was seven and Mae was nine, they developed enough courage together to tell their mother about the abuse. To their surprise, Carrie became extremely angry and said if they told their father she would kill them. She then took them to the cellar of an abandoned school and showed them where she would hide their bodies as well as the knives she would use to cut them up if they told anyone else. This experience was so vivid that Rosalind had nightmares for years about being cut up and buried in that dark cold cellar. Rosalind now believes Carrie thought Ben would blame her for the abuse if he found out, since he was not aware of how often she left the children alone to go out with friends.

The Latency Period

When Rosalind was 12, her parents were divorced. She went to live with her father for a brief period after the divorce because she and her mother were having continuous conflicts. During that time, she learned that Ben had saved a lot of money he had kept hidden from the family. Consequently, he had an upper-middle income lifestyle in contrast to the family's impoverished existence during the years before and after the divorce. Rosalind did not understand how he could hide needed resources from the family. But she did become closer to her father than she had been in the past; while living with him she was able to tell him about the sexual abuse. Ben became very angry and reacted by forcing Ross and Don move out of the mother's house (they were then 21 and 19 at the time).

A few months later, Carrie convinced Rosalind that her father did not need her as much as **she** did. When Rosalind returned to live with her mother, the physical and emotional abuse resumed. Her mother did not want Rosalind and the other children to have friends, so they were socially isolated from their schoolmates. Mae assumed the role of caretaker for the two youngest children with the help of Rosalind. Not having Ross and Don at home relieved some stress from the sexual abuse (Greenwald & Leitenberg, 1989; Daie, Wilztum, & Eleff, 1989). But taking care of the younger children and Carrie led to additional stress (as Carrie's addiction made her more dysfunctional).

It is often during the latency period that some sexually abused children reveal the abuse to someone who is more likely to believe them and to eliminate it (Pilat and Boomhower-Kresser, 1992). This period may be an optimal one for helping youths to resolve the range of effects that result from the abuse. In Rosalind's situation, however, treatment was not provided even though the sibling abuse was eliminated. The following summary of Rosalind's adolescent years illustrates how such situations can continue to be dysfunctional if family treatment is not provided to the youth and to other family members.

The Adolescent Years

Carrie would have Rosalind come to the neighborhood bar where she spent each evening. She did homework while waiting until Carrie was ready to leave, usually late at night. Rosalind was uncertain about why Carrie wanted her there. Rosalind continued to make excellent grades inspite of the daily turmoil at home and spending time in the bar. One night when Rosalind was not feeling well, Carrie asked one of the men in the bar to take her home. Apparently Carrie had told the man he could have sex with Rosalind for $40. When they got to the house, the man tried to rape Rosalind. Ross and Don came by about that time, and when they realized what was happening, they threw the man out.

When Carrie came home and found out what had happened, she flew into a rage. She kept hitting them and throwing things until they were all bruised and bleeding. The police were called by neighbors and as a result of the violence and inadequate supervision, protective services decided that the three younger children should be placed in foster care (Mae was working at the time, and, as an eighteen year old, she was allowed to establish her own household). Rosalind was sent to live with Carrie's brother Darrell and his family in a different town while Kevin and Steve were placed in separate foster homes. Darrell was the brother that Carrie was closest to. He and his second wife had just had another child and were very kind to Rosalind. She thought she had found the "perfect family."

However, Rosalind soon found out that Darrell was an alcoholic and was physically violent toward his wife. After a year, the violence was so traumatic and had escalated to a point where Rosalind began to run away even though Darrell never hit her. Protective services decided that Rosalind, who was seventeen at the time, would be allowed to room with another emancipated minor under the agency's supervision in order to finish her senior year of school. She did not see any of her siblings for approximately five years. Rosalind did well in this alternative sibling subsystem, both academically and socially. She graduated with honors and established a very close and supportive relationship with her roommate that has continued until the present.

These positive outcomes demonstrate Rosalind's resiliency without the benefit of family treatment. She should have received treatment at age twelve when the abuse was revealed, but her treatment did not begin until she was twenty. Rosalind referred herself for treatment when she began to have such vivid flashbacks about her sibling and parental abuse that they interfered with her current life functioning.

A Sibling and Family Therapy Program

Rosalind's case study portrays some of the sibling and parental dynamics that make treatment necessary in violent families. Frey-Angel (1989) underscores the fact that just stopping parents' abuse and violence by providing them with treatment is insufficient. This important step "... may not prevent the children, the next generation, from being clients in the future for the same problem" (p. 106). Children will invariably repeat the abuse in their adult intimate relationships if they are not taught a different way of relating. So it is not surprising that Rosalind later married a man who abused her sexually just as Ross did, and emotionally and physically as her mother did.

It is not only important to provide treatment to the perpetrators and victims of violence individually. Frey-Angel (1989) notes that the learning of new relationship patterns should take place with the siblings together since that is the natural subsystem that has lived through the problem at home. In the next sections, assessment and treatment strategies will be described for sexually abused latency-aged children, their siblings, and the parents. In such programs, the overall goal is to resolve the issues of trust, identity, loss, and differentiation within the sibling subsystem as part of the healing process. Only then can the lifelong relationships between siblings and childhood resiliency be enhanced.

Assessing the Problem

Pilat and Boomhower-Kresser (1992) emphasize that the discovery of child sexual abuse inevitably precipitates a crisis for the victim and the family. This type of crisis facilitates assessment and entry into treatment because the family is more open to change at that point. For instance, when Rosalind revealed to her father that she had been sexually abused, her family probably would have been more responsive to treatment at that time due to the resulting crisis. Assessment should focus on each parent's ability to acknowledge individual responsibility for not having protected the child from victimization, the effects of denying that the abuse has occurred or of doing nothing to stop it (as Rosalind's mother did), or the role of substance abuse in perpetuating the abuse (Brown, 1988; Mayer, 1983).

In terms of siblings, practitioners should also assess the effects of the sibling perpetrator's age and whether or not he or she has been sexually abused (Geiser, 1979). When the perpetrator is five or more years older than the victim the abuse is not considered "natural sex play or experimentation" between siblings. For instance, Ross was eight years older than Rosalind so this was a true abuse situation rather than normal experimentation (deJong, 1989). Moreover, the effects of Carrie's abuse of Ross should be assessed and then focused on during treatment as well as his abuse of Rosalind. Often sibling perpetrators also have unmet dependency needs, inadequate coping skills, unresolved anger, and guilt and shame that should be identified during the assessment (Pilat and Boomhower-Kresser, 1992).

The effects on nonabused siblings should be included in the assessment. Survivors guilt may be a factor if siblings believe they should have been able to protect the victim. Mayer (1985) indicates nonabused siblings may also experience shame from being relieved that the abuse did not happen to them. In Rosalind's family, all of the children experienced Carrie's emotional and physical abuse, but it is not clear how Kevin and Steve were affected by Mae's and Rosalind's sexual abuse. If the family had been involved in treatment, the assessment would need to focus on how the younger children coped with those feelings (Mayer, 1985) if they were aware of the sexual abuse.

Sibling and Family Therapy Strategies

As noted previously, it is important to include sibling therapy for single or multiple sibling subsystems in order to resolve issues identified during the assessment process (see Table 4.1 in Chapter 4). These group modalities can be provided in child welfare agencies where the abuse is usually reported and in family service and child guidance centers. A number of authors have clarified the advantages of using those modalities for children 3–12 years when siblings and issues of violence are involved (Frey-Angel, 1989; Bank and Kahn, 1982; Green, 1981):

1. Siblings are people who can trust each other the most because of their shared experiences.
2. Change is not as threatening when siblings experience new ideas and behaviors together related to changing old relationships.
3. Sibling relationships are most intense during times of stress and change and when parental relationships are not available (this

makes sibling relationships more vulnerable to positive changes in treatment groups).

4. When individual siblings are involved, children of different ages can be seen in the same groups—this heterogeneity creates a system similar to the family for learning about the effects of violence.
5. Because each sibling is born into a different family and has a different vantage point, together they can provide more clarity in reconstructing significant family events including episodes of abuse and the reactions of various members.
6. Siblings come into a group with a common history and will continue to be a subsystem after the group ends, this adds to their initial commitment and to the longevity of changes that occur during treatment that reduce the risk of future abuse and violence.
7. The personal and collective needs of siblings can be addressed in treatment, this can increase their understanding of each other's experiences and current reactions to the work in treatment (e.g., continued denial that the abuse occurred, loyalty to the abusive parent or sibling).
8. These modalities provide new adult role models that expose the children to alternative coping mechanisms, while reducing the threat that treatment raises for parental credibility and lessening the pain from developing a coping style of open communication with siblings during treatment sessions and at home.

A number of effective treatment strategies can be used during sibling and family therapy to strengthen the sibling bond and natural support network. The goal is to build on the natural resiliency exhibited in each situation such as that demonstrated by Rosalind and her sibling subsystem. The interventions are part of a combined strategic and cognitive-behavioral family systems approach. One strategy involves the use of collective storytelling to reconstruct cognitions about the abuse experiences. The group leader can write down the story so that gradually through collaboration the siblings can develop a wholistic and realistic perspective about what happened (Freeman, 1992; Frey-Angel, 1989).

This cognitive-behavioral restorying process helps to identify distortions siblings may have about violent episodes and about each others' reactions. The basis for fears (such as Rosalind's "unreasonable" fears of basements and cellars) can be uncovered and validated. The cognitive-behavioral technique of desensitization or having the individual gradually go into the fearful situation can be useful in resolving such fears (Werner, 1986). This process can help the group members learn to trust their perceptions and feelings along with those of siblings, and thus, can increase self-esteem and a sense of unity. Strengths and examples of resiliency can be revealed as when Rosalind and her siblings collaborated to avoid their mother's abuse.

In addition, the experience can help to explain how parental denial of the abuse or its importance has undermined the children's identity as worthwhile persons and their self-esteem (Pilat and Boomhower-Kresser, 1992). Restorying has one other important advantage in sibling therapy. The cognitive restructuring from restorying is necessary to counteract the memory losses that occur as a coping mechanism among siblings. When the abuse situations have been reconstructed, they provide the opportunity for confronting the perpetrator with the victim's account of these experiences and his or her reactions. The confrontation is necessary for helping the perpetrator to acknowledge and own his or her responsibility for what occurred (Pilat and Boomhower-Kresser, 1992). In Rosalind's situation, as in all abusive and violent families, such an acknowledgement by the parents and Ross could have enhanced her healing process and that of the other siblings.

Group members can learn new ways of expressing anger and other feelings such as empathy through role modeling, games, and interactive exercises. Rosalind commented that she had never experienced anger "below the neck" because it would have been too threatening to her mother and Ross if she had really felt angry. So she "stuffed" her anger and never considered it except as a word in her mind that had no feelings attached to it. Rigid rules about not expressing feelings can be identified and examined by group members in terms of how they are developed to support the family violence. Here strategic family systems interventions can be effective such as prescribing the symptom ("you should not express anger and other feelings until you know it is safe") or reframing ("keeping the family secret is an effort to be loyal to your parents and siblings") (Watzlawick, Weakland, and Fisch, 1974; Papp, 1983).

A similar type of rigidity in sibling roles needs to be the focus of treatment as well. Frey-Angel (1989) points out that siblings often assume rigid roles with each other that tend to replay the parents' abusive roles and relationships. Role playing and games could have helped Rosalind's family discover how sibling roles reflected the parents abusive and distant behaviors with them and each other. More of the same is a strategic family systems intervention that could illustrate over and over again in role plays how sibling's rigid roles make a negative situation worse rather than better (Watzlawick et al., 1974).

In addition to problems from prescriptive roles, siblings from violent families often do not develop the ability to tune into the feelings behind actions or behavior. This includes their own behavior as well as that of others in areas such as empathy. Using stimulus completion stories can be useful for developing empathy. The group leader begins a story designed to elicit certain responses, has the members finish it, and then has them discuss the feelings related to behaviors and events in the story (Freeman, 1992). Another intervention involves using photographs of people interacting (including conflicts and acts of violence) to help siblings to learn about the feelings behind behavior and to generalize that understanding to their family and sibling relationships.

Role modeling and role play are cognitive-behavioral interventions that can help group members to experience and express empathy to each other based on what they have learned from the photographs and storytelling (Werner, 1986). Mirrors are useful too for helping children to see their own affect and to label the underlying feelings related to their behaviors (Frey-Angel, 1989). Similar methods can be used to teach other important social skills such as assertiveness, problem-solving, and accepting feedback. Education about the stages of loss and grief help children to mourn their loss of childhood and innocence due to the sexual abuse (Pilat and Boomhower-Kresser, 1992). Siblings may also need to grieve the loss of their unity when parental abuse hinders their ability to support one another or the loss of contact when they are separated in out of home placements. The latter was certainly a source of loss for Rosalind and her siblings.

Resolving grief from separations and other issues that clarify each sibling's boundaries helps with the important developmental task of differentiation within the sibling subsystem. Bowen (1974) emphasizes this task is as important as differentiation or individuation from the parents. Sibling differentiation can be facilitated in both sibling and family therapy sessions focused on the value of individual differences by teaching effective communication and restructuring family relationships during the sessions. Circular questions help siblings and parents to focus on what is unique about each sibling by having them comment from another family member's perspective (Papp, 1983). Examples of this strategic family systems intervention in the case of Rosalind include the following: (1) To each sibling, "What would each parent say is unique about Rosalind; or (2) To Rosalind, "What areas do you and Ross agree on and what areas do you disagree on"?

Many of these treatment strategies are necessary for helping siblings to handle the core issue of trust: related to themselves, siblings, and adults. In part, trust develops as the siblings break down their isolation from each other by sharing more openly in the group their past experiences and by discovering some common pain and fears along with unique individual reactions (Frey-Angel, 1989). Giving up the defenses that have assisted them in past coping (e.g., denial, hopelessness, and helplessness) and developing new more functional ways of coping also increase trust (e.g., acquiring assertiveness skills increases the responsiveness of others and the predictability of how they might respond).

Although sibling therapy can increase trust among siblings, trust in parents comes only when the violence and other dysfunctional behaviors are eliminated through family therapy sessions. Family therapy should be provided simultaneously with sibling therapy. It is important for the children to observe the parents collaborating positively so that the need for dysfunctional and harmful sibling coalitions is eliminated (e.g., Ross and Rosalind, Don and Mae, Ross and Don). Sometimes the abuse has been so extensive, that family therapy or later family-oriented individual treatment can not repair the lost of trust. Rosalind commented that when she returned to her mother's home at twelve and the abuse resumed, she learned never to trust her mother again although she secretly hoped through the years that Carrie would change.

Rosalind's resiliency in developing trusting relationships with others, however, is demonstrated by her ability to bond with her alternative sibling during adolescence. The opportunity to bond with a substitute sibling may have helped her to mourn the loss of Mae and Steve and might have served as a bridge until they were able to resume contact five years later. The loss of trust in the relationship with Ross has had significant effects on Rosalind's ability to trust men. It has also made her stay distant and cut-off from the males in her family except for Steve and other males in general over her lifetime.

Evaluation Procedures

Many of the intervention strategies used in sibling and family therapy for abuse and violence are also useful in evaluating the quality of treatment. As mentioned previously, practitioners can utilize the collective storytelling strategy to write out the important events in the siblings' family life. Those stories can be illustrated by art work that is done by the siblings periodically. It is important to date the art work so that during and at the end of family treatment, the siblings and parents can be involved in analyzing how the drawings change over time and what they mean in terms of feelings (Frey-Angel, 1989). Their analysis and feedback helps the family and practitioner to monitor if the objectives of treatment are being achieved in a timely manner.

When Rosalind was involved in individually-oriented sibling and family treatment at the age of 20, her initial drawings invariably contained scenes of a dark scary-looking area drawn in black. As her treatment progressed, Rosalind was able to identify the scene as the school cellar where Carrie took her and Mae and threatened to kill them. When her fears were resolved, Rosalind's art work focused on other things rather than that particular scene.

Logs and diaries are useful for helping children write brief notes about flashbacks related to their abuse. These tools aid in treatment and in evaluating how the frequency, content, and childrens' reactions to the flashbacks change as the healing process occurs. They can also help to monitor when treatment is not helping to resolve the flashbacks, or when parental or sibling behavior is inhibiting progress. Logs can be structured or unstructured in terms of what information is recorded and how it is recorded based on the child's age (Bloom and Fischer, 1982). In addition, the logs of children in the same sibling subsystem and in multiple subsystems can be compared to monitor the patterns of positive changes and setbacks.

Finally, scaling can be used to quantify how siblings and parents respond to circular questions or exercises and games designed to help in problem-solving. For instance, in terms of circular questions children can be asked: On a scale from 0 to 10 (0 = not very bad and 10 = awful) how bad a sibling would say the abuse was. The ratings given by the different siblings could be compared and discussed, and changes in their ratings could be monitored over time before and during treatment. In structured exercises and role plays, children could be asked to rate their own and siblings' choices of coping and problem-solving responses to simulated but real family events.

Conclusion

This chapter has identified some of the characteristics of resilient children and sibling subsystems in violent and abusive families. Examples include finding a functional area to excel in leading to individual validation and collaborating as a subsystem to cope with parental abuse. From the author's research and Rosalind's case study in particular, it has been possible to follow this pattern of resiliency over the lifespan of some individuals. Those individuals thrive, rather than just survive. For others, resiliency within the sibling subsystem is not at a sufficient level to maintain individual functioning except at a survival level.

Possibly, sibling and family treatment during childhood may enhance or create more adequate levels of resiliency in individuals and sibships. It is not clear at this point whether some people are born without resiliency or whether it can be learned, but some intervention strategies have been described for addressing other important issues: trust-building, loss, identity, and differentiation within the sibling subsystem.

REFERENCES

Anthony, E.J. (1987). Risk, vulnerability, and resilience: An overview. In E.J. Anthony and B.J. Cohler (Eds.), *The invulnerable child* (3–48). New York: Guilford.

Bank, S. and Kahn, M. (1982). *The sibling bond.* New York: Basic Books.

Bloom, M. and Fischer, J. (1982). *Evaluating practice: Guidelines for the accountable professional.* Englewood Cliffs, NJ: Prentice-Hall.

Bowen, M. (1974). A family systems approach to alcoholism. *Addictions, 21,* 3–4.

Bowlby, J. (1977). *Attachment and loss:* Vol. I. New York: Penguin.

Brown, J. (1988). Common bonds of family tragedy: Alcoholism and child sexual abuse. *Focus, 34,* 18–46.

Cowen, E.L. (1988). Resilient children, psychological wellness, and primary prevention. *American Journal of Community Psychology, 16,* 591–607.

Daie, N., Wilztum, E., and Eleff, M. (1989). Long-term effects of sibling incest. *Journal of Clinical Psychiatry, 50,* 428–431.

deJong, A.R. (1989). Sexual interactions among siblings and cousins: Experimentation or exploitation? *Child Abuse and Neglect, 13,* 271–279.

Finkelhor, D. (1984). *Child sexual abuse: New theory and research.* New York: Free Press.

Finkelhor, D., Gelles, R., Hotaling, G., and Strauss, R. (1983). *The dark side of families: Current family violence research.* Beverly Hills, CA: Sage.

Freeman, E.M. (1992). The use of storytelling techniques with young African-American males: Implications for substance abuse prevention. *Journal of Intergroup Relations, 29,* 53-72.

Frey-Angel, J. (1989). Treating children of violent families: A sibling group approach. *Social Work with Groups, 12,* 95-107.

Geiser, R.L. (1979). *Hidden victims: The sexual abuse of children.* Boston: Beacon.

Green, A. (1981). Child abuse by siblings. Paper presented at the meeting of the American Academy of Child Psychiatry, Dallas, Texas.

Greenwald, E. and Leitenberg, H. (1989). Long-term effects of sexual experiences with siblings and nonsiblings during childhood. *Archives of Sexual Behavior, 18,* 389-399.

Mayer, A. (1985). *Sexual abuse: Causes, consequences, and treatment of incestuous and pedophilic acts.* Holmes Beach, FL: Learning Publications.

Mayer, A. (1983). *Incest: A treatment manual for therapy with victim, spouses and offenders.* Holmes Beach, FL: Learning Publications.

Papp, P. (1983). *The process of change.* New York: Guilford.

Pilat J. and Boomhower-Kresser, S. (1992). Dynamics of alcoholism and child sexual abuse: Implications for interdisciplinary practice. In E.M. Freeman (Ed.), *The addiction process: Effective social work approaches* (65-78). White Plains, NY: Longman.

Pollack, O. and Hundermar, D. (1984). Some unexplored aspects of the sibling experience. *Adolescence, 76,* 869-874.

Taylor, S.E. (1983). Adjustment to threatening events: A theory of cognitive adaptation. *American Psychologist, 21,* 1161-1173.

Watzlawick, P., Weakland, J.H., and Fisch, R. (1974). *Change: Principles of problem formation and problem resolution.* New York: W. W. Norton.

Werner, H.D. (1986). Cognitive theory. In F.J. Turner (Ed.), *Social work treatment: Interlocking theoretical approaches* (91-130). New York: Macmillan.

Chapter 7

COMMUNICATION AND TASK CENTERED FAMILY TREATMENT FOR ADOLESCENT SIBLING LOYALTY AND COMMUNITY VIOLENCE ISSUES

> I guess running track and working in the grocery store kept me out of the gangs. My brother Luiz couldn't understand where I was coming from—he thought I was trying to be anglo. Bob, my older brother, he knew what was happening. He deserved a lot of credit for pulling **himself** back from the edge of trouble.
>
> —Lucky

Hahn and West (1985-1986) indicate that in America, "The ultimate resource..." is the "ability to exert control over others in the street or in the board room" (p. 4). Lucky, as an Hispanic teenager, exemplifies the struggle that ethnic minority youth are confronted with based on the above assumption. They are confronted with media messages that having a good job and the "right contacts" are important vehicles for achieving in America. Yet, these youths are denied access to traditional avenues that are necessary in order for achievement to become a reality (Freeman and McRoy, 1986).

It is not uncommon for youths from the same family to perceive this dilemma differently and to respond to the situation in unique ways. Siblings do grow up in the same sibling subsystem as well as experience a common family milieu and history. They may perceive and respond to racism differently, however, on the basis of individual factors such as intelligence, personality, coping patterns, and other strengths and limitations (Freeman and McRoy, 1986; Szapocznik, Kurtines, and Fernandez, 1980; McShane, 1988; Liu, Yu, Chang, and Fernandez, 1990).

Those differences lead to issues that must be dealt with in the sibling subsystem and in the family, peer group, and community. Some examples of issues needing to be addressed include the handling of loyalty conflicts between siblings, developing a value consensus, choosing an achievement versus an avoidance orientation, and implementing ways to cope with environmental risk factors effectively (see Chapter 1) (Mosatche, Brady, and Noberini, 1983; Klein, Alexander, and Parsons, 1977). This chapter illustrates many of these issues in the case study of Lucky. The focus of this case study is an Hispanic family, but the discussion can be generalized to families of any ethnic background that are experiencing community violence.

A combined communications and task centered family treatment approach is discussed and applied to Lucky's circumstances. The approach involves self- and mutual help strategies for assisting empowered families to decrease violence in their communities and to cope with loyalty conflicts, survivor guilt, and grief related to the loss of siblings and others through violence. Post traumatic stress disorder is described as a frequent reaction to such violence in high risk communities. Useful methods for evaluating this approach, including symptom checklists and community assessment inventories, are described as well.

A Case Study: Lucky

Cesar (Lucky) Ramirez was a 29 year old federal law enforcement officer when he agreed to participate in this author's study of sibling relationships. Two themes evident throughout his interview were sibling loyalty and the family conflicts he had experienced from being achievement-oriented. However, his understanding of these themes presently (how siblings in the same family struggle differently with environmental risks) is in contrast to his lack of clarity during his earlier years. Fox (1985) supports this emphasis on environmental factors for understanding the dynamics involved in the range of responses to adolescence: From developing an achievement orientation to becoming a member of a gang. That author describes gang behavior, for example, as a universal and normal striving by adolescents for adult status coupled with the added social and economic pressures in the current milieu. Lucky's case study illustrates the interaction of these environmental factors with individual and sibling subsystem variables and the family's cultural adaptations.

The Childhood Phase

Lucky's parents met after their families emigrated to the midwest from Mexico (when his parents were young children). The grandparents emigrated for economic reasons. They were attracted to the Midwest by information from other relatives about employment opportunities in the railroad and meat packing industries (see Figure 7.1). Both families settled into a small multicultural community that has maintained its ethnic diversity and relative stability until recent years. This community has continued to be the cultural center for Hispanics or Latinos living in the larger metropolitan area (i.e., for Mexicans, South Americans, Cubans, Puerto Ricans, and other Latinos in the surrounding area). Lucky described the area as the major opportunity for cultural identification and participation in cultural institutions and traditions for the city's Hispanics.

It was this sense of cultural support, identity, and traditions that Lucky remembers from his childhood years. As can be seen from his genogram, he was the third oldest in a family of four boys and two girls. He has always been closest to his brothers Bob and Luiz who are the next oldest and youngest to him in terms of birth order. Lucky described all three of his brothers as "hell raisers" in different ways, even as young children. Alphonso was his father's favorite son, from Lucky's perspective, perhaps because he was the oldest child and the most like their father in temperment. For example, they are both forceful and aggressive, but while easy to anger, they tend to forget about conflicts easily after the fact.

But while their father is quiet generally, Alphonso is outgoing. By the time the latter was eight or nine, he wanted to spend most of his time with friends instead of with the family as the parents expected. He was picked up several times for shoplifting and later for stealing cars. Alphonso would also skip school occasionally for which he would be beaten by Emilio.

Like Alphonso, Bob was outgoing but spent time with Lucky and Luiz as young children, often playing games with them and teaching them to box. Lucky felt Bob gave him a sense of being "okay" as a child. It did not seem to matter to Bob whether Lucky was good at any of the activities they got involved in; Bob was always patient with him. Although Lucky spent some of his time in organized activities (e.g., the boy scouts and a church group), he was more a loner socially. He stuttered as a child and felt very self-conscious about this. His mother, Eileena, gave him mixed messages. She would tell him not worry about things, but then would encourage him to be more outgoing and aggressive like his older brothers, "the way boys are supposed to be."

Their father was not as patient with Lucky's stuttering and shy manner, especially when he had been drinking. Then he would sometimes push

140 Family Treatment

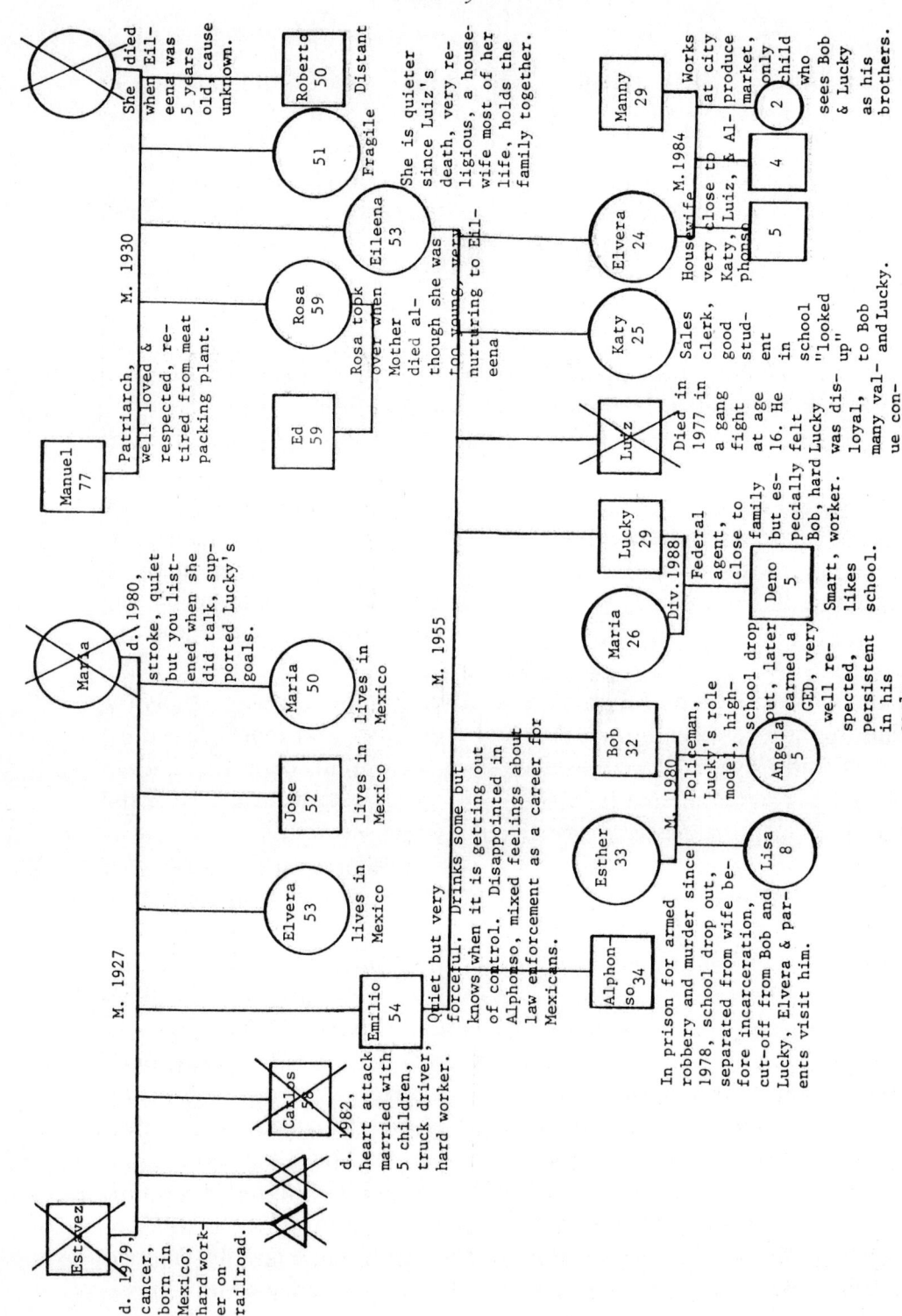

Figure 7.1. Genogram of Lucky Ramirez (1989).

Lucky to box with him, to show him what Lucky had learned from Bob. At those times, Lucky was afraid of his father who would often become angry if Lucky cried or tried to avoid boxing with him. Luiz, a year younger than Lucky, liked their sparring matches and would often jump in and get Lucky "off the hook" by agreeing to box their father instead. If Bob was around he would try and distract their father by getting him focused on some other issue. Although Lucky was a better student in school than Luiz, the latter was more adept socially and physically. He often helped Lucky out of other difficult situations such as disagreements about a game on the school playground. Lucky indicates their two sisters were both quiet when they were young, and spent more time in the house with their mother as it was expected traditionally.

The family was active in the Catholic church and attended regularly. Lucky felt their involvement in the services and traditional celebrations added to their closeness as a family. When he was about ten, his mother began to talk about Lucky becoming a priest because he was a good student and liked going to church. Lucky recalled that in many Hispanic families, it was an honor to have a son or daughter choose the church as a vocation. Lucky's father did not want any of his children to become priests or nuns. He believed some of the priests in Mexico had helped to keep the people poor by discouraging them from getting involved in political causes. Although he attended church, he was also very critical of what went on there. This was a continuing source of tension between the parents since Eileena believed that to question anything about the church was blasphemous.

The parents were in agreement, however, about the importance of their cultural traditions and values. They believed in close family ties with the extended family and that children should be obedient to their parents. Lucky remembers an emphasis on staying out of trouble and avoiding any involvement with the police and other legal matters. This is the reason Alphonso's involvement in minor crimes and he and Luiz's later participation in gang activities were distressful to them (Buriel, 1984). They associated mostly with other Mexicans in the community and had fewer contacts with the caucasian and African-American families living there. When they did have contacts with members of those ethnic groups, the contacts were mostly through the church and community center involving the more long term residents in the community.

His parents were more suspicious of newer residents who lived mostly in public housing and certain other sections of the community. Lucky remembers that at one point, his parents took him out of a boy scout troop when the troop leader decided to move their meetings from the community center to a community room in one of the public housing projects. His mother felt it was too dangerous for him to go to the projects because of the frequent crime and gang activities there. Eileena said the families in the projects did not have the "right values."

The Adolescent Years

Because there was no junior high or high school in the community, when Lucky was 13 he was bussed to a junior high and high school on the same campus outside his community. This school was predominantly caucasian and involved racial tensions between students and what Lucky recognized later as subtle racially-biased messages from the teachers. There was only one Latino teacher in the school and very little of the curriculum and atmosphere was culturally-sensitive in support of the Latino students' adjustment (Vigil and Long, 1981). Alphonso had dropped out of school the previous year when he was sixteen. The year Lucky entered this school, Bob also dropped out. Lucky thinks they both experienced the same cultural confusion he did in going from a multicultural community school in which they were in the majority to a school outside their community in which they were in the minority. But they did not talk about their experiences, perhaps because of the machismo image their father encouraged.

Alphonso had been suspended several times for fighting, smoking, and skipping school. He had also began to use drugs since this was about the time when he became involved in a street gang. Bob was failing in most of his classes. He was not in a gang, but spent most of his time with other youths in the community who were also failing in school. He had not been able to find work because there were very few jobs in the community and public transportation was not available to other areas of the city. Their parents were very concerned and did not want either of them to drop out. When asked about what the school did when the two brothers dropped out, Lucky noted that at sixteen, Alphonso could legally stop going and that probably no one at the school cared when Bob dropped out.

When he was about fourteen or fifteen, Lucky's gym teacher noticed he was a superior athlete in track and encouraged him to try out for the track team. There were very few Hispanic students on the school's athletic teams. One reason was they were all bussed to the school and could not stay for daily practice. The coach was so convinced of Lucky's talents that he made a personal call to the parents and agreed to transport him home each day after practice if he could stay. Lucky believes the factor that convinced his parents was the coach's conviction that doing well in track might help Lucky feel better about himself and end his stuttering.

Lucky feels his life began to change at that point because he had discovered something "I was good at," although he was afraid the coach might discover any time he had made a mistake about Lucky's track skills. In addition to this change, Lucky found a job working evenings in a grocery store near his house. It was owned by an older German man from the community who usually hired caucasian boys to work for him. When Lucky asked Mr. Muehler for a job, he asked Lucky why he should invest the time necessary for training him to work in the store. Lucky was confused by the question, thinking it meant Mr. Muehler would not even consider hiring him. He stumbled through an answer before realizing that the grocer was asking whether he was trustworthy and responsible. Another of Mr. Muehler's questions was what had Lucky done before to demonstrate his persistence. This initial experience with Mr. Muehler was repeated over and over during the next few years. Lucky felt Mr. Muehler made him think about things, and like Bob, he was patient and accepting.

In looking back, Lucky thinks being on the track team and having one of the few jobs available to youths in the community was helpful to him in two ways. He did not have time to get involved with other youths who were in trouble at school and/or involved in gangs. Also the two activities taught him responsibility and discipline, while providing him with a constant source of positive feedback. Lucky also believes he, Bob, Katy, and Elvera were affected positively by his family's traditional cultural values in a way that Alphonso and Luiz were not. Some researchers support this assumption about the role of protective factors in preventing delinquency in youths from high risk communities (Hawkins and Catalano, 1992; Edelman, 1984; Buriel, Calzada, and Vasquez, 1982; Rodriguez and Zayas, 1990).

Lucky experienced conflicts about the path he was on, a path toward achievement that Lucky believed had chosen him rather than the reverse. Luiz had joined a gang when he was fifteen and had tried off and on to get Lucky involved too. They would have frequent arguments about why Lucky "was trying to fit in with the anglos and was ashamed of being

Latino." Luiz said Lucky was being different (disloyal) and that made Luiz look bad with his gang. Padilla (1980) indicates that such acculturation and loyalty conflicts are common among Hispanic siblings and peers (see Chapter 5 for a more detailed discussion about acculturation levels and conflicts among ethnic minority children and youths). Moreover, Lucky believes Luiz was using Alphonso as his model for the criminal activities he was involved in with the gang. Alphonso had continued with his own gang activities over more than three years, exhibiting a tendency noted in the literature for some Hispanic and other minority youths to continue such involvements as they mature (Caetano, 1984; Rodriguez, Burger, and Banks, 1984).

Lucky believes another turning point came when Luiz was killed at age sixteen during a gang fight. His gang members dropped him off at a hospital after he had been shot. He was already dead when he reached the hospital. It was a difficult time for the family because they were uncertain whether Luiz was taken to the hospital right away by the gang members. His killer was never identified and the family received very few details about his death, adding to their grief and rage (Hahn and West, 1986). Lucky believes that Alphonso may have learned information later that he has never shared, but there was never any proof of that.

Some family members experienced self-blame (especially Alphonso) which is a common reaction among siblings (Hogan and Balk, 1990; Pollock, 1986; Schumacher, 1984). Bob was very remorseful to the extent that he gradually turned his life around. He stopped spending time with his friends who were on the fringes of neighborhood gangs though not directly involved. He decided to take GED classes at a community center, and later received his high school equivalency certificate (see Figure 7.1). Eileena was especially affected by the loss of Luiz; she has not resolved her grief over his death or the circumstances involved.

Lucky experienced a sense of guilt and nightmares for months after Luiz died. Those experiences might have been the result of survivors guilt (Eth and Pynoos, 1985) and the arguements about loyalty that he and Luiz had previously. Eventually, Luiz's death **and** Bob's turning his life around reinforced Lucky's efforts to do well in school. As a postscript, Mr. Muehler supported Lucky's plan to go to college and that was a major factor in Lucky's belief that he could do it. Lucky used a combination of scholarship and loans to go to a predominantly white college in another state where he again experienced cultural shock. He indicated what helped him to do well after an initial period of failing academically and socially was the going-away party his family and neighbors had given him. He felt they, and Bob in particular, were depending on him to do well.

An Approach to Handling Community Violence/Sibling Loyalty Issues

Lucky's situation in the previous section indicates the need for a family treatment approach that can effectively address issues related to the sibling subsystem, the family unit, and the community. The losses through violence and family members' reactions to those losses are an important focus for assessment and intervention. Sibling loyalty issues and values clarification related to consensus/conflicts should be addressed as well. When adolescents are involved, the approach must include a focus on the normative tasks such as separation from the family of origin and differentiation within the sibling subsystem (see Chapter 1 on the natural history of siblings).

Theoretical Underpinnings

These developmental tasks and related themes require a theoretical approach that helps practitioners to address them within the context of the family and environment. A combined task centered and communications family treatment approach is appropriate for this purpose. Reid (1986) advises that the task centered component is designed to help "... clients to devise and carry out actions or tasks to alleviate their problems" during developmental and other transitions (p. 267). Those probems can be related to managing social roles, making life decisions, securing resources, and relieving emotional distress such as the grief experienced by Lucky and his family in the loss of Luiz.

The communication component builds on the task centered aspects by considering verbal and nonverbal messages along with the context in which the communication occurs (i.e., within the sibship, family, neighborhood gang, community, and larger environment). This theory is useful because it provides guidelines about how "... people change either naturally or in response to therapeutic intervention" (Nelson, 1986, p. 220). The family systems components are from family systems theory which emphasizes the interrelationships between the different parts of the unit and how a change in one part influences changes in other parts (see Chapter 1). The integration of task centered and communications theories and their application as part of a family treatment approach are evident in the following sections on assessment and treatment/evaluation.

The Assessment Process

Although an initial assessment is needed, the assessment should continue throughout the helping process consistent with the circularity of a family systems approach. Helping professionals in public housing projects, neighborhood crime watch organizations, public schools, and community centers may be able to utilize this approach in their services to families. They may already be involved with families when violent incidences occur or families may be referred to practitioners on the basis of those incidences. The approach to assessment and intervention can take place on two levels: with individual sibships or families and with community groups involving multiple family units.

Assessing Individual Sibships or Families. It is important to involve all family members in the assessment whenever possible, since their reactions to the violence will affect each other and different members may have information that is important in handling those reactions. For example, if Alphonso were not included in the assessment of Lucky's family, the members might not be able to adequately explore their suspicions that he knows more about Luiz' death than they do. It would also be important to know why he is blaming himself for the death and how that reaction is affecting him and the other members.

The process of assessment can be facilitated through the use of several procedures related to development tasks, communication patterns, and symptoms of stress among the members. A life events scale and a symptoms checklist are examples of two useful procedures. A life events scale lists the range of stressful transitions and changes that can occur (e.g., marriage, birth of first child, divorce, death of a sibling, loss of a job, a change in jobs, involvement in a natural disaster, being arrested or a family member is arrested) (Datan and Ginsberg, 1975; Berren, Beigel, and Barker, 1982; Dohrenwen and Dohrenwen, 1980). The members are expected to check off any events that have occurred during the past year. The practitioner can quantify the responses by assigning each response a numerical value and then adding up the total to clarify the cumulative effects. The accompanying discussion is as important as the numerical weighting because any unique circumstances and reactions can be identified. Cultural sensitivity is important in this process. With ethnic minority youth such as Lucky and Luiz, the lack of job availability or being rejected for a job may be as traumatic as a member of another ethnic group losing a job. Helping professionals should explore such environmental and cultural nuances which may be important in understanding the sources of stress and the members' reactions (Freeman and McRoy, 1986).

The symptom checklist is a similar scale with items that indicate whether the person is experiencing Post-Traumatic Stress Disorder (PTSD), for example:

1. Feelings of detachment and estrangement as well as avoidance of significant involvements/activities (numbing).
2. Exaggerated startle responses or hyperalertness.
3. Sleep disturbances.
4. Memory impairment or trouble concentrating.
5. Unwanted thoughts, feelings, and dreams in reaction to environmental reminders of the event (re-experiencing).
6. Marked changes in eating patterns.
7. Escalating feelings of self-blame and guilt about surviving the event (a sense of having done something wrong and being undeserving of survival).

PTSD is a normal reaction to an abnormal amount of stress. The reaction is thought to be problematic if it exceeds one month's duration according to the DSM III–R (American Psychological Association, 1987). However, in situations of repeated violence the person's reactions may be cumulative, and it may be impossible to identify a discrete period of symptomatology. Most authors agree that the intensity of the trauma and its' intrapsychic impact on the survivor are highly subjective and individualized (Eth and Pynoos, 1985; Carmen, Reicker, and Mills, 1984). By formulating the above symptoms and others into a checklist, the practitioner can help clients assess the differential effects of the trauma on the various combinations of members. In the case of Lucky, each of Luiz's siblings had a different reaction to his death, based not only on the issues being addressed in their sibling relationships with him but also on factors/tasks related to their individual development. Therefore, an important step in using a symptom checklist is to help siblings and other family members identify the underlying relationship issues and developmental tasks that may influence their identified symptoms. For Lucky, the issue of sibling loyalty and the task of differentiation from the sibling subsystem may be key areas that have affected his guilt reactions (symptoms).

A third procedure for assessment in these situations is a values clarification grid designed to identify areas of consensus or conflict between different sibling coalitions and across family generations (see Table 7.1). The discussion about entries made on the grid by family members can be useful in clarifying areas of similarities and differences as well as identifying areas to work on during treatment. The grid can be completed by one individual in relation to one or more family members or peers and then comparisons can be made between the different grids. Another use is to have two or more individuals complete the grid together focused on their relationships with each other.

The names of persons who are providing information for the grid should be entered under "Recorder(s)," while the names of other members in the target relationship should be entered under "Focus." Items on the left side of the grid can be modified or items can be added or eliminated based on the situation. The items listed here reflect the developmental tasks of adolescence and issues often addressed during that phase between siblings and between youths and their parents. Had this grid been used with Lucky, several different sibling coalitions could have been assessed. For instance, it would have been possible to assess coalitions involving Bob and Lucky; Bob and Alphonso; Alphonso and Luiz; Lucky and Luiz; or Lucky, Bob, Katy, and Elvera. It might have been useful to assess intergenerationally the parents and the sibling subsystem as well.

Assessing Families in Community Organizations. A beginning step to helping families like Lucky's to enhance the health and safety of their communities is to assist them in assessing the collective and individual family needs. This assessment can be accomplished through the leadership of existing community organizations whose goals include crime reduction, substance abuse prevention, political action, cultural awareness, family preservation, drop out prevention, or economic development (Bowser, 1988; Curtis, 1989; Mitchell & Daniels, 1989; Valencia, Henderson, and Rankin, 1985; Gurak, 1981; Mendelberg, 1986; Rogers and Williams, 1987). Helping professionals may serve as consultants to these organizations or become involved with them through services to individual families. Hawkins and Catalano (1992) recommend the use of community assessment procedures that focus on the following risk factors:

Table 7.1. Values Clarification Grid.

	Date _____
	Recorder(s) _____
	Focus on _____

	Value Consensus	Value Conflicts
FRIENDSHIP/PEERS		
ACHIEVEMENT ORIENTATION (school, career)		
LOVE RELATIONSHIPS (dating, courtship)		
SEPARATION FROM FAMILY OF ORIGIN (parents, siblings, extended family)		
IDENTITY/SELF–ESTEEM (ethnic, gender, sibship, sexual preference)		
SIBLING SOLIDARITY		
COPING PATTERNS RELATED TO RISK FACTORS IN THE ENVIRONMENT		

Environmental Risk Factors

1. Economic and social deprivation (deteriorating and crime ridden neighborhoods).

2. Low neighborhood attachment and community disorganization (few strong social institutions and low surveillance of public places where crimes may occur).
3. Transitions and mobility (high rates of movement between schools or residences).
4. Community laws and norms favorable toward drug use, drug dealing, and other crimes.
5. High availability of drugs and alcohol in the community.

Individual/Family Risk Factors

1. Family history of alcoholism (a higher risk exists for boys).
2. Poor family management practices (e.g., lack of clear expectations or severe and inconsistent punishment).
3. Early antisocial behavior with aggressiveness.
4. Parental drug use and positive attitudes toward use.
5. Academic failure.
6. Low commitment to school.
7. Alienation or rebelliousness.
8. Antisocial behavior in early adolescence.
9. Association with drug-pushing peers.
10. Favorable attitudes toward drugs.
11. Early first use of drugs.

In helping families in community organizations to assess the the risk factors above, a number of important points should be considered. The members should be helped to assess the individual and collective strengths or protective factors that exist. Including the protective factors can provide a more balanced assessment and the foundation on which to build the intervention strategies. This is particularly important in multicultural communities if the families have not developed a positive view of the diversity among themselves (Freeman and Pennekamp, 1988). A number of protective factors were identified in Lucky's case study in terms of his sibship, family, ethnic group, and community as well as individual factors. Those factors contributed, no doubt, to the resiliency of the sibling relationship between Lucky and Bob and to their individual coping patterns.

Also it is important to assess the environment's influence on the individual and family risk factors. For example, the lack of a community high school, support to Hispanic students by some teachers, summer jobs, and public transportation contributed largely to Lucky's and his siblings' level of committment toward school. In addition, the quality of family management practices can be influenced by the availability of parent training resources within poor versus more affluent communities.

Family Treatment and Evaluation

Like the assessment process above, the treatment needs to be focused on sibling therapy and multiple families in community organizations (Table 4.1 identifies the appropriate modalities). The theoretical orientation identified previously should guide the structure and content of this family treatment approach.

Sibling and Family Therapy. It is important to adapt the family treatment approach so that it is consistent with the cultural factors inherent in the work with Hispanic families. Home visits, the use of Hispanic professionals or paraprofessionals as co-facilitators, and bi-cultural effectiveness training for handling intergenerational and intercultural conflicts are examples of culturally-sensitive strategies (Gordon and Arbuthnot, 1988; Juarez, 1985; Szapocznik, Santiesteban, Rios, Perez-Vidal, and Kurtines, 1986). Understanding the role religion and cultural values play in the members' lives is important. The practitioner can help the family see how the interventions being used can be linked with their cultural and religious views.

A major part of the treatment with sibships and individual families can focus on psycho-education about PTSD and the loss and grief process. An informal discussion format is useful at a level appropriate for adolescents (or younger children if there is a greater age variation within the sibship). The members can help to illustrate the symptoms of PTSD and stages of loss and grief on large poster boards. The posters can also help them to apply what they are learning: to identify their changing reactions over time and the similarities and differences among the siblings. In Lucky's sibship, having him describe and help to analyze his nightmares insession might have normalized them and provided him with support from his sibling network. Comparing Bob's and Alphonso's stages of grief and symptoms could have helped them to become more self-aware. It might have enhanced the level of sibling differentiation between them, and thus, the leaving home or separation process that was eminent for Alphonso, Bob, and Lucky.

The life events scale, symptom checklist, and values clarification grid discussed in the assessment section should provide the necessary focus as the participants move back and forth between the task centered educational aspects and communication exercises that can help them to resolve issues and accomplish those tasks. At the same time, helping professionals should assist the members in staying focused on the systemic and contextual factors related to the sibling subsystem, family, and the community. For example, it is important for the practitioner and the brothers and sisters to support Bob's efforts to move from an avoidance orientation (dropping out of school and "hanging out" with potential gang members) to an achievement orientation (finishing school and accomplishing his eventual goal of becoming a policeman). But his success also depends on a mutual change in his roles and those of others within the sibship and family as well as locating outside resources that do not exist in his community (e.g., employment and transportation).

If family therapy is appropriate it can be alternated with sibling therapy in a format that fits the needs in each situation. In addition to some of the strategies described above, it is important to help parents model resolution of the grief process and the handling of PTSD symptoms. Crying and expressing their anger by hitting something appropriate might facilitate the grief process. Desensitization strategies are useful for handling PTSD symptoms: getting more detailed information about Luiz's death and gradually/incrementally handling reminders about the event. A hierarchy could have been developed with Lucky's family and then the tasks undertaken, ranging from reading Luiz's obituary to going to the site of his death (McGlynn, Mealiea, and Landau, 1981; Gambrill, 1981).

Other areas may need to be addressed as well. For example, important adolescent developmental tasks such as separation can be focused on in terms of the parental task, the "letting go." Setting fair and age-appropriate rules about curfews and providing guidance but not demands about education and career choices are two such areas (Freeman and McRoy, 1986).

Moreover, parents' unfinished developmental and grief issues with the previous generation might affect the current family relationships and treatment process. In Lucky's family, Eileena's grief about Luiz's death may be affected by unresolved grief from the early loss of her mother and the role of her sister Rosa as a substitute parent (see Figure 7.1). Emilio may have unfinished issues with his three youngest siblings who decided to remain in Mexico with other relatives when their parents were able to send for them. Communication exercises (identifying underlying feelings in a statement about the relationships) and appropriate tasks (writing a letter to explore issues with the family member) could be assigned to help address/resolve these cultural and developmental issues (Hardy-Fanta and McMahon-Herrera, 1981; Hartman and Laird, 1983).

Evaluation of these sibling and family therapy strategies can be accomplished through the procedures used for the assessment. The symptom checklist can be administered at intake, at several specific time intervals during treatment (e.g., once monthly), and at the point of termination (Levy, 1987; Freeman and Pennekamp, 1988). The checklist provides feedback to family members and the practitioner about the focus, sequence, and timing of changes. Discussions about the feedback can identify what aspects of treatment are contributing to or impeding positive changes (Bloom and Fischer, 1982). Responses to psychoeducation can be evaluated through the family members' increased ability to discuss and apply the material to their reactions correctly.

Their changing skills in identifying areas of value consensus and conflicts is another important way to evaluate the treatment effects. This process includes evaluating how well the members' can accept differences between siblings and between the parents and children. Monitoring the members' progress in accomplishing tasks related to desensitization hierarchies is yet another example of how this treatment can be evaluated. This strategy can identify where a member is stuck in the process and whether a particular task needs to be divided into two or more smaller tasks for particular family members. For example, going to the site of Luiz's death may be too demanding as one task. Instead, it may be necessary to divide this task into several stages over time: driving close to the site but not stopping, going to the site and sitting in the car for a period of time, and then getting out of the car and standing in the area with someone else before going there alone.

Family Treatment at the Community Level. Treatment at the community level involves a series of strategies based on the assessment of risk and protective factors that exist for families in a community. Hawkins and Catalano (1992) indicate it is important for helping professionals to assist community organizations in developing a set of specific goals and objectives designed to mobilize families and the community as a whole over several years. The major mobilization tasks include the following which are then divided into smaller tasks: (1) involving key leaders; (2) forming a community board; (3) conducting a community risk assessment; (4) planning a program, including setting goals and objectives; and (5) establishing a program, institutionalizing it, and evaluating it.

In these situations, the family treatment strategies are applied to multiple families and to the environmental context (public policies and practices) that hinders the growth of those families. Although the emphasis of these strategies is on family units within a community, this part of the approach has implications for sibling relationships. The work of community organizations in reducing the risk factors for families can influence how value consensus and loyalty issues are handled by siblings. Stronger collective messages from families about the importance of an achievement orientation and the negative impact of violence, for example, can make it more likely that siblings will develop a similar consensus among themselves. In addition, it is important for helping professionals to insure that children and youth are involved in community changes that will affect their peer and sibling relationships as well as the overall well being of their families. In this manner, they too are likely to experience the empowerment that the adults in the community are striving for.

These family treatment strategies should be used to help families apply new and expand existing self- and mutual-help skills in changing their lives. For instance the objectives, and thus, the strategies may involve changing the nature of communications about families and the particular community in the media. The self-help skills and social competencies of families in decoding and changing those messages should be a major goal of this type of strategy (Black, 1989; Caplan and Weissberg, 1989; DiClemente, Boyer, and Morales, 1988).

Another focus of the work might be community violence and crime depending on the goals and objectives that have been set. Hawkins and Catalano (1992) note that a number of community strategies can be used to involve families in resolving risk factors. Examples include the following activities: (1) helping to enact local ordinances to ban "happy hours" at bars and restaurants in a community, (2) creating "drug free zones" within a certain radius of schools, (3) instituting crime and drug watches in conjunction with immediate reports of illegal activities to the police, (4) getting cigarette vending machines removed from public places frequented primarily by young people, (5) developing and implementing a school reform plan consistent with the ethnic and learning needs of the community, and (6) reclaiming and cleaning up in parks and housing projects used for alcohol and drug gatherings and other criminal activities (Hawkins and Catalano, 1992; Mitchell and Daniels, 1989; Botvin, 1986; Bracht, 1990; Comer, 1980).

Effective evaluation can be accomplished through two major tasks. First, the community needs assessment can be readministered at a preset time period after the change process has been instituted (e.g., at the end of a three to five year period). Comparisons can be made between the pre- and post-assessments in terms of the various environmental and individual/family risk factors that are present. Greater focus can be placed on high priority areas among these factors, including community violence and media messages that undermine the residents' pride in the community and their ethnicity. Another source of comparison is the focus of the goals and objectives and the actual outcomes. The analysis can determine which of objectives have been achieved by the end of the change/evaluation period and what influenced those outcomes (Patton, 1980).

An impact evaluation is important also. This type of evaluation helps communities to compare pre- and post-statistics related to the well being of families. For instance, in Lucky's community it would be important to compare the pre- and post-school drop out rates related to the impact of school reform (the development of a community school at the secondary level). Another focus of evaluation could be the impact of family and community changes on the arrest records for adolescents' alcohol and drug use, the frequency and intensity of gang activity including violence, and the availability of alcohol and drugs in the community.

Conclusion

The environmental context of sibling and other family relationships is an often ignored component of family treatment. In this chapter, the focus on ethnicity and community risk and protective factors has helped to clarify how the nature of that context can influence family life. Effective treatment by helping professionals should maintain equal focus on the dynamic interaction between the family and this context. Such a balance is consistent with the ecological perspective and the person-in-environment emphasis.

This approach is justified developmentally since it guides practitioners in maintaining a focus on individual and sibship tasks during the adolescent phase. Helping youths to address these developmental tasks in an age appropriate format has implications for sibling relationships currently and over the lifespan. For instance, sibling loyalty issues that are resolved satisfactorily during adolescence can positively influence the process of sibling differentiation and separation from the family of origin. As to the future, effective handling of these issues during adolescence can assist siblings in later phases such as old age when resolved loyalty issues often facilitate a shared process of reminiscence.

REFERENCES

American Psychiatric Association (1987). *Diagnostic and statistical manual of mental disorders* (Third Edition-Revised). Washington, DC.

Berren, M.R., Beigel, A., and Barker, G. (1982). A typology for the classification of disasters: Implications for intervention. *Community Mental Health Journal, 18*, 120-134.

Black, G.S. (1989). *Changing attitudes toward drug use: The first year effort of the Media-Advertising Partnership for a Drug-Free America, Inc.* Rochester, NY: Gordon S. Black Corporation.

Bloom, M. and Fischer, J. (1982). *Evaluating practice: Guidelines for the accountable professional.* Englewood Cliffs, NJ: Prentice-Hall.

Botvin, G.J. (1986). Substance abuse prevention research: Recent developments and future directions. *Journal of School Health, 56*, 369-374.

Bowser, B.P. (1988). Bayview-Hunter's Point: San Francisco's black ghetto revisited. *Urban Anthropology, 17*, 383-400.

Bracht, N. (1990). *Health promotion at the community level.* Newbury Park, CA: Sage.

Buriel, R. (1984). Integration with traditional Mexican American culture and sociocultural adjustment. In J.E. Martinez (Ed.), *Chicano psychology* (Second Edition) (95-129). New York: Academic.

Buriel, R., Calzada, S., and Vasquez, R. (1982). The relationship of traditional Mexican-American culture to adjustment and delinquency among three generations of Mexican-American male adolescents. *Hispanic Journal of Behavioral Sciences, 4*, 41-55.

Caetano, R. (1984). Ethnicity and drinking in Northern California: A comparison among whites, Blacks, and Hispanics. *Alcohol and Alcoholism, 18*, 1-14.

Caplan, M.Z. and Weissberg, R.P. (1989). Promoting social competence in early adolescence: Developmental considerations. In B.H. Schneider, G. Attili, J. Nadel, and R.P. Weissberg (Eds.), *Social competence in developmental perspective* (371-385). Boston: Kluwer.

Carmen, E., Reicker, P.P., and Mills, T. (1984). Victims of violence and psychiatric illness. *American Journal of Psychiatry, 141*, 373-383.

Comer, J.P. (1980). *School power: Implications of an intervention project.* New York: Free Press.

Curtis, K.A. (1989). Help from within: Participatory research in a low-income neighborhood. *Urban Anthropology, 18*, 203-217.

Datan, N. and Ginsberg, L.H. (1975). *Life-span developmental psychology: Normative life crises.* New York: Academic.

DiClemente, R.J., Boyer, C.B., and Morales, E.S. (1988). Minorities and AIDS:

Knowledge, attitudes, and misconceptions among black and Latino adolescents. *American Journal of Public Health, 78,* 55–57.

Dohrenwen, B.S. and Dohrenwen, B.P. (1980). Stressful life events: Research issues. In G.F. Jacobson (Ed.), *Crisis intervention in the 1980s* (57–65). San Francisco: Jossey-Bass.

Edelman, M. (1984). Exploratory study on delinquency avoidance in the South Bronx. *Research Bulletin, 7,* 1–2.

Eth, S. and Pynoos, R.S. (1985). *Post-traumatic stress disorder in children.* Washington, DC: American Psychiatric Press.

Fox, J.R. (1985). Mission impossible? Social work practice with black urban youth gangs. *Social Work, 30,* 25–31.

Freeman, E.M. and McRoy, R. (1986). Group counseling program for unemployed black teenagers. *Social Work with Groups, 9,* 73–90.

Freeman, E.M. and Pennekamp, M. (1988). Joining multi-cultural communities: Building on the positive effects of pluralism. *Social work practice: Toward a child, family, school, community perspective* (99–117). Springfield, IL: Charles C Thomas.

Freeman, E.M. and Pennekamp, M. (1988). The search for patterns: Linking cases and programs. *Social work practice: Toward a child, family, school, community perspective* (164–185). Springfield, IL: Charles C Thomas.

Gambrill, E. (1981). A behavioral perspective of families. In E. Tolson and W. Reid (Eds.), *Models of family treatment.* New York: Columbia University Press.

Gordon, D.A. and Arbuthnot, J. (1988). The use of paraprofessionals to deliver home-based family therapy to juvenile delinquents. *Criminal Justice and Behavior, 15,* 364–378.

Gurak, D.T. (1981). Family structural diversity of Hispanic ethnic groups. *Research Bulletin, 4,* 2–3.

Hahn, L. and West, C. (1885–86). The violent deaths of adult children: Strategies for working with prolonged grief in black mothers. *Journal of Minority Aging, 10,* 1–15.

Hardy-Fanta, C. and McMahon-Herrera, E. (1981). Adapting family therapy to the Hispanic family. *Social Casework, 62,* 138–148.

Hartman, A. and Laird, J. (1983). *Family-centered social work practice.* New York: Free Press.

Hawkins, J.D. and Catalano, R.F., Jr. (1992). *Communities that care: Action for drug abuse prevention.* San Francisco: Jossey-Bass.

Hogan, N.S. and Balk, D.E. (1990). Adolescent reactions to sibling death: Perceptions of mothers, fathers, and teenagers. *Nursing Research, 39,* 103–106.

Juarez, R. (1985). Core issues in psychotherapy with the Hispanic child. *Psychotherapy, 22,* 441–448.

Klein, N.C., Alexander, J.F., and Parsons, B.V. (1977). Impact of family systems intervention on recidivism and sibling delinquency: A model of primary prevention and program evaluation. *Journal of Consulting and Clinical Psychology, 45,* 469–474.

Levy, R. (1987). Single subject research designs. *Encyclopedia of Social Work* Volume 11 (588–593). Silver Spring, MD: National Association of Social Workers.

Liu, W.T., Yu, E.S.H., Chang, C., and Fernandez, M. (1990). The mental health of Asian American teenagers: A research challenge. In A.R. Stiffman and L.E. Davis (Eds.), *Ethnic issues in adolescent mental health* (92–114). Newbury Park, CA: Sage.

McGlynn, F., Mealiea, W., and Landau, D. (1981). The current status of systematic desensitization. *Clinical Psychology Review, 1,* 149–179.

McShane, D. (1988). An analysis of mental health research with American Indian youth. *Journal of Adolescence, 11,* 87–116.

Mendelberg, H. (1986). Identity conflict in Mexican-American adolescents. *Adolescence, 21,* 215–222.

Mitchell, M.A. and Daniels, S. (1989). Black-on-black homicide: Kansas City's response. *Public Health Reports, 104,* 605–608.

Mosatche, H., Brady, E., and Noberini, M.R. (1983). A retrospective life span study of the closest sibling relationship. *The Journal of Psychology, 113,* 237–243.

Nelson, J.C. (1986). Communication theory and social work treatment. In F.J. Turner (Ed.), *Social work treatment: Interlocking theoretical approaches* (219–244). New York: Free Press.

Padilla, A. (1980). The role of cultural awareness and ethnic loyalty in acculturation. In A. Padilla (Ed.), *Acculturation, theory, models, and some new findings* (5–22). Boulder, CO: Westview.

Patton, M.Q. (1980). *Qualitative evaluation methods.* Beverly Hills, CA: Sage.

Pollock, G.H. (1986). Childhood sibling loss: A family tragedy. *Psychiatric Annals, 16,* 309–314.

Reid, W.J. (1986). Task-centered social work. In F.J. Turner (Ed.), *Social work treatment: Interlocking theoretical approaches,* (267–295). New York: Free Press.

Rodriguez, O., Burger, W., and Banks, L. (1984). Crime rates among Hispanics, blacks, and whites in New York City. *Research Bulletin, 7,* 1–2.

Rodriguez, O. and Zayas, L.H. (1990). Hispanic adolescents and antisocial behavior: Sociocultural factors and treatment implications. In A.R. Stiffman and L.E. Davis (Eds.), *Ethnic issues in adolescent mental health* (147–174). Newbury Park, CA: Sage.

Rogers, M.F. and Williams, W.W. (1987). AIDS in blacks and Hispanics: Implications for prevention. *Issues in Science and Technology, 12,* 89–94.

Schumacher, J.D. (1984). Helping children cope with a sibling's death. *Family Therapy Collections, 8,* 82–94.

Szapocznik, J., Kurtines, W.M., and Fernandez, T. (1980). Bicultural involvement and adjustment in Hispanic American youth. *International Journal of Intercultural Relations, 4,* 353–365.

Szapocznik, J., Santiesteban, D., Rios, A., Perez-Vidal, A., and Kurtines, W. (1986). Family effectiveness training for Hispanic families: Strategic structural system intervention for the prevention of drug abuse. In H.P. Lefley and P.B. Pedersen (Eds.), *Cross cultural training for mental health professionals* (125–157). Springfield, IL: Charles C Thomas.

Valencia, R.R., Henderson, R.W., and Rankin, R.J. (1985). Family status, family constellation, and home environmental variables as predictors of cognitive performance of Mexican American children. *Journal of Educational Psychology, 77,* 323–331.

Vigil, J.D., and Long, J.M. (1981). Unidirectional or nativist acculturation—Chicano paths to school achievement. *Human Organization, 40,* 273–277.

Chapter 8

FAMILY GROUP WORK WITH YOUNG ADULTS WHO HAVE SIBLING CONTROL ISSUES

> I had 5 brothers and sisters. We must have been taught—we believed our parents' affection was like a pie. Whatever happened, one of us was bound to get the smallest slice. And that was **not** okay.
>
> —Eric

An overemphasis on sibling differences and competition for parental affection are characteristic of the type of sibling rivalry that Eric and his siblings experienced. Mild forms of rivalry are usually resolved in childhood and adolescence, but this pattern of interaction may continue into old age for some sisters and brothers. Sibling rivalry can be the result of interaction between siblings or various external influences (Ross and Milgram, 1980). For instance, some children develop patterns of coping that involve externalizing the causes of their stress to siblings, leading to an emphasis on the differences between siblings.

Others may learn to pattern their sibling relationships and roles based on models established by their parents. Family stories, secrets, and myths about the parents' sibling relationships can perpetuate indirectly family patterns of either solidarity, neutrality, or rivalry (Byng-Hall, 1988; Karpel, 1980). Caplow (1968) presents a different perspective on how parents may influence whether sibling rivalry develops beyond typical disagreements and differences. He indicates that parents may handle their conflicts and fears about power by vying for support from their children and forming intergenerational coalitions. Such coalitions tend to create or heighten rivalry among siblings (see Figure 1.2 on the consequences of rivalry).

In this chapter sibling rivalry is defined and some of the consequences are discussed, particularly during the developmental period of leaving (the family-of-origin) home. Eric's case study is presented to illustrate some of those consequences and the sibling dynamics that can occur when the problem is at a moderate level. An approach is included for addressing the resulting problems with young adults from 20 to 25 years of age: a family treatment approach involving sibling-oriented groups for multiple sibling subsystems or individuals from different families. Those approaches are described also in terms of appropriate, user-friendly evaluation methods.

Overview of Sibling Rivalry

Definition and Intensity of Sibling Rivalry

Rosenthal and Doherty (1984) indicate that sibling rivalry is more than the "normal" power struggles and healthy competitiveness that occur between brothers and sisters. Mild forms of rivalry include verbal abuse such as put downs, name calling, or the use of profanity as well as more aggressive competition in games, hobbies, or school performance. In comparison, extreme forms involve physical abuse toward siblings at an overt **or** covert level (pushing, biting, hitting, cutting, or killing a sibling). In the most serious situations, the abuser often begins this type of behavior as early as 3 or 4 years of age, with the abused sibling generally being younger than the abuser (Rosenthal and Doherty, 1984). Often such incidences are accompanied by destructive thoughts about siblings that are subsequently acted upon. In some of these extreme situations, parents may covertly condon this behavior or they may have severely deprived the abuser emotionally and/or physically prior to the development of the rivalry (Green, 1981; Steinmetz, 1977).

Developmental and Familial Influences

The rivalry may manifest itself more often or more intensely during transition points of the life cycle, for instance, when a new baby is born into the family, during a parental divorce, or at the point when an individual leaves home during the late adolescence-young adulthood stage (18–25 years generally). Sibling rivalry may tend to heighten during the latter period for several reasons. This developmental transition may create stress because individuals believe they must make the "right" plans and decisions (in comparison to siblings) for developing a career. Issues of identity and boundary setting are often difficult to manage with people in general as well as with siblings because individuals are no longer living within their predictable family structure (see Chapter 3 on changes in sibling solidarity).

Many people experience ambivalence about leaving home during this period. Unresolved sibling rivalries and insecurities about parental affection and supports can intensify the process of separation and leaving home. Individuation from parents **and** from siblings may be more difficult as a consequence (Bowen, 1974). Moreover, older siblings' patterns of leaving home in the past can influence how each of the younger siblings separates from the family of origin (Freeman, Logan, and McRoy, 1987). Typically, according to Allan (1977) and Circirelli (1980) this is also a period when parents have fewer opportunities to mediate the quality of sibling relationships by influencing the frequency and nature of contacts among their children.

A typical response in families with control issues is for individuals to fail to fully individuate from parents and siblings. They may stay connected emotionally to siblings at too intense a level (enmeshment) through rivalry and efforts to control each other. These boundary infringements between siblings may be encouraged by parents because they also help the parents stay in control of their young adult children's lives, frequently through conflicts over money, careers, and selection of dates and spouses. The following case study of Eric illustrates some of these sibling and family dynamics related to rivalry.

A Case Study: Eric

When asked how someone from the outside might describe his family-of-origin, Eric indicated they were known in the southern town where he grew up as "that funny Bennett family." They were respected but were known too as having "their own way of doing things." From Eric's perspective inside the family, the members were overly concerned about how others in the family lived their lives. He believes it was their attempts to control each other that made them "funny" and different to the rest of the town. Eric believes also that this pattern between his father's siblings has become the model for Eric's sibling relationships in the current generation. That pattern can be observed in each section of Eric's case study described below.

Background Information

Eric is a 25 year old caucasian man who is married to Susan and has one child, nine month old Sean. Eric had just opened his own florist shop when he participated in the author's study on sibling relationships.

His father and uncles own several hardward stores in the South, one of which Eric and his brother Carl operated together until the previous year. They had frequent conflicts over how the business should be run, and as a result, Carl succeeded in getting Eric "pushed out" of the business according to Eric. As can be seen from Figure 8.1, there has been a pattern of sibling conflicts over business decisions in Eric's father's family for many years. Also on that side of Eric's family, the pattern in leaving home has been to live within 10–20 miles of each other and to stay involved in how personal decisions are made as well. That pattern is in contrast to Eric's mother's family where the siblings are described as close but not overly involved in each others' lives.

Childhood and Adolescence

In childhood, Eric thought of his father's family as close. They often criticized each other's ways of raising their children and personal decisions such as how to spend money or what church they should attend. For many years, they argued about the family hardware business because they had different ideas about how the business should be operated and refused to listen to each other's ideas. Because they were always together talking about the business, they seemed to be close. Their father Stanley started the hardware business, and when he died, left it and his money to the oldest son Bill. He said Bill was more responsible than his other children. Sam and Horace eventually went to work for Bill and as the business prospered over the years, they expanded by opening several new hardware stores in the state. Henry, the youngest, decided not to go into the family business but opened his own hardware store in the next town.

All of the siblings live within 10 miles of each other, and in one sense, have never left home or become differentiated from the sibling subsystem. Bowen (1974) has noted that this is an important step before an individual can be successful in other significant relationships. In fact, Bill and Sam have always lived next door to each other and have fought about a fence between their property for years. Since much of their energy goes into their unresolved conflicts, none of the siblings has been able to establish positive and warm relationships with their spouses and children (See Figure 8.1). Moreover, Eric believes that they never resolve their disagreements.

Although Blanch, their sister, is not directly involved in the family business she too gets involved in the frequent disagreements. Sometimes

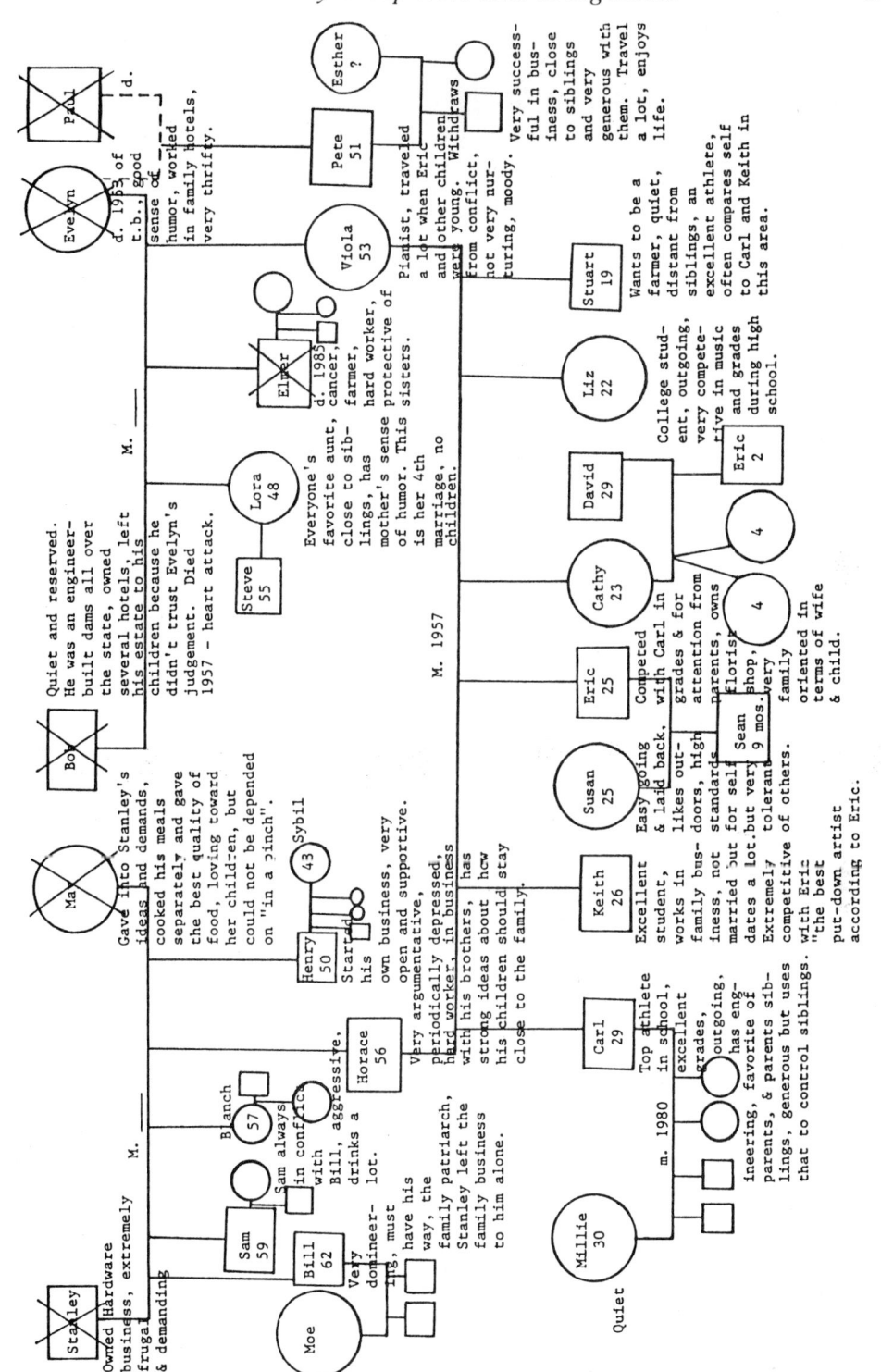

Figure 8.1. Genogram of Eric Bennett (1989).

she takes sides, but at other times she attempts to mediate family arguements whether or not the brothers ask her to do so. Henry seems to be the most differentiated among the siblings, yet is still enmeshed somewhat in the sibling subsystem. He is able to stay out of many family arguements; having his own business has helped him to stay neutral in some instances. In addition, Henry travels a lot, is more tolerant of different ideas, and seems to be less concerned about how his siblings think he should live his life. They refer to him as the spoiled baby of the family who does whatever he wants to.

This pattern of unresolved arguements was also a factor in interactions within Eric's nuclear family. From the time he was about eight years old, Eric remembers that his mother would leave home sometimes when she and his father had arguements. Sometimes she would stay with relatives for a few days, but once she hid in the basement and would come into the house when everyone else was gone. She stayed hidden for several days and Eric remembers being surprised none of them had discovered she was that close by. Many of their fights occurred because Eric's mother was the pianist for a band that traveled to other towns on the weekends. Although Horace did not want her to go on those trips, he would admit they needed the money, especially during the years when the family hardware business was not doing well. At other times when his parents would argue, Eric's mother would not leave but they would not talk to each other for several weeks or months. In looking back, Eric believes Horace's arguements and use of silence to get Viola to stop playing in the band were similar to the tactics used by his father's siblings to control each other.

Eric thinks that because his parents did not get along with each other and often withheld their affection from the children, he and his siblings competed for their attention. He remembers thinking that Carl would always be his father's favorite son because, at four years older than Eric, he could do things Eric could not do. Carl helped his father with the yardwork and went fishing with him frequently. As an adolescent, Carl was able to help out by doing some of the record keeping in the hardware store because he was extremely good in math. All of those things made Carl seem closer to their father and made Eric feel left out.

Eric was a good student in school and used his grades as a way to gain his parents' affection and attention. His parents sometimes praised Carl for his grades but might not say anything positive about Eric's although they both had good grades. At other times, Eric's mother would buy him something he wanted as a reward for his good grades. Or she would buy him things and pay more attention to him or one of the other kids during the periods when she and his father were not talking. Eric was often confused and could not understand what his parents' behavior meant.

Since the parents were never consistent in how they responded, their inconsistencies caused Eric and his siblings to increase the number of ways in which they competed with each other. For example, Carl and Eric not only competed in the grades they earned, they also competed in trying to keep Horace company while their mother was away with the band. Horace often seem to be "down" on the weekends when Viola was away. Eric and Keith were closer in age and they competed for the same friends and as players on the same softball team. Keith always complained their parents cheered more for Eric than for him, and tended to ignore when he played well. Keith, Eric, and Cathy helped their father in a family garden that they grew every year and competed heavily in the same Four-H activities.

Eric started drinking when he was in the eighth grade and continued to drink during high school. While his drinking never got completely out of control, Eric believes he could have become an alcoholic if he had continued to live near his family as a young adult. He drank because of the lack of support and nurturing from his parents and because he did not feel adequate in relation to his siblings. He had peers that he spent time with in high school, but like Eric, they were loners with very little self-esteem. Eric believed he did not really fit in at school just as he did not fit in with his siblings at home.

Young Adulthood

Eric decribed his time away from home during his college years as a period of complete freedom. He continued to do well academically. In setting his own schedule, he felt there was no one to tell him what to do for the first time in his life. Eric had intentionally chosen a college in the midwest far away from his hometown. His father had suggested he obtain a degree in engineering like Carl because he felt Carl had made a very wise career choice. Instead, Eric chose to pursue a degree in English Literature in an effort to be different from Carl, even though he was not particularly interested in that field. He started dating Susan during his senior year and they became very close. He thinks they were drawn to each other because they were so different, and yet, liked each other "without strings or conditions". When he would go home during the summer each year, Eric would work for his family. He said it felt secure in some ways but also it was like being caught in a giant web. Consequently, he always felt better when he returned to school where he had his own "space."

Even though Carl had an engineering degree, his father had encouraged him to go into the family business. Initially, Carl decided to work in the family business until he could find a job in his field. After Carl had been in the family business for about a year, it became clear to Eric that Carl was probably not going to leave although he threatened to do so periodically when family conflicts developed. After Eric finished college, he found himself in a similar position. His father and uncles urged him to come to work for them just until he could find a job in his area. Eric said, "I must have been out of my mind. I let them talk me into working with Carl in one of the stores, and eventually, going into partnership with him."

Carl and Eric stayed in business together for two years although Eric says it never really worked out well. When they got into a particularly prolonged disagreement about the business, Carl went to Bill with only his side of the disagreement. As a result, Bill told Eric it would be better if he got out of the business. The family was divided over this decision, with only Keith and Cathy siding with Eric. At Susan's urging, Eric returned to her hometown where they had gone to college and found a job in a florist shop. A year later, with a loan from Susan's parents, Eric was able to open his own florist shop. He likes what he is doing now because he makes his own decisions, and that is important to him.

Eric describes his relationship with Carl as cut-off and says he is closest to Cathy among his siblings. He and Cathy understand and support each other. They both view the family as too controlling. Carl frequently criticizes their parents when they give money to any of his siblings. When they made the down payment on Cathy's house, he called her and complained, saying her husband should be able to take care of his own family. Eric sided with Cathy by calling Carl and telling him "he was out of line."

Eric feels his relationship with Keith, Liz, and Stuart is neutral. Although Keith supported him in the conflict with Carl and the rest of the family, Eric says there have been too many years when they could not stand one another. He does not think they will ever be close. Eric has visited his parents since he moved away, but feels uncomfortable being around them. Even now, he feels he is always competing for their affection as they continue to compare their childrens' jobs and lifestyles. Eric believes he can never do enough to please them. He loves them but has a lot of anger about how they have encouraged him and his siblings to compete against one another. He has coped with the parents' behavior by moving far away. He makes infrequent telephone calls to his parents and limits contact with his siblings (except Cathy) to ocassional family gatherings. Doing the genogram for the author's research made Eric more aware of some of the positive ways his mother's siblings get along. He was surprised that he has been so focused on his father's family all these years, but thinks it is because they are much more dramatic in their relationships.

A Family Treatment Approach

Eric's comment in the previous section about his continued anger provides clues to his unresolved family issues and his incomplete differentiation from siblings and parents. On the positive side, he has chosen a satisfying business that provides him with a separate identity from his family. He has maintained a close relationship with one of his sisters, Cathy. In addition, Eric describes his present relationship with his wife Susan as a loving and committed one. No doubt these strengths assist Eric in coping with his situation and in keeping his anger at a level that does not interfer with his functioning. Other individuals in similar situations may be less able to cope with the anger, expressing it inappropriately and through displacement toward others outside the family. Moreover, their sibling rivalry may be expressed by indecision in choosing and achieving a satisfactory career or in an inability to maintain on-going intimate relationships as they desire. Thus, they may self-refer or be referred for treatment related to difficulties in anger management, leaving home and emotional cut-offs from the family-of-origin, or career indecision.

Anger Management and Issues of Control

The anger felt by some individuals who, like Eric, experience sibling rivalry may come from a loss of autonomy and control over their lives. Some of them act out their anger while others internalize it (Frey-Angel, 1989). When the rivalry is accompanied by family relationships that also involve efforts to control how the members think and conduct their lives, the anger and loss of individual control may be increased. These individuals may self-refer or be referred by others to mental health and family service agencies for help with anger management. Often they state that others (spouses, children, parents, co-workers, or peers) complain about their frequent episodes of anger and rage. In Eric's case, his wife Susan was concerned about his unexplained angry explosions from time to time. For some clients, these episodes include physical violence to others or themselves or the anger is simply threatening to others toward whom it is directed or who witness these events.

Obtaining a thorough history is important in these situations because the real triggers for the anger are often outside the awareness of the client. The client may believe the anger is related in a general way to some person or situation in his or her current life or that the source of the anger is unknown. Some important questions for exploring sibling rivalry and control issues during the assessment include the following (Freeman, in press; Carter and McGoldrick, 1980; Hartman and Laird, 1983):

1. In what ways were members of your family different from one another?
2. What are some examples of how those differences were expressed?
3. How did other members of the family respond to those expressions at different times?
4. Who was close to whom in the family and how was or is that closeness expressed?
5. Who in the family is distant or cut-off from each other and for what reasons?
6. How much pressure, if any, is there on other family members to respond in certain ways to those distant or cut-off relationships?
7. What are some typical things your mother's (and father's) siblings disagree about?
8. How have your father's (and mother's) siblings handled their disagreements?
9. Under what circumstances and how did your mother's (and father's) siblings leave the family home?
10. Under what circumstances and how did you and your siblings leave the family home?

If Eric had been in treatment, an analysis of his responses to these questions could have helped to explore the sources of his anger and the sibling rivalry that are part of how his family members relate to one another. Simply presenting the questions to clients can encourage them to see patterns they were not previously aware of and to be more objective about those patterns and the related family dynamics. That information is useful for determining what should be the focus of family treatment as well as who should be involved.

Family treatment may need to include sibling-oriented groups for individuals or multiple sibling subsystems from different families. In either type of group the interventions to be used and the group process are similar. The former would have been the treatment of choice for Eric since he does not live in the same geographic area as his siblings. The initial focus can be on helping the members such as Eric to acknowledge their anger and to explore its' dimensions, whether they act out their anger or repress it. Cognitive-behavioral techniques are useful for these purposes (Werner, 1986; Miller and Berman, 1983). One of these techniques is applicable to anger as well as other feelings. It involves having the members close their eyes and gradually relax all the muscles in their bodies. Then they are asked to imagine themselves inside their bodies and to explore where in the body the anger or other emotion is usually located. Once it is located, the next step is to concentrate on that emotion for a few minutes in order to become familiar with it. The members are asked to respond to a series of questions once they have concentrated on the emotion:

1. Where in the body is that emotion located?
2. What color is the emotion?
3. What is its shape? Does it resemble anything else?
4. If it changes shape, is it getting larger or smaller?
5. Does it stay in one place, or does it move around?
6. Under what circumstances does it change in shape, size, or location?
7. When it comes out of the body, what is it like or how is it expressed?

This technique helps the members to demystify their anger and to become more familiar with it. Defining it in this way gives it a predictability that produces a greater sense of control within the person. In addition, using this technique in the group allows the members to hear how others describe their anger, the sources of that anger, and its dimensions. Therefore, the analysis can be used to explore what responses to the questions mean and how the responses and meanings differ for each member. For instance, the color, shape, size, and pattern of change may be interpreted in terms of issues that the different members are bringing to the group. Clients can identify other group members with their siblings (e.g., with Eric's brother Carl), hear the perspectives of those members, and generalize what they have learned to their siblings. In this way, they can increase awareness of their own emotional patterns as well as those of their siblings and other family members. Perhaps Eric might have realized earlier the effects of his father's family's dramatic ways of relating to each other on how he and his siblings get along.

This strategy can be used also by group members while anger episodes are occurring for helping them to cope more effectively and for creating more awareness of the triggers for their anger. Initially, some members may need to use group sessions to tune into past anger episodes and retrospectively analyze the anger before using this strategy **while** the episode is occurring. The opportunity to practice improved ways of coping is an important first step before risking the application of cognitive techniques in the actual circumstances (Berlin, 1980). A second guided imagery technique is designed to provide the members with an alternative to acting out their anger against others or internalizing it in a self-blaming manner. This technique teaches the members to relax by imagining a self-selected scene that is calming and comfortable, and to experience the positive emotions associated with that scene. They are then helped to take the anger or other emotion they have located in their bodies to the peaceful scene when they need to in daily life (Lantz, 1978). The prior association of the scene with feeling calm and in control decreases the anger so that clients can address the situation in a more appropriate manner.

Other useful interventions for helping young adults to cope with and resolve their anger include encouraging them to leave situations temporarily when they sense they are losing control. The leaving can be reframed positively (Papp, 1983) as a "cool down" or time out period designed to assist the person in strengthening his or her self-control. Journaling or keeping a log to express thoughts and feelings is also useful for developing awareness of one's "inner life" and validating feelings that are often shared by other group members. This experience encourages members to understand their siblings may also have shared some of their feelings, but may have expressed or responded to those feelings differently. The knowledge of shared experiences and feelings previously unacknowledged between siblings helps to reduce the sense of being different that maintains sibling rivalry. Finally, doing physical exercises may be useful in reducing stress and tension on a regular basis so that the triggers for anger can be responded to with these alternative coping strategies. In some situations involving anger management, couple therapy may be necessary if sibling group treatment does not resolve the problem or if the negative emotional patterns between a couple have become too ingrained.

Problems in Leaving Home/Emotional Cut-Offs

Just as the anger management problems described above may be related to past and current rivalry/control issues, problems in leaving home are often related to the same family patterns. Some of the assessment questions identified in the previous section include the issue of leaving home. These questions illustrate too the close relationship between separation/individuation and anger from rivalry and control issues. Palazzoli (1985) indicates that often the most "competent" member of the family may be the one who initiates the request for services related to control or leaving home issues. In many ways, if this family member is a sibling, he or she may also be the one who is the most differentiated within the sibling subsystem. In Eric's family, for instance, Eric and his uncle Henry appear to fit that role although it is apparent that Eric still has unfinished family-of-origin business.

Several family treatment interventions may be used to address this issue. Redecision-making is a family treatment intervention that was developed for working with families involving an alcoholic member. Family members are helped to understand their decisions related to addiction or enabling behavior are coping strategies that they can change without invalidating the "rightness" of those decisions at the time they were made (Flanzer and Delany, 1992). In sibling-oriented group sessions, each member can be asked to develop a list of regrets and secondary gains related to rivalry, control, individuation, or other issues to assist in their redecision-making. The group members are expected to raise questions they may have about the list and to brainstorm about missing items or how the list helps in redecision-making. For example, Eric's list might have included the following entries if he had been involved in such a group:

Name: Eric Bennett
Date: May 9, 1989
Issues: too much competition between sisters and brothers and the controlling behaviors of family members

REGRETS	SECONDARY GAINS
1. Lack of closeness to Carl and competition for parents' affection and a career	1. Found my own satisfying career
2. Big family blow-up about the business disagreement with Carl	2. Was able to move away from the safety but controlling behaviors of the family
3. Lack of nurturing from parents and opportunity to be myself—to be different	3. Intentionally chose college far from home where I met and was attracted to Susan whom I might have rejected because she is so different from me and the family
4. Constant argueing and conflicts in my family	4. The family's pattern of controlling each other and handling conflicts has helped me understand how my anger feels to others
5. All the years of feeling inadequate and jealous toward Carl and my other sisters and brothers	5. Gained a better sense of who I am and that finally I am an ok person without regard to what others do and think

The secondary gains side of the list helps group members develop a better perspective of their current functioning and the positive adaptations they have made based on their family experiences. The regrets side of the list can be used by group members to identify what was or is within their control and what is not. They can work toward identifying in which of those areas they did the best they could at the time (redecision-making) and which areas they need to forgive themselves for. That side of the list is useful also for identifying the unfinished business that is within their control.

A number of family treatment interventions can be used to address any unfinished business so that individuation can be achieved and cut-offs can be resolved by group members. The members can be paired to role play situations that demonstrate the emotional and communication patterns between siblings. As sibling "stand-in's," the members can then roleplay how to interact using the reciprocal and complementary roles described in Chapter 5 (Dunn, 1983). Experiencing this type of interaction with a sibling stand-in facilitates the healing process that is necessary for decreasing sibling rivalry and for applying what is learned to actual interactions with siblings, parents, and other significant individuals.

When there are cut-offs, Gestalt techniques such as the empty chair (Blugerman, 1986) and mailed or "no send" letters (Hartman and Laird, 1983) involve talking to the absent sibling, parent, or other relative as though they are there or actually reading the letter. Items included on the regrets side of the list from the redecision-making exercise are usually the focus: the significant events that occurred, how the individual felt, the consequences, and what he or she would have wanted from the sibling or other key person at the time. The group member doing the exercise has to listen too for how the absent family member might respond or feel. It is not uncommon for group members to learn in the treatment group that they are cut-off from family members. They may not recognize they have experienced a cut-off because the normal pattern in their family is to stop talking to various members from time to time.

The members are asked to decide if and when they might attempt to re-establish contact with the sibling or other relative they are cut-off from. Some members may decide the healing process they have experienced in the treatment group is all the change they desire. Others may then use the group to identify and practice how to resolve the cut-off and how to handle the possible rejection by their family member if that occurs.

The same intervention can also be used to "talk to" an absent family member who is still integrated into the family but has achieved an "acceptable" degree of individuation. In the case of Eric, he might talk to uncle Henry or write him a letter to ask how the latter has achieved his individuation and position in relation to his siblings/other family members. The resulting information and insight would then be applied to Eric's life situation, with other group members helping to identify what the information means and how he could use it in the here and now.

In addition to sibling groups for addressing cut-offs and individuation issues, family therapy may be indicated when siblings and parents are available and when the issue involves the entire family. Kahn and Bank (1981) suggest, however, an alternative approach to resolving individuation problems between adult clients and their parents through the use of individual and sibling therapy.

User-Friendly Evaluation Procedures

Many of the interventions described in the previous section are also useful for monitoring and evaluating the effects of sibling groups. For example, group members' journals and logs can be evaluated over time to identify how the triggers, underlying feelings including anger, responses to triggers, and overall handling of target situations change. Clients responses to cut-offs can be evaluated, whether related negative or self-deprecating statements decrease or the cut-offs are resolved. Information about the frequency and nature of sibling and other contacts can be compared from intake to termination, along with the clients' level of satisfaction with those contacts. In fact, a simple self-anchored scale can be used to identify **how** those levels of satisfaction change and what contributes to the changes (for example, in the case of Eric from the previous section) (Bloom and Fischer, 1982):

Name: Eric Bennett
Date: August 21, 1989　　　　　　　　　　　　Type of Contact: telephone
Target: Satisfaction with my contacts with Keith

1	(2)	3	4	5
Awful	So-so	Not so bad	Getting there	Tops

Contributing factors to how I felt about the contact:
  I was already having a bad day when I called Keith, and he said he was real busy at the time. I didn't stop to ask if it was a good time to call.

Other useful evaluation methods not included as part of these interventions involve the use of video taping and problem-solving exercises. The video tapes are useful if they are done during beginning sessions of the group, periodically, and at the point of termination. In this type of format, they can help the members recognize the intensity of their feelings about siblings and other family members and evaluate how those feelings change over time (anger, a sense of rejection, low self-esteem, assertiveness about boundary and control issues, self-acceptance, and expressions of caring). The group members and the practitioner can analyze what aspects of the sibling group interventions contributed to or hindered the positive changes (Berlin, 1980). Video tapes can help to demonstrate changes or the lack of change much more vividly than discussion alone.

Problem-solving exercises can provide similar pre- and post-test data for evaluating the groups (Freeman, McRoy, and Logan, 1987). The typical problem situations that group members present during intake and the first few sessions can be organized into a simple written pre-test. The pre-test can be administered verbally item by item with discussion among the members, or in written form with discussion occurring after the administration. Those problem-solving exercises can be used as a discussion tool periodically over the life of the group. At the point of termination, the items can be reviewed as a verbal or written post-test, with the members analyzing their responses in terms of what they have learned from the group. All of these evaluation strategies are practical for group members in providing relevant feedback, and they are user-friendly and nontime-consuming for practitioners.

Conclusion

This chapter demonstrates the life span implications when sibling rivalry and control issues are not handled effectively in childhood and adolescence. One critical implication is that individuation from the sibling subsystem and parents may be hindered. The lack of differentiation may occur even when the individual leaves the family-of-origin physically. The related emotional separation/individuation may not have taken place.

Yet, even in those situations family treatment sessions can address the unfinished issues and provide opportunities for clients' growth, both as individuals and as members of sibling subsystems. Evaluation is necessary to determine if the healing and maturation that occur in regard to sibling stand-ins during treatment are generalized to actual sibling relationships.

REFERENCES

Allan, G. (1977). Sibling solidarity. *Journal of Marriage and Family, 39,* 177–184.
Berlin, S.B. (1980). A cognitive-learning perspective for social work. *Social Service Review, 58,* 255–266.
Bloom, M. and Fischer, J. (1982). *Evaluating practice: Guidelines for the accountable professional.* Englewood Cliffs, NJ: Prentice-Hall.
Blugerman, M. (1986). Contributions of gestalt theory to social work treatment. In F.J. Turner (Ed.), *Social work treatment: Interlocking theoretical approaches* (69–90). New York: Free Press.
Bowen, M. (1974). A family systems approach to alcoholism. *Addictions, 21,* 3–4.
Byng-Hall, J. (1988). Scripts and legends in families and family therapy. *Family Process, 27,* 167–179.

Caplow, T. (1968). *Two against one: Coalition in triads.* Englewood Cliffs, NJ: Prentice-Hall.

Carter, E.A. and McGoldrick, M. (1980). *The family life cycle: A framework for family therapy.* New York: Gardner.

Cicirelli, V.G. (1980). Sibling relationships in adulthood: A life span perspective. In Leonard W. Poon (Ed.), *Aging in the 1980's* (455–462). Washington, DC: American Psychological Association.

Dunn, J. (1983). Sibling relationships in early childhood. *Child Development, 54,* 787–811.

Flanzer, J.P. and Delany, P. (1992). Multiple-member substance abuse: Exploring the initiative for change in addicted families. In E.M. Freeman (Ed.), *The addiction process: Effective social work approaches* (54–64). White Plains, NY: Longman.

Freeman, E.M. (In press). Women who work outside the home: Multicultural and multigenerational influences on the family adjustment process. In L. Davis (Ed.), *The strengths of women.* Newbury Park, CA.: Sage.

Freeman, E.M., Logan, S., and McRoy, R. (1987). Clinical practice with employed women. *Social Casework, 68,* 413–421.

Frey-Angel, J. (1989). Treating children of violent families: A sibling group approach. *Social Work with Groups, 12,* 95–107.

Green, A. (1981). Child abuse by siblings. Paper presented at the Meeting of the American Academy of Child Psychiatry, Dallas, Texas.

Hartman, A. and Laird, J. (1983). *Family-centered social work practice.* New York: Free Press.

Kahn, M.D. and Bank, S. (1981). In pursuit of sisterhood: Adult siblings as a resource for combined individual and family therapy. *Family Process, 20,* 85–95.

Karpel, M.A. (1980). Family secrets: Conceptual and ethical issues in the relational context. *Family Process, 19,* 295–306.

Lantz, J.E. (1978). Cognitive theory and social casework. *Social Work, 23,* 361–366.

Miller, R.C. and Berman, J.S. (1983). The efficacy of cognitive behavior therapies: A quantitative review of the research evidence. *Psychological Bulletin, 94,* 56–66.

Palazzoli, M.S. (1985). The problem of the sibling as the referring person. *Journal of Marital and Family Therapy, 11,* 21–34.

Papp, P. (1983). *The process of change.* New York: Guilford.

Rosenthal, P.A. and Doherty, M.B. (1984). Serious sibling abuse by preschool children. *Journal of the American Academy of Child Psychiatry, 23,* 186–190.

Ross, H.G. and Milgram, J.I. (1980, September 3). Rivalry in adult sibling relationships: Its antecedents and dynamics. Paper presented at the Annual Meeting of the American Psychological Association, Montreal, Canada.

Steinmetz, S.K. (1977). *The cycle of violence.* New York: Pergamon.

Werner, H.D. (1986). Cognitive theory. In F.J. Turner (Ed.), *Social work treatment: Interlocking theoretical approaches* (91–130). New York: Free Press.

Chapter 9

FAMILY TREATMENT WITH INDIVIDUALS: ACOA'S WITH SIBLING ISSUES AND PEER CONFLICTS IN THE WORKPLACE

> I took the heat off my sister and off my Dad's drinking by staying in trouble all the time. I keep thinking someday they'll thank me for what I did.
>
> —Lisa

When family treatment with ACOA's such as Lisa is focused on unfinished family of origin issues, the process is complicated by many factors. In general, even when all family members are involved in treatment, "the family process is similar to the wind, evident but elusive to capture" (Corrales, Bueker, Ro-Trock, and Smith, 1981, p. 5). Moreover, the predominant strategy with ACOA in particular has been not to involve the parents in treatment directly. The goal is to help ACOA disengage from the family of origin's dysfunctional patterns of addiction and enabling, while beginning to focus more on themselves as individuals (Pape, 1992). And when a more systemic approach to treatment has been utilized, seldom has the treatment included siblings except to identify the series of dysfunctional roles assumed in some alcoholic families (Wegscheider, 1981). Typically, the effects of sibling issues on the relationships of approximately twenty-two million ACOA with coworkers, other peers, or spouses are not addressed either (Freeman, 1989; Ackerman, 1987).

When ACOA are also addicted, another treatment dilemma is presented. Practitioners are confronted with how to address barriers to the client's recovery such as trust and boundary issues within these other relationships, especially in the sibling relationship. Again the difficulty in handling this dilemma is increased when sibling- or family-oriented individual treatment is being utilized without involving those key persons in the sessions. This chapter clarifies ways to handle these treatment dilemmas through the presentation of a case study from the author's research on siblings. The manner in which the sibling relationship affects and is affected by the family dynamics involved in parental alcoholism is highlighted. The influence of those relationships on peer interactions in the workplace and spousal relationships during the period between 25 and 35 years of age is discussed as well. Finally, an appropriate assessment and treatment process is illustrated with data from the case study, along with examples of procedures for evaluating the treatment such as social network analyses.

The Case Study: Lisa

Lisa Masters is a 34 year old caucasian woman who agreed to participate in the author's research on siblings "because I'm still working on myself, and there was a time, not too long ago, when my problems were making it hard for me to keep a job." Her case study is presented below in terms of background information, her childhood and adolescent experiences, and her functioning from young adulthood until the present. She began the interview by indicating that she has been the stabilizing force in her family-of-origin over the years.

Background Information

Lisa is the youngest in a family of two children as can be seen from the genogram that was developed with her during the research interview (see Figure 9.1). She works as a civilian employee for the local police department and is married with two step children who live with their natural mother. Her husband, Lou, is a 43 year old fireman who is a recovering alcoholic. Lisa too is a recovering alcoholic although she combined her alcohol use with cocaine and marijuana. She grew up in the Southwest where both parents' families had lived for two generations. Her parents married when they were 35 years old and neither had been married before. The mother became a homemaker after she got married, but worked in retail sales prior to that time. She was a high school graduate. The father was a college graduate who worked as an accountant for an airline until his retirement when he was 66. He is an alcoholic who drinks mostly at home, but prior to retirement, it was obvious to Lisa that often he had been drinking when he would come home in the evenings.

Childhood and Adolescence

Lisa characterizes her childhood as a period when she had many questions that no one would answer. She wondered why her sister Janice

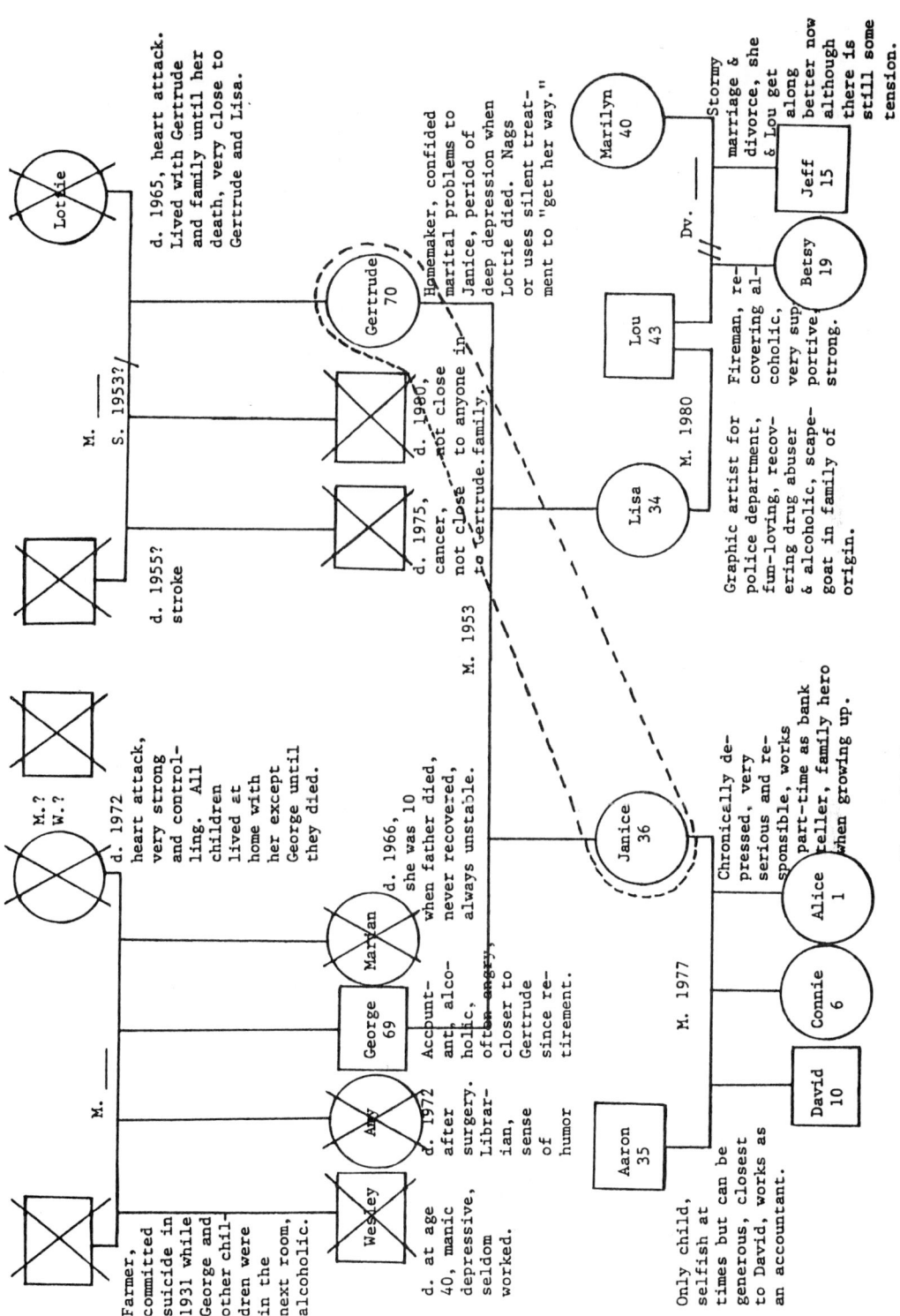

Figure 9.1. Genogram of Lisa Masters (1989).

was withdrawn and angry; later she realized Janice was chronically depressed. Her father drank and was alternately angry and hard to please or very "silly." She could not understand why his behavior was unpredictable from day to day. In subtle ways, her mother used guilt to coerce the daughters to obey her. She made it clear to them, however, that the father did not have a drinking problem although she nagged him about drinking too much when she thought the daughters could not hear her. Whenever Lisa tried to talk with her sister about the parents' behavior during their childhood, Janice would become angry and refuse to talk about the family interactions.

When she was about 10, Lisa learned that the mother had developed a pattern of confiding in Janice about her relationship with the father. Lisa believes Janice may have felt trapped in the middle of the parents problems. Lisa thinks Janice's quandry about how to handle being the mother's confidante contributed to her depression and to her keeping the sibling relationship distant. Consequently, Lisa did not have the natural opportunity to learn how to react to the parents' co-enabling behaviors from her older sister nor to receive her support. Pollak and Hundermar (1984) and other authors have noted that sibling support networks can fulfill a critical quasi-therapeutic role (Janzen and Harris, 1986; Hamlin and Timberlake, 1981), but in Lisa's case, her perceptions were invalidated rather than supported by her sibling and parents.

The parents had similar distant relationships with their siblings. The mother was 14 years younger than her next sibling (she had two brothers) and often remarked that it felt like she was an only child (see Figure 9.1). Lisa said her mother was not close to her brothers for that reason. During the interview Lisa had trouble recalling whether her mother had two or three brothers. Lisa's father's three siblings were not married and lived with their mother until they died in middle and old age. The father would visit them only every 5 or 10 years and Lisa described them as not close.

The maternal grandmother lived with the family from the time the parents got married until she died when Lisa was 10. Lisa had grown very close to her grandmother and received her only nurturing and support from that relationship. Janice, on the other hand, had a very stormy relationship with the grandmother that continued until the latter's death. Lisa recalled being very resentful about Janice's lack of grief when the grandmother died. The mother withdrew from other family members at the time of the death, so Lisa felt she did not have anyone with whom she could discuss her feelings.

Janice was a good student inspite of her depression, while Lisa began to act out more and more in school and at home as she neared adolescence along with earning near failing grades. Lisa started using alcohol and marijuana in high school and "hung around" kids who were also heavy users. Her mother and Janice colluded to keep the father from finding out about her substance abuse. Wegscheider (1981) notes that it is not unusual for family members to be overly concerned about the alcoholic member's reactions to the exclusion of other important issues (e.g., ignoring the consequences of Lisa's substance abuse for her). Lisa remembers feeling that her behavior at school was the one way she could embarrass her sister. She recognized that, ironically, her behavior also kept the parents focused on her rather than on Janice's depression and the father's drinking. Perhaps the underlying communication from Lisa to Janice was similar to the "sibling deflecting message" described by Lewis (1987) (see Chapter 4). That message communicates "I will protect you by deflecting our parents attention away from you".

When she was fifteen, Lisa began to have blackouts that scared her and, as a result, she started to spend time with other youngsters who were not using substances. Then she decided to join the Youth for Christ group that most of those teenagers belonged to and encouraged Janice to join the same group. Involvement in this group enabled Lisa to stop using substances. The sisters began to spend more time together; this was the first time they had been involved in any mutual activities since their preschool period. It was also the first time Lisa felt close to Janice. This relationship compensated for the on-going emotional distance between them and the parents.

Their new alliance allowed them to handle conflicts more effectively with the parents in regard to friendships and curfew. Pollak and Hundermar (1984) describe this as a gang formation role within the sibling subsystem. Lisa remembers that Janice's support during those two years helped her maintain her sobriety and improved her coping with the father's alcoholism and the mother's nagging. Then Janice went away to college and Lisa felt abandoned. The closeness they had experienced previously gradually diminished, especially after Janice married during her college years.

The Young Adult Years Until the Present

Lisa began using alcohol, cocaine, and marijuana during her college years and continued until she was about 26 years of age. Although she had been sober for four years she had not resolved her fears about always being wrong in comparison to Janice. Janice did well in college while Lisa flunked out. When she eventually finished college Lisa believes her family was very surprised. For the first time, she felt she had accomplished something on her own although she was still comparing herself to Janice and wanting her acceptance. After completing college Lisa simply never moved back home; she felt this was an easy way to gain her independence and get away from her father's alcoholism. Janice lived in a different state so Lisa felt "cut-off" from her family since she only visited her parents on holidays and for some other family gatherings.

During this period, Lisa was using alcohol and marijuana heavily. She got married to Lou who was also alcoholic at the time. She thought then that their relationship was good until he went to AA and recovered. Lisa remembers feeling rejected because they were no longer involved in drinking together. She felt she was being judged silently by Lou as inadequate. The conflicts in their relationship became more apparent and escalated as a consequence. Lisa had two friends but found it hard to talk openly about her troubles and she was still cut-off from her family, so she kept all her feelings inside. The family rules about "don't feel, don't talk" reinforced this closed communication pattern (Black, 1981; Kritsberg, 1986).

In terms of employment, she had a series of jobs over the years that she would leave suddenly. In retrospect, Lisa believes she recreated her family and sibling dynamics in each of these work experiences by focusing on the same interpersonal issues of nurturance and acceptance. She felt Janice was more nurtured by the parents and that Janice never fully accepted her. In work situations, Lisa would unconsciously seek out a mentor relationship in which she could be nurtured and accepted while also seeking out a relationship with another coworker who was not likely to accept her. The latter type of relationship always created stress and stormy interactions, causing her to leave each job when the pressure became unbearable. What Lisa identified as unresolved rejection by her parents and Janice led her to recreate a pattern of self-defeating work relationships. Those work pressures and the marital conflicts caused Lisa to enter substance abuse treatment. She had been in recovery for six years at the time of her interview.

The Process of Change

Kritsberg (1986) states that "The alcoholic system will recreate itself generation after generation if the family is not treated" (p. 8). This prediction is important in the situation of Lisa, along with Huberty's and Huberty's (1986) reminder that siblings can silently sabotage treatment and abstinence goals by keeping "... the drug abuser in a dependent, incompetent role" (p. 34). These assumptions about family factors that can strengthen and inhibit change in ACOA are illustrated as assessment, treatment, and evaluation are discussed in this section. The discussion draws upon information from the previous case study of Lisa, and information in Chapters 1 and 4 on systems' dynamics.

Assessment of ACOA

The assessment process with ACOA should include the areas involved in any general assessment. This includes exploration of family and individual factors with added attention to some of the sibling factors identified in previous chapters. Related to the individual factors to be assessed, Pape (1992) suggests that untreated ACOA struggle with several major issues such as a lack of self-esteem, high stress and intensity levels, boundary difficulties, approval seeking, and an inability to trust others. Wegscheider (1981) notes the assessment should be focused on the survival roles that children in alcoholic families are bound to assume in relation to each other and to their parents: the hero, scapegoat, lost child, and mascot. While much of this information is useful for assessing the situations of ACOA such as Lisa, the emphasis is on the problems almost to the exclusion of individual, sibling, and family strengths. Assessment strategies are needed, therefore, to help practitioners identify and build on strengths as well as clarify and help to resolve problems. Some examples include strategies focused on assessing family, sibling, and individual factors. These factors tend to interact dynamically with each other over time.

Family Assessment Procedures. Kritsberg (1986) has developed a classification system that is useful for helping ACOA identify where their family fits and the issues that tend to surface within each category of alcoholic families. The four types are as follows:

1. Type 1: the system is "riddled with active alcoholism in every generation of the family" (p. 2).
2. Type 2: the actively drinking member in the family has stopped drinking but the family continues to operate "in a way that can only be described as alcoholic" (p. 4).
3. Type 3: the active drinking has been removed from the family for one or more generations, but the family dynamics still operate in a way that is still "characteristic of the alcoholic family" (p. 5).
4. Type 4: there is no previous history of alcoholism in the family, but a member of the current generation has become alcoholic and "the children of that generation will be at high risk for alcoholism" (p. 7).

Lisa's family fits in the type 1 category with alcoholism in the paternal grandfather who committed suicide, the father, and Lisa (see Figure 9.1). Although Lisa was not aware of problem alcohol use in the father's three siblings, their closed system with their mother seems characteristic of the alcoholic family described in the type 2 category. Lisa's mother's enabling behavior related to the father's alcoholism is also characteristic of such systems (e.g., denying his addiction, controlling the daughter's through guilt, and failing to nurture them). Assessment of these family factors is useful in the case of Lisa because it becomes more clear how deeply embedded the problem of alcoholism has been across the generations.

To balance the assessment in using Kritsberg's (1986) classification system, it is important to identify the strengths in each situation. For example, in regard to type 1 families it can be beneficial to identify those family members in each generation who have recovered and what resources they used to initiate and maintain their recovery: both the addicted and nonaddicted members. This information could have helped Lisa to reject the family script regarding addiction **and** her sibling role of incompetence. It might have been useful in later treatment for reconnecting her with specific family members and encouraging her to learn about their recovery experience from them (e.g., relatives of Lisa's paternal grandmother).

Expanding the genogram beyond its conventional use can make it more relevant for family assessments with ACOA. Additional questions to be explored with the genogram include the following (Freeman, 1990):

1. Instances of alcohol problems, alcoholism, or family secrets related to alcoholism in a member (e.g., "Uncle Bill fell a lot", "Your grandfather was never able to hold a job for long," "Esther was always the life of the party but never drank at other times," or "My father could really hold his liquor"!).
2. Examples of eating problems including obesity, abuse of other drugs (illegal drugs, prescription medication, or over the counter drugs), workaholism, or sexual addictions across the generations.
3. Patterns in sibling relationships that are repeated from one generation to another, including sibling solidarity, support networks, and role modeling; alcoholism; interpersonal behaviors that are characteristic of alcohol abusers even if alcoholism is not apparent; and sibling ghosts (an individual in the current generation has a sibling and family role similar to a parent's role or that of his/her sibling in the previous generation).
4. Other strengths and positive qualities of family members and the sibling subsystem that counterbalance the effects of the negative intergenerational factors (e.g., what qualities or aspects of relationships should be maintained and what positive reconnections are possible).

For Lisa, helping her to assess that her father was also a workaholic could clarify additional factors that might be affecting her success at work. In addition, Lisa expressed surprise during the interview that he had coped well with retirement. He used exercise (walking) and volunteering his services in a friend's business (at a moderate level) as a way of handling the transition. This information seemed useful to Lisa as a positive model for assessing her current work patterns and how she might prevent herself from becoming a workaholic in the future.

A third family assessment tool for ACOA such as Lisa is the "Substance Abuse Work-Related Assessment Inventory" shown in Figure 9.2 (Freeman, 1989). This inventory is useful for assessing patterns in the parent and previous generations, the sibling subsystem, and the client that reflect the unresolved sibling and family issues discussed previously in this chapter. Moreover, the assessment will identify workplace factors that can maintain problems such as conflictual, enabling, bargaining, and overfunctioning behaviors of co-workers and supervisors (Freeman, 1990) or resources for resolving the problems.

In assessing Lisa's situation, this inventory might have helped her achieve the insights that she later developed about her dysfunctional work relationships and the connection to her unresolved issues with Janice. The inventory could have been useful in pointing out important information that Lisa lacked about family members' work-related experiences. Both positive and negative aspects of those experiences might have been useful for expanding her perceptions about and relationships with Janice, co-workers, and her parents.

Sibling Assessment Procedures. The family assessment tools described above illustrate how many family, sibling, and individual factors interact to affect the problems and strengths of ACOA. In addition to those tools, there are assessment procedures that focus more centrally on clarifying sibling relationships and roles. Pollak and Hundermar (1984) conceptualized three roles for siblings of disabled young adults that are generalizable to siblings in alcoholic families. Freeman (1989) expanded those roles to include three additional roles (#'s 4, 5, and 6 below). These six positive roles can become problematic if siblings become fixed in them or if they are exaggerated during a given period when they are needed. The roles may vary over the life cycle of siblings depending on the developmental issues that need to be addressed (e.g., Lisa and Janice developed the gang formation role during adolescence related to the task of friendship and loyalty). Or the roles may be determined by external events to which siblings must adjust (for example, the quasi-therapeutic role for coping with a parental divorce or the placement of siblings in different foster homes) (See Chapter 2 about the author's research on these roles):

1. The quasi-parental role: adoption of parental concerns by one or more siblings in regard to other siblings.
2. The quasi-therapeutic role: provision of support to one another and being an ally in the developmental struggle of individuation and separation.
3. The gang formation role: strengthening of familial ties among siblings and resulting from a degree of closeness that has been lost in the parent/child relationship.
4. The counter role: acting opposite from a sibling's role to influence the family toward positive change and help siblings cope with parental alcoholism.
5. The positive risk-taking role: modeling by one sibling how the

A. Background Information:

    Date _____

    Completed By _____

1. Name _____

2. Age _____   3. Sex: Male _____

                                    Female _____

4. Education: _____

5. Race: African-American   _____
             Asian-American   _____
             Hispanic   _____
             Native American   _____
             White   _____
             Other   _____

B. Important Relationships and Roles:

	Quality of Relationships (close or distant; nature of contacts, satisfaction with, and frequency of contacts)?	*Roles* (who does what in maintaining or distancing the relationship, past & present)?
1. Between you and your spouse or live-in partner/lover (if applicable):		
2. Between you and each of your siblings:		
3. Between you and your parents:		
4. Intergenerationally: Between your parents and their siblings and between your parents and grandparents:		

C. Work-Related Factors: The Client   Client's Siblings in   Client's Parents/
                                                                      General or Most   Grandparents
                                                                      Significant Sibling

1. Occupations (Begin with current positions).

2. Reasons for Occupational choices and work settings?

3. Addictions (substances, work, and the reverse)?

4. Coping patterns related to work and other areas?

5. Significant work events or experiences (eg., job changes or losses, conflicts, promotions, passovers, other recognitions or rewards, work status)?

6. Work performance patterns or trends?

7. Work attendance patterns and trends?

8. Attitudes and values toward work and how they are manifested?

9. Roles and Relationships with coworkers or colleagues?

10. Roles and Relationships with supervisors/administrators?

11. Interpersonal skills/concerns or problems re: work relationships?

12. Work setting atmosphere or climate re: addictions?

13. Level of overall job satisfaction?

1	2	3	4	5
Unsatisfactory	Barely Satisfied	Mostly Satisfied	Very Satisfied	Extremely Satisfied

Figure 9.2. Substance Abuse Work-Related Assessment Inventory

others can be different in a positive manner in families where there are strong rules for compliance.
6. The neutral/waiting role: provision of covert support and coaching to siblings who take positive risks and learning by observation due to negative family rules and sanctions against change.

A timeline might have been useful for helping Lisa assess changes in her relationship with Janice, the different roles they assumed with each other over the years, and unacknowledged periods of sibling solidarity. For example, Lisa characterized their relationship as distant during the years from early childhood until she was about fifteen. But an analysis of their sibling roles during that period might have revealed how and when those roles changed subtly. It would be interesting to clarify what influenced Lisa to move from a counter role to a positive risk-taking role and at what points in time. It might also be possible to determine if Janice assumed the neutral/waiting role at times, for example, at the point where Lisa first joined the Youth for Christ group. Regarding sibling solidarity, one might question if Janice was actually distant and disapproving at that time if she was able to join and then become close to Lisa.

Unlike this timeline role analysis, Tracy and Whittaker (1990) designed a social network map that includes an analysis of **current** parental, sibling, peer, or other relationships. The analysis of each relationship includes the area of life (work or household), the frequency of support and the type provided (concrete, emotional, or information/advice), the extent the interaction is critical (hardly ever or sometimes), the direction of help, the frequency of contact, and the duration of the relationship. The directions for this network analysis suggest including people who make the person feel good or bad, people who have influenced the way the person made decisions during this time, or others who just played a part in the person's life. Those identified persons are, for good or ill, part of the person's social network (Tracy and Whittaker, 1990). If siblings are omitted, this fact may reveal the existence of unresolved sibling issues. Or if work-related conflicts surface (like in Lisa's situation), those assessment results have important implications treatment and evaluation.

Family Treatment and Evaluation Strategies

Pape (1992) cautions that because of the typical sense of isolation and shame experienced by ACOA, treatment with this client population is best done in the group modality. The group provides the type of acceptance and support that Lisa was seeking in all of her relationships outside the family, especially in her work relationships. This author indicates the group "... allows for re-creation of family-of-origin issues" and becomes temporarily "... the new family of choice" (p. 48). In addition, having members of different ages in the groups helps to create the intergenerational climate of the family and supports the use of Bowen's (1974) family treatment approach focused on individuation and the impact of the family transmission process on current functioning (the transmission of alcoholism and other dysfunctional interactional patterns across the generations).

This intergenerational family treatment approach can be combined with Gestalt Therapy which is useful for bringing to the surface hidden feelings that are typical of families with an alcoholic member (Blugerman, 1986; Steinglass, 1989). Because the presenting problem often does not directly focus on sibling issues, individual and group treatment sessions may need to address the related work or general family issues initially. As treatment progresses, however, some of the sibling-related issues that are affecting those other problems indirectly may need to be explored or allowed to surface.

Treatment/Evaluation of Work-Related Issues. ACOA often seek treatment for work-related problems but assume those problems are not related to their experiences of growing up in an alcoholic family (Freeman, 1989). Although many of them appear to adjust adequately, some of them like Lisa, have been the acting out child in the family. Black (1981) indicates that acting out children in these families "often display delinquent problematic behavior which more adequately typifies the state of the family" (p. 26). They seem to cause dysruptions in their own lives and in the lives of other family members in order to provide distraction from the issue of alcoholism in the family. They may use the same unacceptable behavior they have learned in the family of origin to communicate their feelings to co-workers and supervisors in the adult work world (Freeman, 1989). Black (1981) also notes that they tend to be socially isolated and to develop alcoholism at earlier ages than other ACOA.

Even if an ACOA responds to the experience of growing up in an alcoholic family by becoming overly responsible or a placater, similar patterns in hiding thoughts and feelings tend to occur. They may not act out at work, but the work situation may be stressful and involve the same inner turmoil experienced by ACOA who do act out. Consequently, several important work-related and sibling issues should be addressed in treatment. Pape (1992) notes the importance of helping group members identify the shame-based rules from the family of origin that are often "inhuman, unclear, perfectionistic, controlling, and steeped in a denial system so that children can never do enough, cannot measure up or be successful enough to feel good about themselves". Talking about family experiences and the members' feelings and thoughts in the group helps to externalize the shame. It also can affirm what the members have experienced growing up and their reactions to those experiences (perhaps for the first time). Homework assignments are often a useful technique during this process. Writing down the old shaming messages or writing down their strengths or things they like about themselves are examples of how members can be taught to affirm themselves (Lerner, 1985; Whitfield, 1987).

Another important treatment issue is the dysfunctional roles the members have assumed at work and the emotional turmoil they are experiencing as a result. A strategy for addressing this issue involves having group members compare the roles identified on their Work-Related Inventory (see Figure 9.2) with the sibling and family roles revealed by their genograms. In this way, group members can help each other identify how they may be acting out their "fixed" and unproductive roles from the family of origin at work (Pape, 1989). The strategy of role expansion can be used to help them shift out of those fixed roles and to take on positive roles they may have developed at one time with siblings (Freeman, 1989). In the case of Lisa, the gang formation role that she and her sister adopted during adolescence could be useful as a model for how to develop positive alliances with co-workers. Furthermore, group members can be encouraged to identify and demonstrate for each other their experiences with positive sibling and work roles.

Ideally, siblings should be included in individual and group sessions in order to address the real life unresolved or present-oriented sibling issues revealed by the assessment (see Table 4.1, Chapter 4). The impact on Lisa's and Janice's current relationship might be stronger if Janice were present to discuss and relive their positive **and** negative role experiences. If having the sibling present is not possible, an alternative could be to use a Gestalt technique such as the "hot seat." Lisa could be asked to talk to an empty chair as though Janice were present to re-experience their conflicts and solidarity at an emotional level (Blugerman, 1986). Zinker (1977) identified another useful Gestalt strategy: having Lisa physically act out repeatedly the polarities of gaining acceptance and revealing her unexpressed feelings of anger related to Janice and her co-workers.

In other situations, group members can act as "stand-ins" by portraying siblings or co-workers in role plays, sculpting, and other family treatment exercises (Pape, 1992). Moreover, the group relationships can become a model for how to resolve boundary and trust issues with siblings, co-workers, parents, and other significant relationships. Analysis of the effects of the members' changing roles and relationships with each other in the group can provide further learning about how to change sibling, parental, and work relationships. It is often helpful for clients to supplement this work in sibling-oriented individual and group treatment sessions with involvement in Al-Anon family groups developed for ACOA (Cutter and Cutter, 1987; Al-Anon Family Groups, 1988).

Evaluation of these individual and group sessions should be an ongoing process from the point of intake and assessment. The use of the Work-Related Assessment Inventory and the Social Network Analysis should help in identifying the severity, frequency, and duration of the work-and family-related problems. This information, according to Bloom and Fischer (1982), constitutes the baseline rates of the target problems. For instance, it might be possible to have Lisa count the frequency of conflicts with a particular co-worker and to rate her level of coping with those conflicts on a scale of 0 to 5. On this self-anchored scale (Bloom & Fischer, 1982), 0 could represent being out of control verbally or physically while 5 could indicate being able to identify her feelings and to either remove herself from the situation or to resolve it as previously agreed in treatment. Similar methods could be used to obtain baseline data on relationships with siblings and other family members.

This information can serve as a guide for developing measurable objectives that clarify how much change is desired in the target areas and relationships (Freeman, 1985). One objective in Lisa's situation could involve her and Janice identifying at least two instances in the past when they have been helpful to each other. Simply discussing this topic provides an opportunity for positive interaction (they are required to brainstorm and join each other in order to complete the task). Such an objective could, when accomplished, help in clarifying what those experiences were like and how the sisters' could be supportive to one another in the future. Any changes in their ability to support each other could then be monitored and evaluated through updating the social network analysis periodically in terms of the frequency and quality of contacts (Tracy and Whittaker, 1990).

Treatment/Evaluation of Family-Related Issues. In addition to these work- and sibling-related issues, ACOA frequently are referred to treatment because of problems with their spouses and parents. They may have generalized their problems in not being individuated from parents and siblings into relationships within their families of choice. That process may be manifested through self-blame or through blaming the addicted or enabling parents and siblings (Pape, 1992). In Lisa's situation, she generalized the nonacceptance from her sister Janice and the parents into her relationship with her husband Lou. Initially, she interpreted Lou's recovery as an **unspoken** condemnation of her continued addiction. As he progressed in his recovery and began to talk more openly about his feelings and how he was experiencing his recovery, Lisa felt he was more openly judging her to be inadequate. Although her interpretation of Lou's reactions to her could be accurate in part, it is also possible that she was restating to herself the same shame messages she had received in the past from Janice and the parents (Wegscheider, 1981; Black, 1981).

Consequently, a major focus of treatment for family issues is on the approval seeking and low self-esteem of ACOA. Pape (1992) indicates that ACOA tend to equate doing with being so that their self-esteem is based on performance. Criticism about their behavior is taken as a criticism about their personhood (Black, 1981). This pattern of giving power to others to determine their self-esteem creates the sense of resentment and "rebellion" described by Lisa. It also creates boundary difficulties; ACOA may share too much information about themselves too soon to fellow employees, friends, or dates (Pape, 1992).

One goal in family treatment with individuals, couples, or groups is to help ACOA distinguish what is rightfully their responsibility and what is that of their parents. For instance, it is the parents who are responsible for the alcoholism and for failing to protect and nurture the child. It is the "child" who was the victim of the childhood pain that was experienced.

It is also that child who needs nurturing and validation in treatment in order to let go of the past. But it is the adult who needs to set goals and work toward becoming the person he or she wants to be currently and in the future. This treatment strategy of separating responsibility for the past and present is the beginning of Bowen's (1974) process of individuation and identity formation.

Because siblings have gone through the family experiences together, individuation from each other is often another focus of treatment (see Chapter 3, Figures 3.1 and 3.2 on sibling tasks at this stage). Bowen (1974) supports the need for individuals to differentiate from the sibling subsystem while maintaining a personal relationship with siblings. Identifying how siblings coped differently and the consequences for each choice in a neutral rather than blaming climate is a useful way to begin this process. Working through stages of loss and grief related to the parental and sibling relationships often allows ACOA to identify what stages they have been in and are currently experiencing: denial, shock, rage, depression or sorrow, and acceptance (Pape, 1992). Teaching the stages and assigning homework assignments related to them is an effective family treatment strategy.

For example, Lisa could benefit from knowing when she or Janice were in the stage of rage or depression and how they reacted then as a way of understanding their past relationships. Lisa might be encouraged to identify the stage of loss and grief she was in at critical periods in her life: when Janice left for college versus when Lou began his recovery process. In this manner, she could be helped to understand how her unresolved loss experience with Janice was affecting her reactions to Lou's recovery. Then she could take on an insession assignment to express the related thoughts and feelings (a communication exercise with Lou, the empty chair exercise with him if he was not present, or a family sculpting exercise with group members). She might also be asked to do a homework assignment focused on a similar task (a "no send" **or** mailed letter to her parents or to Janice) (Blugerman, 1986).

Evaluation of sessions focused on family issues can be documented simply by using methods similar to those used for work-related issues. The genogram is useful as a monitoring tool because it can be updated periodically with new information resulting from homework assignments. It can be updated too, with a different color entry and date, as perceptions and relationships change between the client and significant others. Changes in the genogram and the social network analysis overtime can be evaluated against the measurable goals that have been set in those areas. An additional advantage of treatment sessions for couples is Videka-Sherman's and Reid's (1985) format for having three individuals evaluate the extent to which each objective is achieved (e.g., Lisa, Lou, and the practitioner rate each objective on a scale from 1—"no progress toward goal", to 7—"goal completely achieved").

Conclusion

Some ACOA are able to enter treatment on their own or to use self-help groups and other means to begin the healing process necessary for overcoming their experiences of living with an alcoholic parent. Whether or not they request treatment for that issue, they may seek treatment at a later period when other aspects of the problem manifest themselves. In both instances, family treatment focused solely on the adult child and parent relationship may be insufficient. Siblings should be included because they influence the pattern of coping adopted by each child in relation to the parents. Furthermore, those patterns and unresolved issues from previous sibling and parental relationships can affect later adjustments with co-workers in the workplace and love relationships. Because the manifestation of those sibling issues is often indirect, practitioners will need to be skillful in exploring these connections.

When possible, siblings, spouses, parents, and even co-workers may need to be involved in family treatment sessions. In this regard, practitioners should be creative in where groups are conducted. The workplace may be appropriate because at least 10% or more workers are likely to be ACOA. Using creative homework assignments for face-to-face contacts between siblings and other relatives during holidays and family gatherings is another important strategy for addressing past, current, or future tasks. Finally, Gestalt strategies that do not require the presence of relatives who are deceased or otherwise unavailable may be needed to help ACOA begin the healing process.

REFERENCES

Ackerman, R.J. (1987). A new perspective on adult children of alcoholics. *EAP Digest, 11,* 25-29.

Al-Anon Family Groups (1988). *Who are the members of Al-Anon and Alateen?* New York: Al-Anon Family Group Headquarters.

Black, C. (1981). *It will never happen to me.* Denver, CO: M.A.C. Printing & Publications Division.

Bloom, M. & Fischer, J. (1982). *Evaluating practice: Guidelines for the accountable professional.* Englewood Cliffs, NJ: Prentice-Hall.

Blugerman, M. (1986). Contributions of gestalt theory to social work treatment. In F.J. Turner (Ed.), *Social work treatment: Interlocking theoretical approaches* (69-90). New York: Free Press.

Bowen, M. (1974). A family systems approach to alcoholism. *Addictions, 21,* 3-4.

Corrales, R., Bueker, J., Ro-Trock, L., & Smith, B. (1981). *Family systems theory: An introduction to systemic thinking.* Unpublished monograph. Kansas City, MO: The Family Institute.

Cutter, C.G. & Cutter, H.S.G. (1987). Experience and change in Al-Anon family groups: Adult children of alcoholics. *Journal of Studies on Alcohol, 48,* 29-32.

Freeman, E.M. (1990). Assessment of substance abuse problems: Implications for clinical supervision. *The Clinical Supervisor, 8,* 91-108.

Freeman, E.M. (1989). Adult children of alcoholics: Study of parental, sibling, and work relationships. Paper presented at the 34th Institute on the Prevention and Treatment of Alcoholism. Pontault-Combault, France: International Council on Alcohol and Addictions.

Freeman, E.M. (1985). Multiple group services for alcoholic clients. In E.M. Freeman (Ed.), *Social work practice with clients who have alcohol problems* (119-138). Springfield, IL: Charles C Thomas.

Hamlin, E.R. & Timberlake, E.M. (1981). Sibling group treatment. *Clinical Social Work Journal, 9,* 101-110.

Huberty, D.J. & Huberty, C.E. (1986). Sabotaging siblings: An overlooked aspect of family therapy with drug dependent adolescents. *Journal of Psychoactive Drugs, 18,* 31-41.

Janzen, C. & Harris, O. (1986). *Family treatment in social work practice.* Itasca, IL: F.E. Peacock.

Kritsberg, W. (1986). *The adult children of alcoholics syndrome: From discovery to recovery.* Pompano Beach, FL: Health Communications.

Lerner, R. (1985). *Daily affirmations for adult children of alcoholics.* Deerfield Beach, FL: Health Communications.

Lewis, K.G. (1987). Bulimia as a communication to siblings. *Psychotherapy with Families, 24,* 640-645.

Pape, P.A. (1992). Adult children of alcoholics: Uncovering family scripts and other barriers to recovery. In E.M. Freeman (Ed.), *The addiction process: Effective social work approaches* (43-53). White Plains, NY: Longman.

Pape, P.A. (1989). Your boss is not really your parent. *EAP Digest, 13,* 37-43.

Pollak, O. & Hundermar, D. (1984). Some unexplored aspects of the sibling experience. *Adolescence, 29,* 869–874.

Steinglass, P. (1989). *The alcoholic family.* New York: Basic Books.

Tracy, E.M. & Whittaker, J. (1990). The social network map: Assessing social support in clinical practice. *Families in Society, 71,* 461–470.

Videka-Sherman, L. and Reid, W.J. The structured clinical record: A clinical evaluation tool. *The Clinical Supervisor, 3,* 45–61.

Wegscheider, S. (1981). *Another chance: Hope and health for the alcoholic family.* Palo Alto, CA: Science & Behavior Books.

Whitfield, C.L. (1987). *Healing the child within.* Deerfield Beach, FL: Health Communications.

Zinker, J. (1977). *Creative process in gestalt therapy.* New York: Brunner/Mazel.

Chapter 10

SIBLING THERAPY FOR INTERGENERATIONAL CARETAKING ISSUES IN MIDDLE-AGE SIBLINGS

> My father was an only child. He spent most of his life wondering why his parents didn't have other children. So I always felt lucky that I had sisters. And if I'd been asked whether either of them might not be there for our parents in the end, I'd have said it couldn't happen.
>
> —Larry

Research has shown that family reciprocity and support are most critical during periods of crises. Cicirelli (1980) notes that adult siblings often provide these requirements to each other during crises because such resources may not be available in other relationships (e.g., from spouses or children). Sibling relationships may be particularly supportive during those times because of their "... durability, blood ties, the similarity of background and experience of siblings, and social expectations for that role (Mosatche, Brady, and Noberini, 1983). Moreover, when the crisis is related to the health and safety of their elderly parents, there is a need for siblings to not only support each other but to collaborate in the care that is needed. Both assumptions imply that reciprocity between siblings is essential during those times.

A number of barriers can prevent these family resources from being available for use. Unresolved sibling issues, along with long-term parent-adult child conflicts, may block participation and collaboration by some members (Sutton-Smith and Lamb, 1981; Cicirelli, 1977). The lack of opportunity to observe and learn from other parental caretaking units may be another barrier. A failure to include extended family members or substitute siblings in the unit as needed when some siblings do not participate can also create problems. (See Chapter 1 regarding philosophical assumptions about substitute or alternative sibling relationships.) Cicirelli (1985) explains that rigid role proscriptions and boundary infringements may be the result when the caretaking unit does not function well, while a strengthened sibling bond can be one outcome of a positive parental caretaking experience.

How then can adult children manage these sibling or parent/child issues and also address their own developmental tasks? Those tasks involve handling generativity and accepting biological, psychological, and social changes in their own lives (see Table 1.1 in Chapter 1). The current chapter includes a discussion of these developmental tasks and sibling issues within the context of Larry's case study. Typical settings in which professionals encounter families needing this type of help and the paths to help are described. Sibling therapy with an intergenerational perspective is discussed in terms of two goals: (1) to enhance collaboration in developing a sibling caretaking unit/plan and, (2) to work on underlying parent-adult child or sibling issues that are affecting the process. Sibling contracts are one of several methods that are included for evaluating this work over time.

Larry: A Case Study

Larry Winters is a 46 year old caucasian male who works as a computer programmer. His divorce occurred four years before he participated in the author's research on sibling relationships, but he pointed out that he and his ex-wife, Jean, continue to have unresolved issues with each other. Jean is still very bitter about the divorce which was initiated by Larry. Larry feels Jean was too close to her family; the couple had many conflicts about that issue and others over the years. Her bitterness about the divorce shows up in a lack of cooperation in planning a visitation schedule and constant complaints about the amount of child support.

Larry thinks the divorce has caused him to put more time and energy into other relationships that he probably ignored when he was married. When he got divorced his family members did not provide much support to him, perhaps assuming he was handling the divorce well. That experience made him feel disconnected and alone, particularly in terms of the lack of sibling support (Leigh, 1982). As a result, he has become more concerned about the quality of his relationships with his family of origin, friends, and his children (see Figure 10.1). Examining his family of origin relationships lately has reminded him of the larger picture and some related family dynamics. For instance, he had forgotten how much his sister, Ernestine, has been cut-off from the other members since she left home at age 17. The roots of Ernestine's cut-off and other relationship dynamics are apparent in the discussion of Larry's case study in the next section.

Childhood and Adolescence

Larry indicates that he and his sisters were not close as children, nor were his sisters close to each other, possibly due to the eight year difference in their ages. The three children usually got along with one another. Larry said he was a quiet child who could entertain himself. He liked to read and could play with his toys alone for extended periods even as a young child. His father called him "the old man" because of those characteristics. Larry grew up on his parents' farm and soon became used to both of them being very busy. His mother was a school teacher in addition to working on the farm.

Ernestine was more demanding as a child; she liked a lot of attention and seemed to resent it when their parents were busy with other things. She did not like helping out on the farm unless it was a chore she liked doing. In contrast, Larry would volunteer to help out because he liked doing things with his father. At the time, Larry thought Ernestine was a pest but now wonders if she needed something different from their parents that they did not understand. When Jan was born, Larry remembers Ernestine was very happy to have a baby sister. Ernestine played with Jan when the latter was an infant but then began to spend less time with her as she grew older. From the beginning, Jan was very friendly and outgoing. She liked following her siblings and parents around and trying to do things with them, which is typical of youngest siblings (Dunn, 1983). She was an entertaining child, often doing and saying outrageously funny things. Like Larry, when she was old enough, Jan would volunteer to do chores around the farm.

Gilbert, their father, was a hard working farmer who seldom relaxed. He was very intense about the farm and his views about how things should be done. Once when he thought a mistake had been made in the taxes assessed on the farm, he wrote letters and talked to every elected official he could identify. He became very upset when he was not able to get the taxes reduced. Two years later he ran for the county assessor's office and won. When Larry was young, he often used that experience as an example of how one person can make a difference (making the tax assessment process more equitable), when confronted with an injustice. Their mother called this his "frontier mentality—pulling the wagons into a circle and digging in for a long fight." Gilbert was also very thrifty

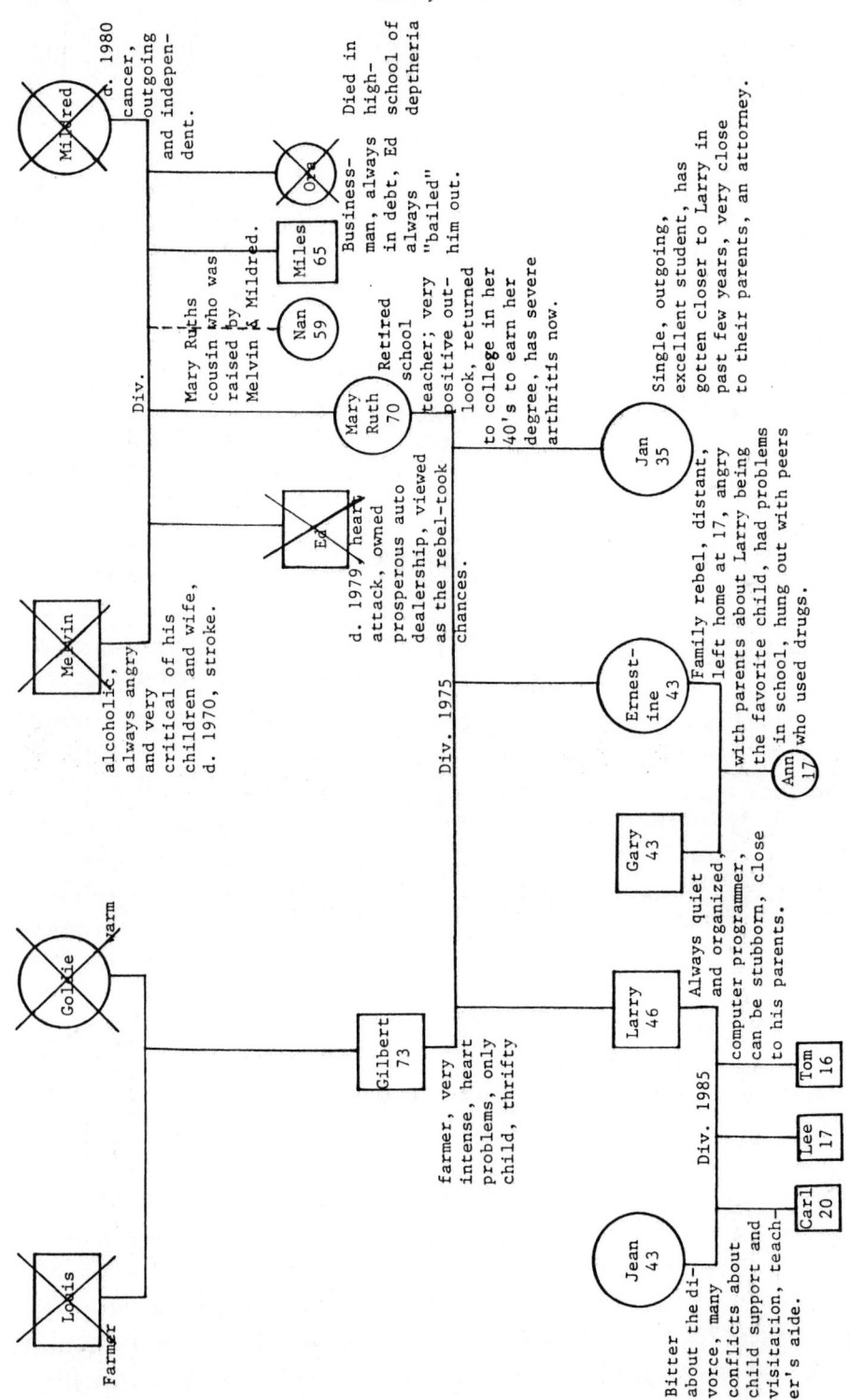

Figure 10.1. Genogram of Larry Winters (1989).

according to Larry. To get money from him required a well thought out plan, and often that did not work.

Larry indicated that their mother has always had a positive outlook. She worked as a teacher without her degree for years, and always said she would finish college when the children were older (she did finish when she was in her 40's). In thinking about his childhood, Larry believes his mother's positive outlook was reflected more in how she did things rather than in what she said. She promised little but kept any promise that she made. She completed her responsibilities on the farm and in her teaching job without complaints. She was not affectionate physically but Larry says he and his sisters knew that she loved them. His most comforting times often occurred late at night as a child, when he would hear the faint sounds of his parents talking together pleasantly in their bedroom. They might be talking about the farm or how their day had gone.

Gilbert was an only child in a small extended family. He had several cousins that he called infrequently, otherwise he had little contact with his family. Both of his parents died before Larry was born. Mary Ruth was very close to her two brothers, Ed and Miles. They lived in nearby towns and would often spend holidays with their sister's family. Mary Ruth was also close to her cousin Nan who had been raised by Mary Ruth's parents after Nan's parents were divorced. She and Mary Ruth considered themselves sisters, especially after a younger sister died at an early age (see Figure 10.1).

Larry and his sisters went to school in the next town. Although he would not have minded having his mother as his teacher, he was never in her class. Having her there in the same building affected his peer relations though. He was teased a lot by the other students because his mother was considered a hard teacher. Larry was generally well behaved in school and did well academically. Occasionally if he became stubborn about something, his teachers would threaten to call in his mother. Larry felt this situation was always humiliating and embarrassing for him. He could not understand why his teachers were not more aware of his feelings. When he entered the high school across town, other students stopped teasing him so Mary Ruth's being a teacher did not matter. He developed some close friendships, three of which he has maintained to the present. Larry was a good athlete and a member of the football team. He dated periodically but did not have a steady girlfriend until his senior year.

Ernestine was a minor behavior problem in elementary school. She would sometimes get into trouble for not completing her work or talking in class when she was not supposed to. She usually managed to get passing grades but would do just enough to get by. When she reached high school, Ernestine began to spend time with friends who skipped school and used drugs. She became harder for their parents to control; she would come home later than her curfew and she continued to spend time with two friends her parents had said she could not be with. There were daily arguments between Ernestine and the parents about her behavior. Now and then Larry would try to talk with her about staying away from this fast crowd of students, but she would not listen to him. Ernestine resented his taking the parents' side in their arguments rather than siding with her.

When she was sixteen, Ernestine ran away from home and was gone for several weeks. When she returned, she admitted that she had started using marijuana and LSD shortly before she ran away. After being away over night, she had been afraid her parents would be angry if she returned home. Then too, her friends had induced her to stay away by saying her parents probably did not care whether she returned or not (Freeman, in press). Ernestine and their parents went for counseling with their minister for several weeks, and for awhile Ernestine seemed to be doing better. Then she began going out with an older boy who had dropped out of school. The next year she became pregnant. When she told her parents, they insisted she give up the baby for adoption when it was born. Ernestine refused to agree to adoption, so her parents said she had to leave home. Ernestine went to live with Nan, their mother's cousin who lived across the state (see Figure 10.1). Although Ernestine had a miscarriage several months later, she told her parents she would never return home.

The Young Adulthood Period

Larry went to college for two years but dropped out to help his father on the farm when Gilbert had a heart attack. He worked the farm for five years until he became concerned that his father was becoming too dependent on him. Larry thought his life was not his own anymore; he wanted to find an area of work he was more interested in. He hesitated in talking to Gilbert because he was afraid the subject would be too stressful for Gilbert's health. So Larry talked with his mother about his concerns and she approached Gilbert about hiring someone else to do some of the farm work. This arrangement allowed Larry to work part time in town and to enroll in a vocational school. He met Jean while taking computer classes and they began to date on a regular basis. When they got married a year later, Larry moved from the family farm and rented a house for them in town. At age 26, this was his first time to leave home, except for his two years in college.

Larry felt he needed to become more independent from his family, so he consciously refrained from asking for help from them during the early years of his marriage. He felt Jean was too close to her family and tried also to encourage her to become more independent. But after he and Jean began having children, Larry noted his in-laws became more involved in their lives and Jean became less concerned about discouraging their interference. His in-laws questioned how they raised the children and whether he was trying hard enough to get ahead. They wanted him to go to work for his father-in-law as a salesman, but Larry decided to stay with his job as a computer programmer.

Larry saw little of his sisters during those years. Ernestine lived out of state by then and seldom wrote or visited their parents. Larry only heard about Ernestine indirectly from Nan, or his parents occasionally. Ernestine had married by then and had one daughter. Jan was in college and then law school, so she was home on the farm only on holidays and during school breaks. Although Larry sometimes thought about the limited contact he had with his siblings and other family members, his current family obligations and work consumed most of his time.

The Middle Adult Years

In thinking about his experiences, Larry believes something momentous happened every decade of his life. When he was a teenager, Ernestine ran away from home and then got pregnant; when he was in his twenties, his father had a heart attack; and when he was in his thirties, he was very depressed for about a year about his marriage and a lack of job advancement. When Larry was 42 years old, his closest friend, Tim, committed suicide. Tim had been one of Larry's friends since high school. Tim was very likeable and outgoing socially. A drinking problem led to his divorce, after which he began to drink even more. He began to have problems in his work as a policeman; he was suspended twice. He shot himself right after the last suspension. He had given a party that he had planned before the suspension, and after everyone had left the party, he shot himself. Larry believed he must have missed some clues about the suicide, so he blamed himself for Tim's death for a long time.

Although all of these situations have been difficult for Larry, he believes part of the problem is that he does not handle transitions very well. Philosophically, Larry can see that he has grown from these unfortunate experiences.

As noted previously, after his divorce Larry began to work on improving his relationships with his parents and friends. Once when he was on a business trip in the town where Ernestine now lives, he called and then went to visit her family. Larry found it difficult to relate to Ernestine. They had a hard time finding something in common to talk about. And it felt too uncomfortable to talk much about things they had done while growing up, because he wanted to stay away from her problems during their teenage years. He sensed that Ernestine might still resent him for not taking her side in past arguments with their parents. Larry noticed that although they were together for about three hours, Ernestine did not ask about or mention their parents or Jan.

When he participated in the author's study, Larry had just begun realizing how much his parents' health was gradually deteriorating. Gilbert's heart condition had worsened but he was continuing to do farm work his physician had warned him not to do. Mary Ruth has severe and crippling arthritis which greatly limited her mobility. The arthritis is painful for her even with the use of medication. It is difficult for the two of them to prepare meals and do other necessary tasks. Jan and Larry have debated how to discuss with the parents concerns about their health and safety on the farm. Larry visits his parents at least once or twice per week, while Jan goes to see them every other weekend from the town where she lives about 125 miles away. Nan visits Gilbert and Mary Ruth frequently. She cooks and freezes meals to prevent them from having to cook daily.

Jan and Larry have called Ernestine to inform her about their parents' current health conditions, but she does not initiate contact with them or their parents in return. She has told Jan and Larry to do what they think is best for their parents, and will not commit herself to a visit because of a busy schedule at home. Jan and Larry resent her lack of involvement. They wonder if she cares what happens to their parents or how much her input is needed.

Larry is also worried about his relationship with his three sons, two of whom have taken their mother's side in the divorce—Lee and Tom (see Figure 10.1). Larry has recently become a tutor for young children in his church, partly to make up for the mistakes he feels he made with his sons and also in order to contribute something to his church and community. His concerns for his parents have encouraged him to serve as a substitute driver for the organization that helps to prepare and deliver meals to elderly shut-ins. Larry's own health is changing; he recently has been diagnosed with high blood pressure and is on medication. This health condition has changed his eating habits and other aspects of his life style such as leisure activities during this midlife period (Wasserman, 1983). Larry also feels disoriented in terms of his social status as a divorced man; in the role reversal with his parents; and in trying to re-establish closer ties with his siblings, his sons, and friends (Hetherington, Cox, and Cox, 1982; Lieberman, 1978; Mosatche et al., 1983).

An Intergenerational Approach to Sibling Therapy

Helping professionals may encounter individuals such as Larry in the previous case study as they attempt to integrate expectations from their changing physical, social, psychological, and family domains during midlife. The cumulative effects of many changes occurring in sequence or simultaneously can make handling them extremely difficult. Wasserman (1983, p. 119) notes that "Erik Erikson has conceptualized the normal ego crisis as "generativity versus stagnation whereby the middle-aged person is primarily interested in guiding the next generation." The alternative is for the individual to become stagnant and unfulfilled developmentally, if he or she is unable to generate and guide the younger generation.

McCullough (1980) presents a different perspective for describing the disorientation and conflicted statuses of individuals like Larry during midlife, labelling them "the sandwich generation." The latter concept is useful because it describes more fully the multiple generational obligations that emanate not only from the younger generation as noted by Erikson (i.e., from children). The individual often must respond to obligations from the middle generation (spouse and siblings) and from the older generation as well (parents and other extended family members) (McCullough, 1980). Many times, such individuals may not request help directly until their situations reach a point of crisis.

Therefore, practitioners in hospitals, home health care agencies, and adult day care facilities may need to develop strategies for early identification of and intervention with these potential clients (Germain, 1984). For instance, the family members of all elderly admissions in those settings could be interviewed from the point of first contact for an assessment of needs. Or other organizations that typically encounter such families prior to the point of crises could be contacted by these practitioners for joint case finding activities (Germain, 1984; Golan, 1986). This includes churches and synagogues, HMO's and EAP's that serve the adult children in those families, multipurpose neighborhood community centers, meal sites for the elderly, specialized housing developments for the elderly, and senior citizen centers. Helping professionals will also need to develop crisis-oriented strategies to integrate with family treatment when such clients are served during periods of crisis. In either situation, the focus will need to be on enhancing collaboration within the sibling caretaking unit and addressing unresolved issues that can disrupt the work of that unit.

Enhancing the Sibling Caretaking Unit

Assessment of Needs. In many situations, middle-aged siblings may have a pattern of managing their issues within the subsystem over time without long-term residual effects. In other instances, the need to collaborate in developing and implementing a caretaking plan can provide an opportunity to work through sibling issues that could become barriers to the plan. These typical and normative situations can be assessed by helping professionals in three ways (Hartman, 1984; McCullough, 1980; Mosatche et al., 1983):

1. An ecomap can be used to assess who is available for forming and collaborating as a caretaking unit, beginning with spouses of the aging parent, siblings of the initial referee, alternative or substitute siblings, and others.
2. The seven life periods can be used to assess how the family has coped with normal transitions and crises in past in the older, middle, and younger generation, particularly regarding the tasks of the midlife years.
3. The current strengths and needs related to the older generation should be assessed to determine the caretaking plan, the role of the members, and any actual or potential barriers to the plan.

During the ecomap assessment, the practitioner can introduce the concepts of the sibling caretaking unit and differential participation by the members. In the previous case study, for instance, the initial referee might be Larry based on contact with a social worker or other helping professional at the meal site where he volunteers. Other potential points of entry to the service system might be through the minister at the church where he participates in tutoring children, staff in the HMO where he receives medical services for his high blood pressure, or staff in the EAP where a seminar on caretaking with elderly parents might encourage his participation.

The idea of a caretaking unit can accomplish two important steps during assessment: (1) It can normalize the stressful situation and the crisis aspects if the situation has reached that level, and (2) It indicates that the intergenerational obligations can be shared beyond the initial referee. In turn, the concept of differential participation in the unit is useful in a related way. This concept implies that each potential member of the unit can not only contribute something, but in different ways. In this manner, the concept broadens the social support network to include others who might not have been considered previously (Scott and Roberto, 1984; 1987; Suggs and Kivett, 1986-87).

With Larry as the initial referee, the ecomap would identify the primary members of the caretaking unit (the first five individuals identified below). The analysis could help to clarify the relative strengths which each of Larry's parents bring to their marital partnership, and the involvement of others at differential levels (e.g., Nan as a substitute sibling from the parent generation) (Dorfman and Mertens, 1990). In addition, Ernestine's statements that Larry and Jan should make the decisions could be reframed as an indication of her role as a consulting, rather than actively involved, sibling. Part of the assessment would be to determine what she might contribute in that role given her prior work experience in a hospital.

Ecomap Analysis   Date_____
                                                       Caretaking Unit_____

INDIVIDUAL	NATURE OF CONTACT	TYPE OF SUPPORT
1. Larry	Visits 1 or 2 times per week.	Emotional, home maintenance, safety, medical care, financial.
2. Jan	Visits 2 or 3 times per month-weekends.	Emotional, personal grooming, financial, house cleaning, social activities.
3. Nan	Visits 2-3 times per month-during the week.	Emotional, house cleaning, food purchasing/meal preparation.

4. Gilbert	Daily at home.	Organizes their social activities, does the laundry.
5. Mary Ruth	Daily at home.	Emotional anchor, monitors their medical regimen.
6. Minister	Visits once monthly, provides transportation to church, has staff telephone twice monthly.	Spiritual and emotional support.
7. Ed & Miles	Telephone on irregular basis.	Emotional support, encourage life review of Gilbert and Mary Ruth.
8. Ernestine?		

This ecomap analysis can be supplemented with the other types of assessments noted. In assessing the prior handling of transitions within the family, McCullough (1980, p. 177) notes the importance of clarifying how the older generation has dealt with "issues of autonomy, responsibility, and connectedness" with respect to the next or middle generation. This part of the assessment is useful in decreasing the crisis aspects of the situation, because it highlights instances of effective problem-solving and resource management (Golan, 1986). Utilizing the seven life periods developed by Mosatche et al. (1983) provides a framework for exploring this area with the initial referee and then with the primary members of the caretaking unit (see Figure 1.2 in Chapter 1 regarding normative issues that are handled in the sibling subsystem).

In Larry's middle generation, two of the siblings represent polarized experiences in handling separation from the family of origin. Larry had a prolonged transition and Ernestine experienced an abrupt and unfinished transition in which family connections were severed on a long-term basis. Both experiences were influenced in part by childhood and then current dynamics in the family. McCullough (1980) indicates a common process for parents who cut-off from one child is to cling to one or several of the other children in the family. Moreover, Larry seems unaware of how responsibility, autonomy, and connectedness have been managed in his parents' families of origin generally and especially during the midlife period. These aspects could be clarified through the analysis of past coping with transitions within the two families.

A third assessment procedure is for the practitioner to help the members to focus on current strengths and needs in a family. This type of assessment with Larry's family could indicate that the parents' basic needs are being met adequately, but that more comprehensive coordination and planning for future needs are required. One or two of the primary caretakers might be identified as the informal "case manager"(s) who could be encouraged to coordinate the different types of assistance or social supports being provided (Auslander and Litwin, 1988; Biegel, 1985). Often it is important to utilize the assessment process to identify more than one person or to identify an alternative case manager. This type of plan helps to spread the responsibilities and insures that none of the members handle the primary work alone.

Sibling Therapy as Family Treatment. This modality of family treatment is consistent with the previously identified developmental tasks of the midlife phase (see Table 1.1 in Chapter 1). Data from the three assessment procedures noted in the section above provide the foundation for this intergenerational family treatment approach involving the primary members of the sibling caretaking unit. The initial referee would be asked to include the other primary members of the caretaking unit in the assessment/treatment process. McCullough (1980) and Hartman and Laird (1983) stress the importance of multiple intergenerational family strategies. Some examples include encouraging contacts with the intergenerational family; detriangulating relationships, especially between siblings; establishing relationships with the dead; connecting cut-offs and unfinished business to current life crises; going with resistance, altering roles, and spreading the problem.

For example, several related strategies might have been used with Larry and his caretaking unit if they had been involved in treatment. After the assessment and agreement about the make-up and roles of the primary caretaking unit, the practitioner might focus on the need to coordinate present supports and plan for future needs. Detriangulation might be used to change the unspoken rules in the family about when and to whom each member could communicate (Hartman and Laird, 1983). Jan and Larry might be helped to develop a series of issues related to caretaking that they would like to consult with Ernestine on. Rather than talking to her through the parents or Nan, they would be encouraged to contact her directly on a regular basis. Furthermore, they would make it clear that they do not expect her to respond by initiating contact with them because of her busy schedule. This strategy of going with resistance makes the covert intergenerational behavior between the siblings and between the parents and Ernestine more overt (Papp, 1983). The goal is simply to update Ernestine, utilize her as a listener, and to free themselves from a set of powerful and rigid family triangles.

Alternating roles might be useful in addition for strengthening the work of the caretaking unit. In Larry's family, several rigidly proscribed roles are apparent between the siblings. Larry has been the responsible achiever, Ernestine has acted out as the irresponsible scapegoat, and Jan has been the entertaining youngest distracter (see Chapter 1 for a discussion of sibling roles). These proscribed sibling roles have made it difficult for the siblings to be multidimensional in each developmental phase and to change over time as opportunities for growth have presented themselves. Perhaps Jan and Larry have been able to overcome their role proscriptions more effectively than Ernestine, although each has achieved a different level of resiliency and adaptation.

But Huberty and Huberty (1986) have indicated the difficulty scapegoated siblings' experience when attempting to change their roles if other siblings do not shift their roles at the same time. Larry might be encouraged to identify the secondary gains from being "the good sibling" ("I'm better off and more responsible than my siblings"), and to admit when he has felt inadequate as most people have at various times. He might share with Jan and then Ernestine his belief that he has difficulty handling transitions and the traumatic events he has experienced each decade. The practitioner might help Jan identify examples of how she could shift her sibling role in tandem with Larry's changing role (Huberty and Huberty, 1986). She could take on the more responsible role in the caretaking unit, both as the casemanager and as the initiator of contacts with Ernestine.

It would be important to help the caretaking unit decide how to involve the parents in this role alteration process, since powerful forces for maintaining the intergenerational dynamics could cause them to sabotage the change (Hartman and Laird, 1983). It might be useful, for example, for brother and sister to make one of their calls to Ernestine in the presence of the parents and Nan. The older generation could directly observe these important role alterations. Then a discussion about Larry's and Jan's new perceptions about the three siblings' roles might help to change how the roles are perceived by the parents. This would be an example of spreading the problem without blaming anyone: essentially indicating that the cut-off is everyone's problem rather than Ernestine's the parents', and that it is hurting everyone.

Working on Unresolved Issues/Barriers

The Assessment Process. The above assessment and family treatment process is useful when unresolved issues are not interfering with the development and implementation of the sibling caretaking unit. When such barriers do exist, the three assessment procedures discussed in the previous section can help to reveal the nature and impact of the barriers. For instance, the ecomap would certainly reveal cut-offs and intergenerational triangles such as those involving Ernestine which affect the formation of the caretaking unit. The assessment of the family's past coping with transitions should help to clarify which transitions have been managed effectively and the pattern of coping in the sibling subsystem and family as a unit. Unfinished transitions to young adulthood such as Ernestine's and a similar sibling polarization between Mary Ruth's brothers could be identified as other potential barriers. Ed was described by Larry as the rebel who took chances ("the good guy") and Miles as the mismanager whom Ed continually bailed out financially and emotionally ("the bad guy"). Their sibling relationship may be a ghost for sibling relationships in the current middle generation (Freeman, in press). Resolution of these barriers would be important for enhancing the development and implementation of a caretaking plan.

Sibling Therapy for Unresolved Issues. In situations involving the unresolved sibling and intergenerational issues noted above, the family treatment strategies described in the previous section would need to be broadened. Often these issues can inpede the development of an effective caretaking unit and resolution of losses experienced by siblings from the changing health status of the elderly parents and their eventual deaths (McCullough, 1980). Mosatche et al. (1983) indicates that siblings may react differently to these loss experiences, while Hartman and Laird (1983) note the importance of focusing treatment on the management of those losses.

In addition, the presence of other unresolved losses can exacerbate siblings' reactions to the current losses related to the parents. In sibling therapy with Jan and Larry, the focus would need to be on a series of unresolved losses: including the loss of the relationship with Ernestine from the cut-off between the siblings, Larry's friend, Tim, through suicide, the relationship with Larry's sons and ex-wife from the divorce, and the recent changes in Larry's health and lifestyle. Information about these losses should be considered in light of data from intergenerational patterns of handling loss from the assessment. During sibling therapy, the practitioner should focus on ways to resolve losses while keeping in mind the examples of ineffective resolution used by family members in the past.

One strategy could be an insession exercise with Jan, Larry, and Nan to discuss their losses and to ask for what they need from each other in terms of support. Other strategies might include homework assignments such as a face to face contact between Larry and his sons to discuss the alienation he is feeling, or the technique of establishing connections with the dead involving a letter from Larry to Tim on his feelings about their relationship. Larry's statement about not handling transitions well supports assumptions about the unfinished quality of his losses. Larry could be encouraged to continue his efforts to work on his developmental tasks: coming to grips with his changing health and social status and working on generativity through volunteer activities and the caretaking of his parents.

Other strategies could help Jan and Larry get in touch with the unresolved pain that Ernestine may have experienced during her childhood and separation from the family. The practitioner might encourage them to role play events between them as siblings and between Ernestine and their parents to reexperience how all of them felt. This strategy of reenacting important intergenerational and development events could clarify Ernestine's current resistance to being included in the caretaking unit. Nan might be helpful in describing sibling relationships in the older generation. The use of storytelling about those relationships could identify how sibling roles in the middle generation (Larry and Ernestine) are influenced by the relationship between Ed and Miles, for example (see Figure 10.1).

Evaluation of Intergenerational Sibling Therapy

Evaluation of the above family treatment strategies can be accomplished through several practical procedures. First, the ecomap analysis utilized during the assessment is effective for evaluating changes in the membership and activities of the sibling caretaking unit from the point of intake to termination. Changes can be made in the ecomap and analysis with different colored pens and dates of revisions (Freeman, 1984). For instance, a shift in Jan's role from the distracter to the informal casemanager could be noted in the analysis as well as a shift in Ernestine's role from uninvolved to consultant. Larry's opportunity to take a lesser role and the growth and learning from that experience between the siblings could be noted also.

The use of scaling and sibling covenants are other practical evaluation procedures. Scaling can be used during family treatment to identify differences in the amount and type of change perceived as possible by members of the caretaking unit. This procedure can be done along several dimensions initially and then again periodically to monitor how perspectives of the members change as treatment is provided (Bloom and Fischer, 1982; Freeman, in press). For example, Jan, Larry, and Nan could have been asked to rate individually, the following dimensions on the scale below:

1. How much would the family have to change in order for the cut-off with Ernestine to be resolved?
2. How well are the primary members of the caretaking unit working together collaboratively?
3. To what extent will the barriers identified affect how well the primary members of the caretaking unit continue to work collaboratively?
4. To what extent does the father want the three siblings and Nan to plan together how to best assist the couple at this stage of their lives?
5. How much does the mother want the three siblings and Nan to plan how to best assist the couple at this stage of their lives?

1	2	3	4	5
Not at all	A little	Somewhat	Very much	A great deal

Discussions about the members' rationales for their ratings and the similarities/differences between them over time provide feedback on which perceptions of the members change, how, and the reason (Bloom and Fischer, 1982). This process of monitoring changes in how the members do scaling on particular dimensions over time is useful for developing a covenant between the members of the caretaking unit. The covenant helps to spell out what tasks and activities the members agree will be accomplished by whom and how often. The covenant represents a value consensus among the members about their family priorities and obligations (Miller, 1990).

The informal casemanager then helps the members of the unit to monitor how well the plan is working and when adjustments are needed in the covenant (e.g., when a member's responsibilities change in other areas or the needs of the elderly parents change). The covenant can be revised and updated as often as the need arises. It provides on-going feedback to the caretaking unit about the members' supportive activities, and therefore, may reduce the likelihood that burnout will occur. It is a practical tool for the practitioner to use in helping the members re-live the process of caretaking (their growth experiences) and resolve their losses when the death of a parent occurs (Mosatche et al., 1983).

Conclusion

The interrelationship between tasks of the sibling subsystem and the family's developmental life cycle has been explored in this chapter. The focus has been on the midlife phase or between the stage of launching children/moving on and the stage of the family in late life as described by McCullough (1980). Both current and unresolved individual and sibling issues may influence whether the siblings can effectively collaborate in planning for the health and safety of elderly parents. The family's history of coping with transitions may affect the collaborative process and how well those issues are addressed. The work of the sibling caretaking unit is critical, not only for assisting elderly parents in their last stage of the family and individual life cycle. The members of the caretaking unit benefit as well from the opportunity to grow through their collaborative work and from resolving their subsystem and individual issues. Thus, their own generativity may be enhanced and the sibling bond may be strengthened.

REFERENCES

Auslander, G.K. and Litwin, H. (1988). Social networks and the poor: Toward effective policy and practice. *Social Work, 33,* 234-238.

Biegel, D.E. (1985). The application of network theory and research to the field of aging. In W. Saver and R. Coward (Eds.), *Social support networks and the care of the elderly* (251-273). New York: Springer.

Bloom, M. and Fischer, J. (1982). *Evaluating practice: Guidelines for the accountable professional.* Englewood Cliffs, NJ: Prentice-Hall.

Cicirelli, V.G. (1985). The role of siblings as family caregivers. In W.J. Sauer and R.T. Coward (Eds.), *Social support networks and care of the elderly* (93-107). New York: Springer.

Cicirelli, V.G. (1980). A comparison of college women's feelings toward their siblings and parents. *Journal of Marriage and the Family, 64,* 11–117.

Cicirelli, V.G. (1977). Relationships of siblings to the elderly person's feelings and concerns. *Journal of Gerontology, 32,* 317–322.

Dorfman, L.T. and Mertens, C.E. (1990). Kinship relations in retired rural men and women. *Family Relations, 39,* 166–173.

Dunn, J. (1983). Sibling relationships in early childhood. *Child Development, 54,* 787–811.

Freeman, E.M. (In press). Substance abuse treatment: Continuum of care in services to families. In E.M. Freeman (Ed.), *Substance abuse treatment: A family systems perspective.* Newbury Park, CA: Sage.

Freeman, E.M. (In press). Developing alternative family structures for runaway, drug addicted adolescents. In E.M. Freeman (Ed.), *Substance abuse treatment: A family systems perspective.* Newbury Park, CA: Sage.

Freeman, E.M. (1984). Multiple losses in the elderly: An ecological perspective. *Social Casework, 65,* 287–296.

Germain, C.B. (1984). *Social work practice in health care: An ecological perspective.* New York: Free Press.

Golan, N. (1986). Crisis theory. In F.J. Turner (Ed.), *Social work treatment: Interlocking theoretical approaches* (296–340). New York: Free Press.

Hartman, A. (1984). Diagrammatic assessment of family relationships. In B. Compton and B. Galaway, *Social work processes* (52–59). Homewood, IL: Dorsey.

Hartman, A. and Laird, J. (1983). *Family-centered social work practice.* New York: Free Press.

Hetherington, E.M., Cox, M. and Cox, R. (1982). Effects of divorce on parents and children. In M.E. Lamb (Ed.), *Nontraditional families: Parenting and child development* (230–245). Hillsdale, NJ: Erlbaum.

Huberty, D.J. and Huberty, C.E. (1986). Sabotaging siblings: An overlooked aspect of family therapy with drug dependent adolescents. *Journal of Psychoactive Drugs, 18,* 31–41.

Leigh, G.K. (1982). Kinship interaction over the family life span. *Journal of Marriage and the Family, 44,* 197–208.

Lieberman, G.L. (1978). Children of the elderly as natural helpers: Some demographic considerations. *American Journal of Community Psychology, 6,* 489–498.

McCullough, P. (1980). Launching children and moving on. In E.A. Carter and M. McGoldrick (Eds.), *The family life cycle: A framework for family therapy* (171–198). New York: Gardner Press.

Miller, P.D. (1990). Covenant model for professional relationships: An alternative to the contract model. *Social Work, 35,* 121–125.

Mosatche, H., Brady, E., and Noberini, M.R. (1983). A retrospective lifespan study of the closest sibling relationship. *The Journal of Psychology, 113,* 237–243.

Papp, P. (1983). *The process of change.* New York: Guilford.

Scott, J.P. and Roberto, K.A. (1987). Informal supports of older adults: A rural-urban comparison. *Family Relations, 36,* 444–449.

Scott, J.P. and Roberto, K.A. (1984). Older rural parents and their children. In W.H. Quinn and G.A. Hughston (Eds.), *Independent aging* (182–193). Rockville, MD: Aspen.

Suggs, P.K. and Kivett, V.R. (1986–87). Rural/urban elderly and siblings: Their value consensus. *International Journal of Aging and Human Development, 24,* 149–159.

Sutton-Smith, B. and Lamb, M. (1981). *Sibling relationships: Their nature and significance across the lifespan.* Hillsdale, NJ: L. Erlbaum Associates.

Wasserman, S. (1983). The middle-age separation crisis and ego-supportive casework treatment. In F.J. Turner (Ed.), *Differential diagnosis and treatment in social work* (119–128). New York: Free Press.

Chapter 11

COGNITIVE-BEHAVIORAL FAMILY TREATMENT AND RET: SIBLING ISSUES AND LIFE REVIEW IN THE ELDERLY

> There was a time when I couldn't accept the fact that my brother was gay. I'd always hoped he would come to his senses and give up that lifestyle... Now that he's older and sick, I'm not sure what I think about it. One positive point though, we've never interfered in each other's lives.
>
> —Simon

Although the psychological, biological, and social aspects of aging are acknowledged as important, less attention has been directed toward how dominant societal values such as age bias and homophobia affect an individual's adjustment to the aging process (Freeman, 1984). In fact, Estes (1985) indicates this deemphasis on the effects of societal values is based on the perception that aging is an individual problem. As part of the individual's intimate environment, however, siblings and other family members have an important role to play in the aging process (as a reflection of society in general). Bank and Kahn (1982) assume that even when siblings are no longer in contact, they continue to influence one another for a lifetime.

When they are in contact, siblings can sometimes allow social comparisons such as sibling rivalry, the issue of homophobia, and a lack of individuation to block the life review process. These barriers prevent siblings age 65 and above from working toward an improved relationship with each other. In a positive vein, siblings can support each other in a shared life review and period of reminiscence. This analysis of the meaning of their significant life experiences is a critical developmental task. It offers the elderly a last chance to resolve their sibling issues and to do a final weighing of their regrets and joys about those relationships over the years (Moss and Moss, 1989). Moreover, when the health of one sibling causes this life review process to begin earlier than usual, the opportunities for preventing future stress in other members of the sibship are enhanced.

What is the best approach to utilizing these opportunities when siblings seem to be "stuck" as Simon is, often unaware of their ironic and conflicting attitudes? Should treatment be focused on the individual, the sibling subsystem, and/or on their other important relationships? These questions are addressed in this chapter through a description and analysis of Simon's case study. Appropriate family treatment strategies are discussed involving a cognitive-behavioral and Rational Emotive Therapy perspective. Individual and sibling therapy are recommended for facilitating the life review process and for resolving sibling issues including homophobia. Cognitive exercises and a log for chronicling the life review stages are useful for evaluating the effects of treatment on these attitudes and relationships.

Simon: A Case Study

Simon is a fifty-eight year old, single caucasian man living in the Midwest. He works as a factory supervisor for a greeting card company. When he agreed to participate in this author's study, he was very focused on his relationship with his older brother, Forrest, who has multiple sclerosis (MS). They had not been close until the past year when Forrest's physical condition greatly deteriorated. Until that time, Forrest worked as an addictions counselor. For many years, Simon viewed Forrest's being gay as a personal choice: as his way of continuing the long term conflicts with their parents. This caused Simon to remain distant in his relationship with Forrest over the years. Simon's genogram indicates that his closest sibling relationship has been with a younger sister, Carol, since childhood (see Figure 11.1). In fact, Simon noted several times that he and Carol always felt as though they were twins.

Several factors may be influencing Simon's current struggle in supporting Forrest's exploration of the meaning of his life (see Chapter 1 for a discussion on the natural history of sibling relationships and the handling of normative issues in those relationships, along with Chapter 3 on siblings' developmental tasks and themes over the lifespan). These factors include the close social support network between Carol and Simon and the negative attitude their older sister, Alma, has toward Forrest. The quality of the relationship between Simon and Forrest during their childhood and subsequent years is a factor as well.

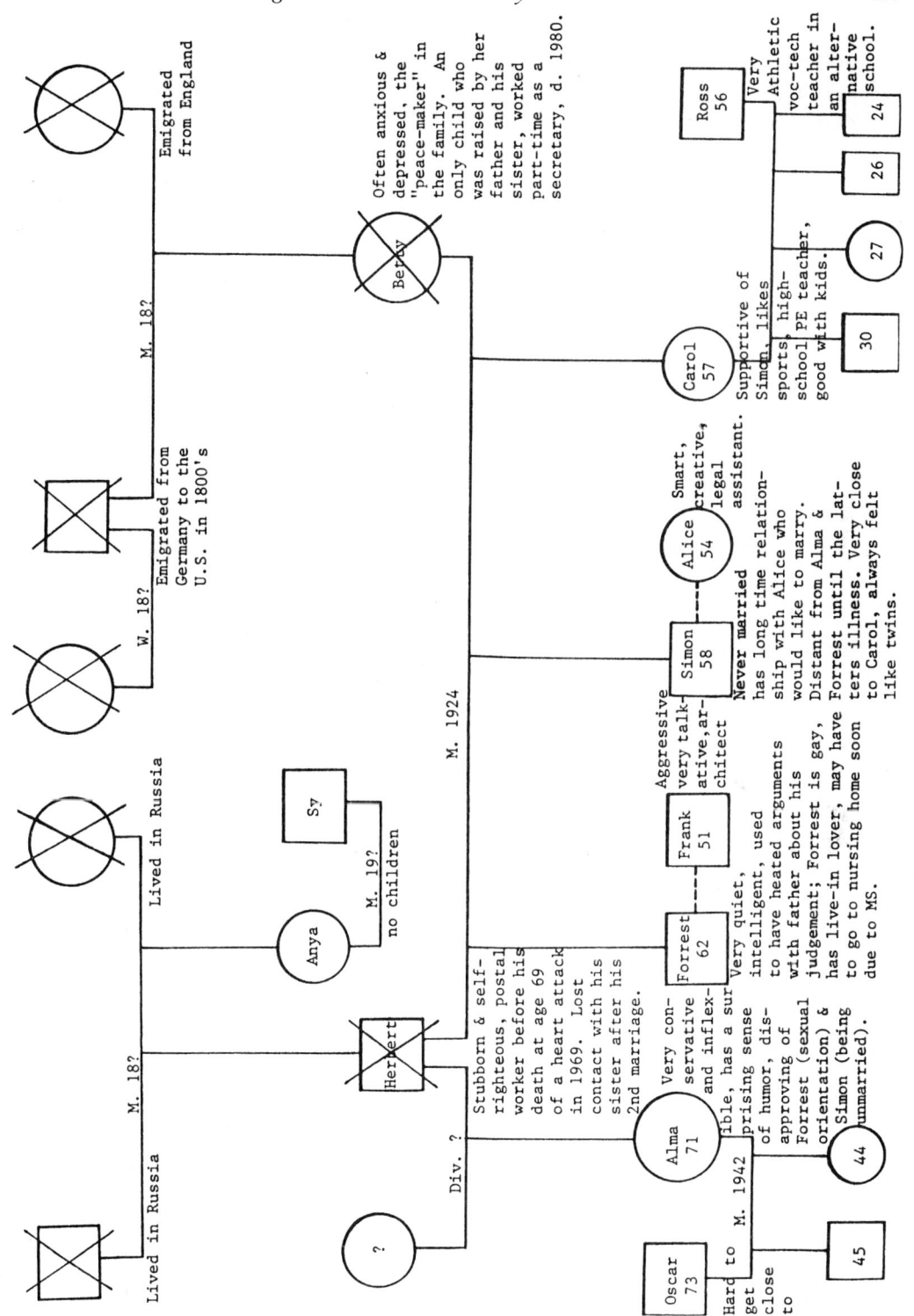

Figure 11.1. Genogram of Simon Walton (1989).

Childhood and Adolescence

Some of Simon's earliest memories of his family life involve his father's anger. Herbert's anger did not seem to be predictable or responsive to anything Simon and his siblings could do at the time. Forrest was frequently the brunt of the father's anger, generally because Herbert was disappointed in something he had done or said. Their mother had a lot of anxieties and was often depressed, which was expressed by the father as, "Your mother is tired again today." At the time, Simon did not connect his father's anger with his mother's being "tired," but now wonders if his parents' behaviors were somehow complementary (Rhodes, 1986). Simon wonders also whether their father's frequent criticisms of Forrest subtly encouraged Simon to not get close to Forrest. One of Simon's coping strategies was to stay out of sight around the house as much as possible. When he was older and had more freedom, he continued this pattern by staying away from home through an "over" involvement in school activities.

Simon described Forrest as the model scapegoat who had perfect timing. He knew how and when to get the most dramatic reactions from their father. He would often ask their father trick questions or senseless riddles to get him upset. Or he would leave chores until the last possible minute before doing them. Herbert's pattern as a critical parent was a corollary for Forrest's pattern of continuous agitation (Rhodes, 1986). Herbert would get home before their mother during the elementary school years. As soon as he would enter the house he would say something like, "Why does this house always look like a pig sty?" Then he would order the children to clean the house and monitor closely what they did. Simon mentioned they were never certain if they understood exactly what he wanted them to do or if they just did not do the work well. Eventually, Herbert would give up, but he was seldom pleased with the outcomes. Forrest called their father "the warden" when he was not around, and after a time, Simon and Carol did too. Although Alma was sometimes there when Herbert got home, his displeasure and anger tended to be directed toward the younger children—Forrest, Simon, and Carol.

Simon and Carol were only eleven months apart in age. They spent a lot of time playing together, so they had a close relationship from an early age. When they were young, they believed they could read one another's minds and that they thought exactly alike. Even when they were older and knew they were not twins, they have continued to feel a strong and intangible bond between them (Bank and Kahn, 1982). In school, they both were above average students, following in the wake of Forrest who was known to be outrageous and disruptive in his behavior. Forrest did average work, but his grades might have been even better if it had not been for his behavior.

Because Alma was much older, she seemed like a second mother to Simon. She was usually very busy studying while she was in high school. Then too, she worked part time during those years and during the period when she attended business school. When her mother and father were divorced, they decided Alma would live with him because her mother "was too young to raise a child alone." Alma was six when her father married Betty, and the latter raised Alma as her natural child. Alma did not have contact with her biological mother after the divorce.

Alma's role in the family depended on her step mother's changing behavior. In looking back, Simon views his mother as a curious mixture of dependence and independence. Apparently when she was depressed she stayed in bed (she was never in treatment for the depression as far as Simon is aware of). Alma helped out around the house more during those periods. Also Betty would talk about her work problems with their father; she had a lot of anxiety about not having good relationships with her co-workers. Simon remembers her asking their father what she should do. Usually, his advice was not to worry about what her co-workers said or did, and to just do her job.

On the other hand, if she really wanted to do something Betty was surprisingly persistent. She did not drive for many years; she used to complain about how restricted she felt as a result. Betty decided to learn how to drive, but driving was extremely difficult for her. She ended up taking the driving test six times before she eventually passed it. Simon was very proud of her at the time. He indicated it was one of the few times as an adolescent he felt he understood either one of his parents. Otherwise, it seemed he was always second guessing them or looking for ulterior motives. For example, when he and Carol were fifteen and sixteen, their parents decided the two of them could go visit their sister Alma in another state for the summer. Simon and Carol were hesitant about going because their parents suggested it and they assumed it would be an awful experience. But it turned out to be good for the two of them. They got to know Alma in a different way (they learned she had a great sense of humor) and Simon was able to be away from home legitimately for weeks.

They went to visit Alma and her family for the next two summers. It was during this period that Carol decided she wanted to become a teacher. As far as she knew, no one in their family on either side had gone to college. Carol was often the mediator in family conflicts by then, so it did not seem unusual for her to want to be different or to take risks. And having decided to become a teacher, she was very persistent in her plan. She sent away for information about different colleges and asked her school counselor for help in completing her applications. The counselor was able to help Carol explore scholarships and other forms of assistance. Their parents were supportive, but they could only help a little financially. Simon was also supportive, often cheering Carol up when she would question whether she should continue to aim for college. His goal, in comparison to Carol's, was to find a job as soon as he finished high school so he could gain his independence.

The Young Adult and Middle Adult Years

During the next few years, Simon's contacts with his family consisted mostly of holiday celebrations except for Carol. He and Carol kept in frequent contact by telephone and occasional letters. Often when they talked for a few minutes they were able to give each other an emotional lift. They seemed to know intuitively when the other was not doing well or needed support. Staying in contact was not easy since Carol was busy in college and later in raising a family while teaching. Simon had several close relationships with women over the years that involved a lot of his time. Also he wanted to get ahead in his employment, so he worked very hard and took several noncredit management courses at the local community college. He was promoted twice to different supervisory positions. Although the company he works for describes his current job as a mid-management position, in actuality he functions as a level II supervisor.

Simon enjoys his work, but he has been frustrated in the limited advancement he has been able to make. Many of the truly mid-management positions in his company are occupied by college educated personnel. His father had a similar experience in his work as a civil servant in the post office. He was forced to take early retirement from his supervisory position after the post office decided to require a college degree for positions at that level. He was very bitter about being passed over and forced to retire.

When he was about forty-eight years old, Simon began going out with Alice with whom he has had his closest relationship (see Figure 11.1). She is the first woman he has taken with him to family celebrations on holidays. Although he knows Alice would like to get married, Simon is not sure he is ready to make that type of commitment. He would like to keep their relationship the way it is currently. Before they died, his parents disapproved of his being single, they wanted him to "grow up" and get married. Alma has always thought he should be married too instead of "wasting his life" in a series of different relationships.

Forrest was in his thirties when he told his parents he was gay. After he left home and moved out of state, his contacts with the family had been very infrequent. Simon knew generally that he had become an addictions counselor after successfully overcoming a drinking problem. Their parents were proud of Forrest for turning his life around, although they thought he was the cause of many of his problems. Apparently, he had made one of his infrequent visits and during the time got into an argument with their father about not being married and settling down. Simon suspects Forrest told them he was gay in anger and as a way of having the last word. The parents told Alma about Forrest's announcement but did not tell the other siblings.

Several months later, Herbert called Forrest to suggest he not visit his parents when Alma was there because she and her husband felt uncomfortable around gays. When Herbert casually shared this conversation with Simon, he seemed surprised that Simon did not know how Alma felt about gays or that Forrest was gay. Although Simon was somewhat shocked, he thought Forrest's way of sharing this information and the related family turmoil were totally in character. He and Forrest have not talked directly about his being gay, but Simon has told him many times that he tries too hard to be provocative. Ironically, Simon thinks he and Forrest do not interfere in each other's lives even though they have been outspoken about their reactions to each other. Generally, their only contacts have been for family celebrations at their parents' home over the years (see Chapter 3 for a discussion on the low end of the sibling solidarity continuum related to maintaining the kinship network).

Forrest has had a long time relationship with Frank who continued to be supportive after Forrest was diagnosed with MS. Alice believes that Forrest has AIDS and is simply saying he has MS to keep the family from knowing the truth. Carol has tried to mediate on Forrest's behalf, but this has not been successful with Simon and Alma who remain distant from

Forrest. Simon wonders if part of the problem is that they have never had a good model of sibling relationships. Their mother was an only child who was raised by her aunt and father after her mother died at an early age. Their aunt was considered somewhat strange in that she claimed to be psychic, so they could never take her seriously as a pseudo grandmother or sister to their grandfather. Their father had long been estranged from his only sister who did not approve of his divorce or the cut-off from Alma's biological mother. Hartman and Laird (1983), Rhodes (1986), and Bowen (1976) have noted this pattern of intergenerational cut-offs and the predictive effects on current family relationships in general. In addition, Freeman (1989) found similarities between the types of sibling relationships parents have and the sibling relationships of their children (see Chapter 2 for a more detailed discussion on this issue).

The Young Elderly Phase

As Forrest's physical condition deteriorated, he began to initiate more contacts with Simon, perhaps as a way to resolve some of the issues confronting them as brothers. Another factor may be the developmental tasks that are confronting Forrest (see Table 1.1 in Chapter 1 regarding the tasks of accepting one's own mortality and struggling with the meaning of one's life experiences). According to Cicirelli (1977), siblings can influence how these tasks are managed and the elderly person's feelings and concerns about life in general. Forrest's physical condition may have led to an earlier than usual attempt to address these developmental tasks of old age **and** a need for additional family support from his sibling network (Cicirelli, 1990; Brubaker, 1990).

Out of guilt about their past differences and concern for Forrest's health, Simon has tried to be responsive to those attempts. But he notes that he is angry too because he believes Forrest has wasted his life and his talents. Like their parents, Simon blames Forrest for most of his problems: "He chose the hard way to do everything". Simon realizes this is not what Forrest needs to hear at this point in his life, so rather than be openly disapproving, he tries hard to be neutral. But he finds it hard to be positive. Forrest has tried to mend his relationship with Alma as well, but Simon thinks his highest priority is for him and Simon to have a close relationship.

Forrest may be confronted with going to a nursing home soon, since the hospital introduced this as a future possibility during his last hospitalization. Simon wonders if Frank will continue to be there for Forrest as things get worse. The situation has made him think more seriously about his relationship with Alice and what his own old age may be like. He thinks his participation in the author's study has helped him to face some hidden thoughts and fears about his family life, especially about his relationship with Forrest. He is not sure what to do about the situation however.

A Family Treatment Approach for Sibling Issues and Developmental Tasks in the Young Elderly

Simon's case study in the previous section has clarified how long term family relationships can affect the feelings and concerns of the elderly as noted by Cicirelli (1990) and Freeman (1984). Such concerns are part of the normative developmental process of aging and should be viewed from that perspective by practitioners in nursing homes, senior citizens housing, church outreach programs for the elderly, hospitals, and visiting nurses associations. When more severe problems arise, additional specialized counseling services may be needed (see Chapter 1 for a discussion about normative and problematic responses to developmental tasks within sibling relationships).

Assessment of Normative and Problematic Aging Issues

Monk (1983) contrasts the process of growth in the elderly with the process during the preceding stages of life. He indicates in the elderly "this growth proceeds through integration rather than expansion and is concerned with the constant imperative to seek out the meaning of life and affirm its value, even in the face of life's impending termination" (p. 130). The assessment, family treatment, and evaluation procedures used by practitioners with the elderly should be focused on this type of growth as the main criterion of effectiveness. These procedures should also be used in an integrative manner. For instance, the ecomap can be used during assessment to conduct a social support analysis as well as to evaluate the effects of treatment. Such procedures are useful whether the work begins and ends with individual sessions or then progresses to joint sessions with siblings and other significant persons.

Freeman (1984) has recommended that one ecomap be completed with the individual based on the current circumstances and that a second retrospective ecomap be completed based on the situation prior to the transition. In Simon's case, Forrest might be referred to the social worker at either the hospital or the visiting nurses association. He might be identified as needing support for handling the recommendation that he will eventually need inhome nursing services or placement in a nursing home. Therefore, the second ecomap could be completed on each brother's social supports prior to the onset of Forrest's illness and the related debilitating changes in his life. Then the before and after ecomaps could be compared for each brother and between the brothers as part of the assessment (Freeman, 1984).

Getting in touch with the series of changes and what they mean in the person's life is often another aspect of the assessment (Goetting, 1986). The practitioner could help Forrest identify his various losses and connect them with the feelings he might be experiencing: including increased vulnerability, fear, anger, sadness and grief, or regrets about things he has done or not done. Making these connections helps with normalizing the process during the assessment and on-going family treatment. If assessment occurs in the presence of a sibling or a significant other such as Frank (see Figure 11.1), the process may increase the others' awareness, and thus, the amount of social support provided to Forrest. The process may also be helpful in identifying how the thoughts or cognitions and beliefs of others in the environment may be affecting the identified client's ability to cope with changes associated with aging (e.g., Simon's possible rational or irrational fears about Forrest's dependency on him).

Practitioners can use attitude checklists focused on the aging and dying process as an additional assessment procedure. These procedures are equally useful during the evaluation of treatment. Such checklists are effective for clarifying the client's and significant others' pre-treatment attitudes/biases/fears about aging, dependency, role flexibility, self-esteem, preferred coping styles, transitions, death education, available social supports, strengths, and concerns (Freeman, 1984; Rhodes, 1983). Again, the discussions about the individual's responses to this type of checklist are as much a part of the assessment as the written responses themselves. In discussing the responses, the individual's distorted thoughts or cognitions, negative self-talk statements, irrational assumptions, and musturbatory language (should's and ought's for others) may be assessed as well as connections between the responses.

Family Treatment Strategies

The assessment process described above should be closely integrated with the recommended family treatment approach involving cognitive behavioral and Rational Emotive components. Such an approach emphasizes that the principal determinant of emotions, motives, and behavior is an individual's thinking. Thinking is socially determined according to these theories, so a focus is extended to social systems such as the sibship, family unit, immediate environment, and experiences in general (Werner, 1986; Jaremko; 1986; Dryden and Ellis, 1986). Thus, this type of family treatment seeks to expand or modify the distorted thinking of the client and significant others "until perception more nearly approximates reality" (Werner, 1986, p. 93). As noted previously, this approach can be provided in sibling therapy or sibling-oriented individual therapy. If the spouse or lover of the identified client is available and the assessment indicates the need, couple therapy may be an appropriate service as well.

In most situations, the focus of family treatment with the elderly should be to facilitate the type of growth described in the previous section. This can be achieved by three principal means during treatment. First, information gathered from the ecomaps and the attitude checklists can be used to educate the person regarding his or her beliefs about his or her stage of development. Education about the series of dramatic changes in all life domains during the aging process is helpful. Providing information about how individuals react to those changes through identifiable stages of loss and grief normalizes this process (Kubler-Ross, 1970; Freeman, 1984). Discussions about previous individual and familial patterns in handling losses may facilitate changing any dysfunctional patterns.

In addition, Maultsby and Gore (1986, p. 172) recommend education about the ABC model of life experiences where the following analysis can be made of any experience or event:

- A = The activating event or experience (what a person notices or perceives to have happened).
- B = The person's beliefs or evaluative thoughts about the event or those perceptions.
- C-1 = The person's emotions that are triggered by his or her beliefs or evaluative thoughts (not the event or perceptions about the event).

C-2 = The person's actions or physical behaviors triggered by beliefs or evaluative thoughts.

The assumption is that external events alone such the loss of physical strength that Forrest has experienced do not cause peoples' emotional or physical reactions (their feelings or behavior). Instead, those reactions are the result of the ideas they have come to believe (Dryden and Ellis, 1986). In family systems language, what individuals have come to believe is influenced by relationships within their sibling networks, families, and other systems (Rhodes, 1986). Thus, in family treatment, clients can use the ABC model of life experiences to expand and modify their cognitions, beliefs, and other aspects that are negatively affecting their ability to cope with the aging process. An example is Forrest's belief that he must develop a closer relationship with Simon. This belief may be a part of the bargaining stage of loss and grief: if he works harder at having a good relationship with Alma and his brother than in the past, his health might improve (Freeman, 1984).

Moreover, clients can be helped to identify when the cognitions and beliefs of family members and others are barriers to their coping. Simon's homophobia is one example along with his assumption that he must approve of Forrest's lifestyle in order to feel positive about him. In that regard, treatment should be focused on helping Forrest to "give up" demands that others must change in order for him to be happy and to use imagery and relaxation to manage stress from those relationships (Werner, 1986). Often in concentrating only on what is within their control to change, clients' stress can be reduced automatically. Ironically, change may occur in the other person (Simon or Alma) because the demand for change has been removed.

A second principal treatment strategy is the use of the life review process. Walsh (1980) has described a family life review technique in which the members reminiscence about their family life history. Similarly, practitioners can assist siblings in a shared life review or reminiscence: "in exploring developmental periods of particular emotional import, evoking crucial memories, responses, and understanding" (Walsh, 1980, p. 207). It may be important for Simon to understand what it was like for Forrest to be gay **and** the "perfect" scapegoat during adolescence (identity and individuation issues). Forrest could learn about the fears underlying Simon's need to hide from their father's anger and Forrest's provocations (within the family and sibling systems) as a young child. The brothers' emotional cut-off from each other during earlier stages may have led to distorted cognitions and frozen snapshots of each other and their current relationship. Walsh (1980) notes that shared reminiscence can facilitate the resolution of cognitive distortions. The process also helps to resolve the developmental tasks of acceptance of each members' life and death and the involvement of significant family members who are central to that resolution.

This life review process can be enhanced by a journal to highlight the major life events and relationships identified during treatment. Journaling helps to concretize the insights and newly developed rational cognitions about those events/relationships over time (Bordon, 1992). The writing can be done between sessions by each client and then reviewed during subsequent sessions. The format of the journal can be completely unstructured or the clients can decide how to structure the entries in their separate journals and what aspects are to be shared insession.

In the case of Forrest and Simon, this process can help Simon to enhance on-going life reviews as he ages and to prevent problems by addressing unfinished issues currently in his relationship with Forrest and their other siblings. When Forrest dies, his journal could be his memorial to Simon and the other siblings if it were made available to them. Journals are useful too for helping clients to identify which aspects of the past can and cannot be changed as part of the resolution process (Walsh, 1980) (See chapter 8 for a discussion about a similar format for journaling about regrets and secondary gains in sibling relationships).

Aspects of the past that can be changed are the focus of the third principal family treatment strategy that can be used with the elderly. Unfinished issues with siblings, parents, spouses, children, and other relatives or friends may be identified through the life review and journaling process. For instance, Forrest may need to resolve his anger toward his deceased parents regarding their homophobia as well as other issues. His unaddressed fears about whether Frank will stay with him through his illness and death is another area for work. Simon's lack of commitment in relationships except with Carol may be yet another unfinished issue revealed by the life review process.

Cognitive behavioral homework assignments involving systemic changes would be useful for these purposes. Thought stopping involves shouting "stop it" to oneself to turn off memories and fears about unpleasant events. This strategy might be useful for helping Forrest to manage his fears that Frank will soon leave him. It could be combined with behavioral rehearsal and role playing for practicing how he might talk to Frank about under what circumstances the latter might stay or leave the relationship. Including Frank in several couple therapy sessions might prove useful in exploring and resolving this and other barriers in their relationship. The use of metaphors could help Simon to develop an alternative view of close relationships. This strategy could allow him to resolve any irrational beliefs and fears that are affecting his relationship with Forrest, Alma, and his girl friend, Alice (see Figure 11.1).

Evaluation of Family Treatment

Evaluation of these family treatment interventions can include an on-going analysis of the current (pre-treatment), retrospective, and post ecomaps for identifying changes in the client's social support networks (Freeman, 1984). Analysis of the pre and post attitude checklists can help practitioners determine the effectiveness of the treatment in changing key attitudes (Levitt and Reid, 1981). For example, it would be important to evaluate whether Simon's and Forrest's attitudes about dependence and social supports from each other had changed and how. Similarly, clients' journals can be used to clarify whether growth has occurred toward greater integration and the pattern of change. Both written and verbal comments about the person's views of his or her life and the meaning identified are important criteria for evaluating whether the treatment has been effective. Comments that reflect this type of growth include the following: "I did the best I could"; "although everything I wanted in life didn't happen, I achieved some important things"; "my brother and I don't agree on everything, but we know where we stand"; "we may never be close siblings, but things are better between us now."

Evaluation of clients' increasing skills in utilizing relaxation exercises for coping with stress is another useful source of feedback. Clients' self-reports about the level of satisfaction in using such exercises are an important corollary in evaluating changes in their skills. Satisfaction can be evaluated informally through verbal feedback or formally through a self-anchored scale with which the client rates numerically his or her level of satisfaction (e.g., 0 = very unsatisfied and 7 = very satisfied) (Bloom, 1982; Freeman and Pennekamp, 1988). These scales allow clients to self-monitor as part of the evaluation process, so their use can enhance client involvement and change negative beliefs about personal power (Jaremko, 1986). This benefit is especially important in family treatment with the elderly who have often loss control in many areas of their lives (Brubaker, 1990; Monk, 1983).

Maultsby and Gore (1986) have identified other self-monitoring tools that can facilitate evaluation with the elderly. Those authors suggest that the following questions can help clients to analyze any event or experience during treatment. Clients can use the questions to monitor their progress in being more rational and in control during and after treatment if follow-up contacts are possible (p. 182).

1. Is my thinking here based on obvious fact?
2. Will my thinking here help me protect my life and health?
3. Will my thinking here best help me achieve my short- and long-term goals?
4. Will my thinking here best help me avoid my most unwanted conflicts with others?
5. Will my thinking here best help me habitually feel the emotions I want to feel?

Conclusion

The quality of the final stage of life discussed in this chapter is influenced by all of the previous developmental stages and family relationships. As noted in Chapter 1, sibling relationships are the most enduring of all relationships over the lifespan. As with other relationships, however, this important support network changes in each stage of development. It provides a final opportunity to reflect on and change life circumstances during the aging process. In one sense, some aspects of the life review process are individually focused (e.g., identity and the acceptance of one's mortality). But in another sense, sibling and other family relationships are the context in which those individual issues develop and must be resolved. Thus, it is difficult to separate the overlap and influence of siblings even in this final stage of life. This fact of influence is true whether the sibling bond is strong or nonexistent and whether siblings are living or dead.

REFERENCES

Bank, S. and Kahn, M.D. (1982). *The sibling bond.* New York: Basic Books.
Bloom, M. and Fischer, J. (1982). *Evaluating practice: Guidelines for the accountable professional.* Englewood Cliffs, NJ: Prentice-Hall.

Bordon, W. (1992). Narrative perspectives in psychosocial intervention following adverse life events. *Social Work, 37,* 135–144.

Bowen, M. (1976). Theory in the practice of psychotherapy. In P.J. Guerin (Ed.), *Family therapy: Theory and practice* (45–59). New York: Gardner Press.

Brubaker, T.H. (1990). An overview of family relationships in later life. In T.H. Brubaker (Ed.), *Family relationships in later life* (13–26). Newbury Park, CA: Sage.

Cicirelli, V.G. (1990). Family support in relation to health problems of the elderly. In T.H. Brubaker (Ed.), *Family relationships in later life* (212–228). Newbury Park, CA: Sage.

Cicirelli, V.G. (1977). Relationships of siblings to the elderly person's feelings and concerns. *Journal of Gerontology, 32,* 322–330.

Dryden, W. and Ellis, A. (1986). Rational-emotive therapy (RET). In W. Dryden and W.L. Golden (Eds.), *Cognitive-behavioral approaches to psychotherapy* (129–168). London, England: Harper and Row.

Estes, C.L. (1985). Austerity and aging in the United States: 1980 and beyond. In M. Bloom (Ed.), *Life span development: Bases for preventive and interventive helping* (377–388). New York: Macmillan.

Freeman, E.M. (1989). Adult children of alcoholics: Study of parental, sibling, and work relationships. Paper presented at the 34th Institute on the Prevention and Treatment of Alcoholism. Pontault-Combault, France: International Council on Alcohol and Addictions.

Freeman, E.M. (1984). Multiple losses in the elderly: An ecological perspective. *Social Casework, 65,* 287–296.

Freeman, E.M. and Pennekamp, M. (1988). The search for patterns: Linking cases and programs. *Social work practice: Toward a child, family, school, community perspective* (164–185). Springfield, IL: Charles C Thomas.

Goetting, A. (1986). The developmental tasks of siblingship over the life cycle. *Journal of Marriage and The Family, 48,* 703–714.

Hartman, A. and Laird, J. (1983). *Family-centered social work practice.* New York: Free Press.

Jaremko, M.E. (1986). Cognitive-behavior modification: The shaping of rule-governed behavior. In W. Dryden and W.L. Golden (Eds.), *Cognitive-behavioral approaches to psychotherapy* (31–60). London, England: Harper and Row.

Kubler-Ross, E. (1970). *On death and dying.* New York: Macmillan.

Levitt, J.L. and Reid, W.J. (1981). Assessment instruments for practice. *Social Work Research and Abstracts, 17,* 13–20.

Maultsby, M.C. and Gore, T.A. (1986). Rational behavior therapy (RBT). In W. Dryden and W.L. Golden (Eds.), *Cognitive-behavioral approaches to psychotherapy* (169–195). London: Harper and Row.

Monk, A. (1983). Social work with the aged: Principles of practice. In F.J. Turner (Ed.), *Differential diagnosis and treatment in social work* (129–144). New York: Free Press.

Moss, S.Z. and Moss, M.S. (1989). The impact of the death of an elderly sibling: Some considerations of a normative loss. *American Behavioral Scientist, 33,* 94–106.

Rhodes, S.L. (1986). Family treatment. In F.J. Turner (Ed.), *Social work treatment: interlocking theoretical approaches* (432–453). New York: Free Press.

Rhodes, S.L. (1983). A developmental approach to the life cycle of the family. In M. Bloom (Ed.), *Life span development: Bases for preventive and interventive helping* 30–39). New York: Macmillan.

Walsh, F. (1980). The family in later life. In E.A. Carter and M. McGoldrick (Eds.), *The family life cycle: A framework for family therapy* (197–220). New York: Gardner.

Werner, H.D. (1986). Cognitive theory. In F.J. Turner (Ed.), *Social work treatment: Interlocking theoretical approaches* (91–130). New York: Free Press.

Epilogue

THE FAMILY TREATMENT PROCESS: WHY EVALUATE?

> Sometimes my sister and I can talk together, but mostly we don't get along with each other at all ... And I don't think our relationship has gotten any better over the years, although I don't have any way of knowing that for sure.
>
> —Ralph

> I appeal to you ... Measure, evaluate, estimate, appraise your results, in some form, in any terms that rest on something beyond faith, assertion, and illustrative case.
>
> —Dr. Richard Cabot

A key assumption of this book is that evaluation and family treatment should be integrated to improve the quality of practice in this area. Ralph, a participant in the author's study of sibling relationships, and Dr. Richard Cabot (1931) have approached the question of an integrated evaluation process from two important perspectives. As a family member, Ralph questions how he can evaluate whether his relationship with his sister has really changed. Dr. Cabot strongly suggests that evaluation of practice is a critical task for helping professionals, and that it should be based on some type of meaningful and objective criteria to be useful.

From both of these perspectives, those of family members and helping professionals, evaluation is a valuable process. The benefits of evaluation have been documented by many researchers, ranging from greater client involvement to increased professional accountability to enhanced practice effectiveness (Tripodi and Epstein, 1980; McFall, 1977; Bloom and Fischer, 1982; Freeman, in press). If this assumption about the benefits of evaluation to general practice is accurate, the process may be even more beneficial to the family treatment field. What aspects of family treatment make evaluation valuable for quality practice in this field?

Evaluation of Family Treatment

Evaluation and the Complex Social Environment

For a number of obvious reasons, family treatment may be more complex than some of the other forms of treatment such as individual counseling. Rhodes (1986) notes that the goal of family treatment is to influence "the functioning of the family as a group as well as each individual family member" (p. 432–433). Furthermore, when the sibling subsystem is included in the list of other subsystems that must be considered (e.g., the marital, parental, and extended family subsystems), another layer of complexity is added to this multi-level assessment and treatment process. And as family treatment is acknowledged to be complex, evaluation of this form of treatment must be equally complex. Consider the evaluation issues embedded in the following practice situations which reflect the increasingly complex social environment of families:

- An HIV positive mother attempts to sell her newborn infant in a bar to obtain money for drugs. When she is arrested, a background check indicates she is a prostitute and an IV drug user. Her brother agrees to have the child placed in his home by protective services. The court requires the sister to have substance abuse treatment after a jail term and during her probation. The brother has many questions for the substance abuse family counselor about whether he can do the caretaking for his sister and how he will know if her many needs are being met (Evaluation of mandated substance abuse counseling and a new type of young adult sibling caretaking unit, with the added stress of a sibling with the AIDS virus or ARC [AIDS-related complex] and the many consequences).
- A man and his family lose their home due to an employment lay-off and the economic downturn. They move into public housing with his brother's family. When the Housing Authority discovers they have moved in, the manager threatens to evict the brother's family because this type of move-in is against policy. The brothers request help from an emergency assistance housing agency in the community, indicating that the stress of the threatened eviction of both families has caused conflicts between them (Evaluation of community risk and protective factors—including the adequacy of housing—and the impact of those factors on a sibling support network's collaboration and problem-solving process).
- A couple with infertility problems goes to a family service agency for marital counseling. They are having conflicts about whether they should allow the wife's sister to become a surrogate parent for them. The husband has concerns about how such a plan could affect their relationship with his wife's sister and the child. He feels the two sisters are too close already and that his sister-in-law might attempt to interfere in how the couple raises the child. The couple indicates that since they probably cannot agree on this issue, counseling with

the agency's psychologist may not work for them (Evaluation of the clients' progress through the family life cycle stage of a couple having a first child with added boundary issues related to sibling solidarity and the new technology of surrogate parenting. Also evaluation of family prevention strategies for helping the couple anticipate and address future relationship barriers between them and the sister if they decide to have a surrogate parent).

- A high school student who participates in a peer counseling program tells the school social worker who serves as the program consultant that she has concerns about a younger brother. The brother has a developmental disability and has just entered middle school where the educational and social demands are very different. His sister is concerned that the requirements may be too difficult for him because his elementary school did not have a transition program. She indicates she will know that her brother has made the transition when she is no longer worried about him (Evaluation of changes in intangible functions of the sibling subsystem such as a shift from a quasi-parental to a quasi-therapeutic sibling role. Also evaluation of how the risk and protective factors in the school environment change as a result of treatment related to the natural transition of moving from elementary to middle school).

- The four adult children of an elderly man in the hospital have been asked to decide whether they want to have their father resuscitated if he stops breathing. The father has inoperable cancer and is on a feeding tube. The brothers and sisters ask the hospital chaplain and social worker for advice in making their decision. One sister does not believe they should even consider a "no code" order, because they do not know if their father has accepted his impending death. She has had conflicts with her father and siblings in the past that have not been resolved (Evaluation of changes in the sibling caretaking unit's ability to balance its efforts in addressing current versus unresolved issues as needed during the collaborative process. Also evaluation of how supportive aspects of the hospital environment {technology for quality of life versus survival} are used by the sibship to collaborate).

These examples illustrate a number of evaluation issues that are influenced by the present complex social environment. For instance, the situation involving the HIV positive mother indicates the difficulties practitioners may have in identifying the needs of siblings and other relatives who become caretakers for individuals with the virus. Early identification is important because it offers the opportunity for practitioners to help caretakers assess and evaluate the use of their resources based on priority needs.

However, many hospitals, substance abuse treatment programs, and mental health centers that serve clients with AIDS or ARC do not have staff especially trained in family treatment and evaluation. This gap can be a barrier in providing effective family treatment and meaningful evaluations of the work. For example, the brother in that situation could easily become overwhelmed without some practical, user-friendly methods for evaluating his efforts in addressing the competing needs of his family, his sister, and the sister's child. Those methods would need to be useful to him in the future, during treatment or after it ends, as the combination of needs change.

Evaluation Principles and Guidelines

These case examples of current family treatment situations involve a number of common patterns and issues related to evaluation. These commonalities and others noted throughout the chapters of this book reflect the need for a set of generalizable evaluation principles. Such principles should be consistent with the complexities of the present social environment and the nature of the family treatment process. Of necessity, these principles are interrelated, and they help in the process of integrating evaluation with treatment. In this manner, evaluation is not simply an addendum to family treatment, but is an important part of the integrated whole. The principles are also related to Cabot's (1931) emphasis on objective criteria and the need to make the evaluation meaningful to family members in terms of the changes they desire.

1. To achieve maximum integration of evaluation and family treatment, utilize a combination of structured and unstructured assessment procedures. Structured procedures are useful as the foundation for treatment and as pre/post measures of important characteristics of the sibling subsystem and related issues (Chapters 5 through 11).
2. The use of cognitive maps and other graphic methods facilitates evaluation because they help to monitor visually changes in subsystems (e.g., sibships) that are the focus of treatment. The environmental and other aspects revealed by these maps may be affecting current or unresolved sibling or parent-child issues (see Chapters 5, 7, 9, and 10, for example).
3. The benefits of cognitive maps can be enhanced if some objective criteria can be developed to guide a formal analysis of the contents of the maps. The ecomap analysis of the sibling caretaking unit in Chapter 10 is one example.
4. The selected evaluation should help to focus on the diversity within the sibling subsystem, family unit, or extended family network, for example, focus on ethnic or personal identity exer-

cises for evaluating changes in those developmental areas with children and how age differences affect responses in children (see Chapter 5).
5. Evaluation of environmental risk and protective factors should be completed during the assessment, while family treatment is occurring, and at the point of termination through the use of community assessment procedures, a life events scale, or a work-related assessment inventory. The evaluation should clarify how family members may be influenced by and cope with the social context differently in comparison to each other, how each member copes over time, and how the environment changes. The evaluation may also clarify when prevention is possible and necessary (Chapters 7 and 9).
6. Important changes related to the family's culture and ethnicity can be monitored through the use of a cultural ecomap or values clarification grid. These tools help to evaluate how sibling acculturation coalitions and generational cultural patterns change as needed in response to family treatment (Note Chapters 5 and 7).
7. Evaluation of specialized psychoeducational programs should be consistent with the goals of such programs, including loss and grief, sexual abuse, and post traumatic stress disorder (PTSD). For instance, evaluation of psychoeducation for loss and grief in family treatment should focus on the pattern of movement through the stages of loss and grief and how the progress of different members of the sibship or family unit affects the others (Chapters 6, 7, and 11).
8. Time-oriented evaluation methods are useful in documenting for siblings and other family members changes in their relationships over time because they identify small and incremental changes in one part of the subsystem/system that can trigger more dramatic changes in another part (See the discussion on the use of logs, diaries, covenants, and cognitive maps in Chapters 6, 7, 9, and 11).
9. Changes in feelings and affect are important aspects to evaluate in family treatment based on their importance to how members of the sibling subsystem relate to each other over time. These intangible changes should be monitored through the use of more objective measures such as self-anchored scales, attitude checklists, and scaling procedures described in Chapters 6, 10, and 11).

Evaluation and the Life Span Perspective

The principles discussed in the previous section provide guidelines that are generalizable to a broad range of family treatment situations. This book was designed to clarify the process of family treatment in regard to sibling relationships across the life span. Thus, evaluation must be viewed from this perspective as well. This means the procedures for evaluating family treatment should be sensitive to the lifespan developmental tasks and themes of siblings that have been identified by many researchers (Mosatche, Brody, Noberini, 1983; Goetting, 1986; Freeman, 1989; Cicirelli, 1985). Table 12.1 provides an example of how evaluation is linked to those developmental themes and tasks at each of the life stages. For example, identity is a primary task during the middle childhood period, so the use of identity and self-esteem exercises for evaluating changes in these areas is very relevant.

Table 12.1. Evaluation and the Life Span Perspective.

Age Range	Developmental Tasks	Evaluation Methods
Middle Childhood (4–7 years)	Identity	Pre/post sibship identity exercises
Latency (8–12 years)	Individuation	Comparison scaling by siblings
Adolescence (13–19 years)	Value consolidation	Value clarification grid for siblings
Young adulthood (20–25 years)	Establish/maintain a separate household	Pre/post problem-solving exercises
Adulthood (26–39 years)	Consolidate lifestyle choices	Work-related family assessment inventory
Midlife (40–55 years)	Generativity	Ecomap of sibling caretaking unit
Old age (56 and above)	Life review/resolution	Journal on shared sibling life review

Conclusion

Helping professionals should work toward integrating evaluation and family treatment as much as possible to enhance the quality of their practice. The systems perspective that is evident throughout this book provides a useful framework for an ecologically-based evaluation process. For this reason, attention to the complex social context as part of treatment and evaluation is extremely important. The sibling and family examples in this chapter support the need for family treatment and evaluation to be sufficiently broad to address important aspects of the environment. Those aspects are strongly influencing the natural history and developmental tasks of sibling relationships currently. For example, the substance abuse and AIDS crises indicate that the use of sibling caretaking units and the developmental task of generativity may occur earlier in the natural history and life cycle. As the focus of family treatment is modified to consider these emerging needs, so must evaluation shift to accommodate these important changes.

REFERENCES

Bloom, M. and Fischer, J. (1982). *Evaluating practice: Guidelines for the accountable professional.* Englewood Cliffs, NJ: Prentice-Hall.

Cabot, R.C. (1931). Treatment in social casework and the need of criteria and of tests of its success or failure. *Proceedings of the National Conference of Social Work.*

Cicirelli, V.G. (1985). Sibling relationships throughout the life cycle. In L. L'Abate (Ed.), *The handbook of psychology and therapy* (177–214). Homewood, IL: Dorsey.

Freeman, E.M. (In press). Single system research in family-focused alcohol treatment: A strategy of empowerment. In E.M. Freeman (Ed.), *Substance abuse treatment: A family systems perspective.* Newbury Park, CA: Sage.

Freeman, E.M. (1989). Adult children of alcoholics: Study of parental, sibling, and work relationships. Paper presented at the 34th Institute on the Prevention and Treatment of Alcoholism. Pontault-Combault, France: International Council on Alcohol and Addictions.

Goetting, A. (1986). The developmental tasks of siblingship over the life cycle. *Journal of Marriage and The Family, 48,* 703–714.

McFall, R.M. (1977). Parameters of self-monitoring. In R.B. Stuart (Ed.), *Behavioral self-management: Strategies, techniques, and outcomes* (196–214). New York: Brunner/Mazel.

Mosatche, H., Brady, E., and Noberini, M.R. (1983). A retrospective lifespan study of the closest sibling relationship. *The Journal of Psychology, 113,* 327–243.

Rhodes, S.L. (1986). Family treatment. In F.J. Turner (Ed.), *Social work treatment: Interlocking theoretical approaches* (432–453). New York: Free Press.

Tripodi, T. and Epstein, I. (1980). The use of client self-monitoring. *Research techniques for clinical social workers* (121–133). New York: Columbia University Press.

AUTHOR INDEX

A

Abend, S., 12, 30, 64
Abramovitch, R., 12, 104
Ackerman, R.J., 179
Adler, A., 76
Alexander, J.F., 73, 77, 93, 138
Allan, G., 36, 55, 66, 163
Allen, J.A., 85
Allen-Meares, P., 92
Anderson, D., 86
Anspach, D.F., 53, 54
Anthony, E.J., 6, 8, 26, 27, 29, 41, 43, 77, 119, 124
Arbuthnot, J., 151
Atkinson, D., 110
Attneave, C.L., 114
Auslander, G.K., 213

B

Baker, B.L., 11
Balk, D.E., 24, 144
Ball, E.S., 53
Bank, S., 3, 4, 12, 15, 21, 31, 36, 43, 53, 67, 73, 74, 75, 76, 77, 79, 83, 86, 110, 123, 128, 175, 221, 225
Banks, L., 144
Barker, G., 146
Beigel, A., 146
Bendor, S.J., 80
Bengston, V.L., 50
Bennett, J.C., 73
Berkovic, S., 11
Berlin, S.B., 172, 176
Berman, J.S., 171
Berren, M.R., 146
Berry, J., 102, 113
Betsa, N., 79

Biegel, D.E., 213
Blacher, J., 11
Black, C., 25, 184, 192
Black, G.S., 154, 195
Bloom, M., 6, 92, 133, 153, 176, 194, 217, 234, 239
Blugerman, M., 67, 175, 192, 194, 196
Boomhower-Kresser, S., 87, 125, 127, 128, 130, 131
Bordon, W., 233
Bossard, J.H.S., 53
Botvin, G.J., 154
Bowen, M., 8, 74, 76, 120, 131, 163, 164, 192, 196, 228
Bowlby, J., 22, 23, 24, 122
Bowser, B.P., 148
Boyer, C.B., 154
Bracht, N., 154
Brady, E., 4, 6, 8, 9, 31, 50, 51, 53, 54, 56, 57, 58, 59, 60, 138, 201, 209, 210, 212, 215, 244
Brett, K.M., 24
Briggs, K., 115
Brody, G.H., 80
Brown, J., 127
Brown, R.A., 86
Brubaker, T.H., 228, 235
Bryant, B., 30
Bueker, J., 179
Bultena, G.L., 50
Burger, W., 144
Buriel, R., 141, 143
Burke, M., 80
Byng-Hall, J., 161

C

Cabot, R.C., 239, 242
Caetano, R., 144

Calvino, I., 115
Calzada, S., 143
Campbell, S., 56, 57, 59
Cantwell, D.P., 74, 76
Caplan, M.Z., 154
Caplow, T., 76, 161
Carmen, E., 147
Carter, E.A., 170
Catalano, R.F., Jr., 3, 143, 148, 153, 154
Chang, C., 137
Chestang, L., 102
Cicirelli, V.G., 4, 9, 51, 53, 54, 56, 57, 110, 163, 201, 228, 229, 244
Clark, M.L., 93
Comer, J.P., 154
Compher, J.V., 4
Corrales, R., 179
Corter, C., 12, 104
Coward, R.T., 50
Cowen, E.L., 8, 26, 119
Cox, M., 209
Cox, R., 209
Crockenberg, S., 30
Cunningham, C.E., 79, 93
Cunningham, L.J., 93
Curtis, K.A., 148
Cutler, N.E., 50
Cutler, P., 78
Cutter, C.G., 194
Cutter, H.S.G., 194

D

Daie, N., 125
Daniels, D., 29
Daniels, S., 148, 154
Datan, N., 146
Davis, L.V., 6
deJong, A.R., 128
Delany, P., 173
DiClemente, R.J., 154
Doherty, M.B., 162
Dohrenwen, B.P., 146
Dohrenwen, B.S., 146
Dorfman, L.T., 49, 211
Dryden, W., 231, 232
Dunn, J., 4, 11, 28, 31, 36, 80, 92, 101, 103–104, 109, 110, 113, 174, 203
Dyer, L., 24

E

Edelman, M., 143
Edward, J., 8
Eleff, M., 125
Ellis, A., 231, 232
Epstein, I., 239
Erikson, E.H., 23
Estes, C.L., 221
Eth, S., 144, 147

F

Faunce, E.E., 3, 75
Feldman, G.C., 4
Feldman-Rotman, S., 56, 57, 59
Felsman, J.K., J.K.
Fernandez, M., 137
Fernandez, T., 137
Finkelhor, D., 25, 119, 120
Fisch, R., 66, 114, 130, 131
Fischer, J., 92, 133, 153, 176, 194, 217, 234, 239
Fishbein, H.D., 12
Flach, F., 26
Flanzer, J.P., 173
Fox, J.R., 138
Freeman, E.M., 4, 7, 8, 11, 12, 24, 25, 30, 31, 37, 38, 43, 47, 68, 73, 81, 83, 86, 87, 89, 91, 92, 93, 101, 102, 109, 110, 111–112, 115, 129, 131, 137, 147, 150, 152, 153, 163, 170, 176–177, 179, 186–187, 192, 193, 194, 206, 215, 216, 217, 221, 228, 229, 230, 231, 232, 234, 239, 244
Frey-Angel, J., 120, 124, 127, 128, 129, 130, 131, 132, 133, 169
Friedrich, W.N., 11

G

Gallimore, R., 104
Gambrill, E., 152
Garrison, C., 6
Geiser, R.L., 128
Gelles, R., 120
Germain, C.B., 6, 209, 210
Gerson, R., 86
Ginsberg, L.H., 146
Giordano, J., 114
Glynn, T.J., 75

Goetting, A., 4, 9, 12, 15, 25, 47, 50, 53, 54, 59, 230, 244
Golan, N., 210, 212
Goldenberg, H., 6
Goldenberg, I., 6
Gordon, D.A., 151
Gordon, J.U., 115
Gore, T.A., 231, 235
Goudy, W.J., 50
Grajek, S., 9, 28, 29
Grater, H., 28, 30
Green, A., 128, 162
Greenbaum, L., 115
Greenberg, M.T., 11
Greenfield, G., 12, 64, 66
Greenwald, E., 125
Gurak, D.T., 148

H

Hahn, L., 87, 137, 144
Hamlin, E.R., 73, 74, 78, 91, 182
Hardy-Fanta, C., 153
Harris, O., 75, 83, 85, 182
Hartman, A., 6, 67, 85, 86, 88, 89, 90, 112, 114, 153, 170, 175, 210, 213, 214, 215, 228
Hawkins, J.D., 3, 143, 148, 153, 154
Heer, D.M., 29
Hegar, R.L., 24
Henderson, R.W., 148
Hepworth, D., 6
Hetherington, E.M., 209
Hill, R., 102
Hogan, N.S., 144
Holmes, I., 115
Hotaling, G., 120
Huberty, C.E., 80, 81, 82, 86, 89, 92, 185, 214
Huberty, D.J., 80, 81, 82, 86, 89, 92, 185, 214
Hundermar, D., 28, 36, 37, 62, 123, 182, 183, 188

I

Ihinger-Tallman, M., 50
Itzkowitz, J.S., 79, 80

J

Janzen, C., 75, 83, 85, 182
Jaremko, M.E., 231, 234
Jones, J.W., 87
Juarez, R., 151

K

Kahn, M., 3, 4, 12, 15, 21, 31, 36, 43, 53, 67, 73, 74, 75, 76, 77, 79, 83, 86, 110, 123, 128, 175, 221, 225
Karpel, M.A., 88, 161
Keith, P.M., 50
Kendrick, C., 11, 104, 110
Kim, U., 102, 113
Kivett, V.R., 49, 50, 211
Klein, N.C., 73, 77, 93, 138
Koch-Hattem, A., 80
Koegel, R.L., 79
Kritsberg, W., 25, 184, 185–186
Krout, J.A., 47
Kubler-Ross, E., 231
Kurtines, W.M., 137, 151

L

Laird, J., 6, 67, 85, 86, 88, 89, 90, 114, 116, 153, 170, 175, 213, 214, 215, 228
Lamb, M.E., 49, 51, 201
Landau, D., 152
Landesman, T., 87
Lane, B.A., 92
Lantz, J.E., 172
Larson, M., 6
Lerner, R., 193
Lee, G.R., 50
Leigh, G.K., 47, 50, 202
Leitenberg, H., 125
Levitt, J.L., 234
Lewis, K.G., 80, 81, 86, 89, 92, 183
Leventhal, G., 66
Levy, R., 153
Levy, S., 79, 80
Lieberman, B.L., 209
Light, P., 104
Lindsey, J.D., 11
Litwin, H., 213
Liu, W.T., 137

Lochner, B.T., 102, 110, 112
Long, J.M., 142
Logan, S.L., 86, 102, 111–112, 163, 176–177

M

Mangen, D.J., 50
Manns, W., 102, 111, 112, 115
Marquis, R.E., 56, 57, 59
Marshall, V.W., 50
Martin, E.P., 114
Martin, J.M., 114
Martin, R.R., 109
Maultsby, M.C., 231, 235
Mayer, A., 127, 128
McCollum, E.E., 64, 66, 67
McCullough, P., 209, 210, 212, 213, 215
McFall, R.M., 239
McGlynn, F., 152
McGoldrick, M., 86, 114, 170
McKeever, P., 3, 4
McMahon-Herrera, E., 153
McRoy, R.G., 86, 101, 102, 111–112, 137, 147, 152, 163, 176–177
McShane, D., 137
Mealiea, W., 152
Mendelberg, H., 148
Mertens, C.E., 49, 211
Milgram, J.I., 47, 50, 54, 161
Miller, H., 77
Miller, J.Y., 3
Miller, N.B., 74, 76, 77
Miller, P.D., 217
Miller, R.C., 171
Mills, T., 147
Minde, T., 102, 113
Minuchin, S., 4, 31, 74, 77
Mitchell, M.A., 148, 154
Mok, D., 102, 113
Monk, A., 229, 235
Morales, E.S., 154
Mordock, J.B., 77
Morton, G., 110
Moriarty, A.E., 26, 27
Mosatche, H., 4, 6, 8, 9, 31, 50, 51, 53, 54, 56, 57, 58, 59, 60, 138, 201, 209, 210, 212, 215, 244
Moss, M.S., 221
Moss, S.Z., 221

Munn, P., 80, 92
Murphy, L.B., 26, 27
Murphy, R., 102, 110, 112

N

Nelson, J.C., 6, 145
Noberini, M.R., 4, 6, 8, 9, 31, 50, 51, 53, 54, 56, 57, 58, 59, 60, 138, 201, 209, 210, 212, 215, 244
Nulman, E., 3, 96

O

O'Neill, R.E., 79
Ornic, K., 11

P

Padilla, A., 144
Palazzoli, M.S., 78, 178
Palmer, N., 11, 12, 30, 31
Pape, P.A., 179, 192, 193, 194, 195, 196
Papp, P., 130, 132, 172, 214
Parsons, B.V., 73, 77, 93, 138
Patterson, G., 77
Patton, M.Q., 92, 155
Pearce, J.K., 114
Pearlin, L., 6
Perez-Vidal, A., 151
Perlin, M., 28, 30
Pennekamp, M., 25, 43, 91, 92, 93, 111, 150, 153, 234
Pepler, D., 12, 104
Pfouts, J.H., 77
Phinney, J.S., 102, 110, 112, 113
Piaget, J., 23
Pilat, J.M., 87, 96, 125, 127, 128, 129, 131
Plomin, R., 29
Pollak, O., 28, 36, 37, 62, 123, 182, 183, 188
Pollock, G.H., 144
Powell, B., 29
Powell, T.H., 79, 80
Powers, E.A., 50
Pratt, T.C., 77
Pulakos, J., 28
Pynoos, R.S., 144, 147

R

Ranieri, R.F., 77
Rankin, R.J., 148
Reicker, P.P., 147
Reid, W.J., 145, 197, 234
Riskin, J.M., 3, 75
Rhodes, S.L., 6, 23, 43, 85–86, 224, 228, 232, 240
Roberto, K.A., 211
Rodriguez, O., 143, 144
Rogers, M.F., 148
Rose, S.D., 6
Rosen, W., 53
Rosenberg, B.G., 56
Rosenberg, E., 78, 79, 92
Rosenberg, G.S., 53, 54
Rosenthal, P.A., 162
Ross, H.G., 47, 50, 54, 161
Rotheram, M.J., 113
Ro-Trock, L., 179
Rule, S., 79, 80
Ruskin, N., 8

S

Salzberg, C.L., 79, 80
Santiesteban, D., 151
Scarr, S., 9, 28, 29
Schacter, F.F., 30, 56, 57, 59, 80
Schibuk, M., 80
Schreibman, L., 79
Schumacher, J.D., 144
Scott, J.P., 50, 54, 211
Shore, E., 56, 57, 59
Shorkey, C.T., 53
Simon, B.K., 91
Smith, B., 179
Spradley, J., 32, 33
Steelman, L.C., 29
Steinglass, P., 192
Steinmetz, S.K., 162
Stewart, D.A., 11
Stone, G., 116
Stone, R.K., 30, 80
Stoneman, Z., 80
Strauss, R., 120
Stream, H.S., 22, 23
Strobino, J., 78

Sue, D., 110
Suggs, P.K., 50, 211
Sutton-Smith, B., 56, 201
Szapocznik, J., 137, 151

T

Taylor, S.E., 8, 26–27, 119
Terrell, P., 91
Timberlake, E.M., 73, 74, 78, 91, 182
Tolman, R., 6
Tracy, E.M., 86, 191, 195
Tripodi, T., 239
Turrini, P., 8

V

Vaillant, G.E., 8
Valencia, R.R., 148
Vasquez, R., 143
Videka-Sherman, L., 197
Vigil, J.D., 142

W

Walsh, F., 232–233
Wasserman, S., 209
Watzlawick, P., 66, 114, 130, 131
Weakland, J.H., 66, 114, 130, 131
Weatherley, D., 12, 64, 66
Weber, J., 6
Wegscheider, S., 25, 179, 183, 185, 195
Weisner, T.S., 104
Weissberg, R.P., 154
Werner, H.D., 131, 171, 231, 232
West, C., 87, 137, 144
Whitfield, C.L., 193
Whittaker, J., 86, 191, 195
Williams, W.W., 148
Wilson, J., 11
Wilztum, E., 125
Work, W.C., 8

Y

Yu, E.S.H., 137

Z

Zayas, L.H., 143
Zinker, J., 194

SUBJECT INDEX

A

Adolescence, case study examples and issues related to, 126–127, 142–145, 164–167, 180–184, 203–206, 224–226
Adult children of alcoholics (ACOAs), 179–199
Adulthood phase, case study examples and sibling issues related to, 184–185, 207–209, 226–228
Advocacy (*see* Systems advocacy)
African-Americans (*see* Ethnicity)
AIDS, family treatment and evaluation issues related to, 240–242
Anger management, assessment of and treatment for, 169–173
Art work, as examples of evaluation tools, 116
Assessment, ACOA issues in terms of, 185–191; appropriate tools for, 86–87, 146, 149, 189–190, 210–213; collaboration within the sibling caretaking unit, 210–213; culturally-oriented types of, 111–113, 146; issues of control and anger, related to, 169–171; overview of process with siblings, 86–87; sibling caretaking unit related to, 229–230; sibling incest issues related to, 127–128; violence, consequences of, 146–151
Attachment theory, related to children in general, 22; related to siblings, 22–23; applied to stressful family conditions, 24, 122

B

Boundaries (*see* Family system boundaries)

C

Childhood phase (*see* Early or late childhood)

Child sexual abuse, involving sibling perpetrators, 119–135; sibling subsystem healing process in regard to, 87–89
Children of Alcoholics Screening Test (CAST), overview of use with siblings, 87
Cognitive-Behavioral theory (*see* Family treatment)
Communication family theory (*see* Family treatment)
Community development, related to sibling and family therapy, 148–151, 153–154
Coping patterns, maladaptive generalizations of, 24
Crisis theory, applied to sibling subsystems, 6
Cultural ecomap, guidelines for use with siblings, 87
Culture (*see* Ethnicity)
Culture-specific treatment, applied to family network therapy, 110–116; in terms of sibling and family therapy, 145–154

D

Developmental tasks, related to adulthood, 50–54, 59–62; resources for addressing, x
Developmental themes, effects on sibling activities in childhood, 39–41; related to adulthood, 50–54, 59–62
Developmental theory, applied to sibling subsystems, 6, 23
Diagnostic and Statistical Manual III, Revised (DSM III-R), PTSD, related to, 147
Differentiation, level of, defined, 8; sibling subsystem, related to, 12, 131–132
Diversity, within the sibling subsystem, 11–12

E

Early childhood, case study examples and sibling issues related to, 105–106, 122–124, 138–142, 164–167, 180–184, 203–206, 224–226

Ecological perspective, applied to sibling subsystems, 6

Ecomap, applied to cultural issues, 112–113; as an example of an evaluation tool, 115–116, 210–213, 229–230; overview of use with siblings, 86

Educator role, related to multidisciplinary work on sibling issues, 93

Ethnicity, developmental themes related to, 53; expansion of family treatment in consideration of, 83–85; family and sibling roles related to, 38–39; identity development related to, 102–104; sibling acculturation issues in African-Americans, 101–117, in Hispanics, 137–157; issues of bi-culturality in terms of, 112–113; tools for assessment of, 87, 111–113, 148–151

Ethnographic research, definition of, 32; efficacy of, 32–33; examples of, 32–42, 57–66

Evaluation, in regard to sibling and family network therapy, 115–116; in terms of sibling therapy, 133–134, 153, 155, 234–235; in terms of sibling groups, 176–177, 192–197; life span perspective related to, 244; principles and guidelines for, 242–243; related to intergenerational sibling therapy, 216–218; rationale for and issues related to, 239–245

F

Family culture, effects on sibling roles, 38–39
Family cut-offs, treatment related to, 175
Family dysruptions, definition of, 8; examples of, 8, 25
Family issues, definition of, 8
Family relationships, definition of, 6
Family roles, definition of, 7; where unit alcoholism exists, 25; related to birth order, 28–29

Family structure, definition of, 6
Family system boundaries, definition of, 6
Family systems theory, part of conceptual framework related to sibling subsystems, 6
Family therapy, common framework for treatment, xi; definition of, 85–86; historical summary of, 75–82
Family treatment, aspect of family network therapy, 113–116; cultural diversity, related to, 83–85; general guidelines for, 87–90; modalities useful for, 83–86; rationale for, 82–83; theories related to, cognitive-behavioral, 129–132, 171–173, 231–234; communication, 6, 145–155; problem-solving, 113–115; Gestalt therapy, 192–197; intergenerational, 192–197, 213–216; Rational Emotive Therapy, 231–234; strategic, 129–132; task centered, 145–155; theoretical framework, overview of, 83–86
Fictive kin, definition of, 84–85

G

Gender, effects on siblings' mutual aid, 49; effects on male identity, 139–141
Genogram, as an example of an evaluation tool, 115–116; examples of, 107, 121, 140, 165, 181, 204, 223; overview of use with siblings, 86
Gestalt therapy (*see* Family treatment)

H

Hispanics (*see* Ethnicity)
Homophobia (*see* Sexual preference)

I

Identity, ethnic and racial acculturation outcomes associated with, 102–103; overview of ethnic and racial aspects of, 101–103; sibling and familial influences on, 103–105
Individuation (*see* Differentiation)
Intergenerational family systems theory (*see* Family treatment)

Subject Index

L

Late childhood, case study examples and sibling issues related to, 124–125, 138–142, 180–184, 203–206, 224–226
Latency period, case study examples and sibling issues related to, 125
Life history grid, overview of use with siblings, 86
Life review, shared process with siblings, 228–235
Life span perspective, related to sibling issues and treatment, 13–14; role of siblings related to, 3–4

M

Medical model, limitations of, xi; underlying the crisis paradigm, 24
Middle childhood, case study examples and sibling issues related to, 106–110, 124–125

O

Old age, 228–230

P

Parentified children (*see* Substitute parental roles)
Post-traumatic stress disorder (PTSD), assessment and treatment of, 147–155
Premature role transitions, 24
Prevention, aspect of family treatment, 42–43; aspect of treatment with adult siblings, 67–68; professional roles related to, 92–93; related to family network therapy, 113–116
Practitioner roles, leadership activities related to, 90–93
Problem-solving family theory (*see* Family treatment)
Protective factors, benefits of, 3

R

Race (*see* Ethnicity)
Rational Emotive Therapy (*see* Family treatment)
Reframing, as an opportunity for growth, 11
Research-practitioner role, activities related to, 92–93
Resiliency, 26–28; applied to system/subsystem culture, 41–42; common characteristics of, 26–27, 119; definition of, 8; historical background of, 26; literature, focused on, 21; types of, 7, 27–28; prevention, related to, 43
Resources, informal ones related to families, 7–8; formal environmental sources, 8
Risk factors, value in use of, 3; examples of, 149–151
Role theory, applied to sibling subsystems, 6

S

Self-help activities, x; related to treatment of adult siblings, 68
Separation from family of origin, assessment and treatment of, 173–175
Sexual preference, expansion of family treatment in consideration of, 83–84, 221–237; sibling supports related to, 63–64
Sibling bond, quality of, ix
Sibling caretaking unit, purpose of, 8, 9; transitions related to, 47; management of issues that interfere with, 210–216
Sibling coalitions, 8, 122–127
Sibling deidentification, definition of, 56; factors affecting, 56–57
Sibling interactional patterns, related to adulthood, 54–57
Sibling proximity, impact on frequency of contacts, 58–59
Sibling relationships, across the adult life span, 48–57; impact of earlier sibling relationships, 62–64; autonomous functions of, 21, 31; conceptual framework related to, 6–9; consequences, management of, 11–15; elderly, patterns of, 49–50; historical context of, 22–28; philosophical assumptions about, 4–6; natural history of, 9–10; normative issues, x, 9, 10, 11–12, 22–23, 36; problematic issues, 12–15, 23–25; examples of, 73; including sexual abuse, 122–134

Sibling rivalry, 30–31; childhood influences on adult handling of, 161–178; factors affecting, 30; lack of emphasis on positive factors, 30; impact on adult caretaking unit, 47
Sibling roles, 37–38
Sibling solidarity, 31–32; continuum of, 55–56
Sibling status variables (or birth order), 3; types of, 28–30; research on, 28–30
Sibling therapy, rationale in terms of group work, 128–129
Social support networks, characteristics of elderly siblings' networks, 49–50; extended family networks, x; treatment approach related to, 110–116; related to siblings, 6, 8, 15; tools, appropriate for analysis, 86; uniqueness of the sibling network, ix, 4
Strategic family systems theory (*see* Family treatment)
Strengths perspective, related to conceptual framework of sibling relationships, 6
Stress and coping theory, applied to sibling subsystems, 6, 24
Substitute parental roles, adopted by siblings, 7, 24
Symptom checklist, appropriate situations for use of, 87

Systems advocacy, professional roles for accomplishing, 90–91

T

Task-centered family systems theory (*see* Family treatment)
Theories (*see* Family treatment)
Timeline, overview of use with siblings, 86
Treatment, implications related to adult siblings, 66–68

V

Violence, sibling coalitions related to, 122–127, 137–148

W

Workplace issues, impact of sibling relationships on, 187–190, 192–195

Y

Young adulthood, case study examples and sibling issues related to, 167–168, 184–185, 206–207, 226–228

DATE DUE

DEC 2 2 1997			
APR 2 1 1998			
AUG 2 1 1998			
ILL: 9359246 Pieragostini, N. Due: 4-4-99			
DEC 1 4 2001			

Demco, Inc. 38-293